The New Latin American Mission History

Latin American Studies Series

Series Editors Michael C. Meyer, John D. Martz, Miguel León-Portilla

The New Latin American Mission History

Edited by Erick Langer and Robert H. Jackson

University of Nebraska Press
Lincoln and London

© 1995 by the
University of Nebraska Press
All rights reserved
Manufactured in the United
States of America
⊖ The paper in this book meets the
minimum requirements of
American National Standard for
Information Sciences—
Permanence of Paper for Printed
Library Materials,
ANSI Z39.48-1984.

Library of Congress Cataloging-
in-Publication Data
The new Latin American mission history
/ edited by Erick Langer and Robert H.
Jackson.
    p. cm.—(Latin American studies
series)
Includes bibliographical references
and index.
ISBN 0-8032-2911-9 (hard : alk. paper).—
ISBN 0-8032-7953-1 (pbk. : alk. paper)
1. Catholic Church—Missions—Latin
America—History. 2. Indians—
Missions—Latin America—History.
3. Evangelistic work—Latin America.
4. Latin America—Church history.
I. Langer, Erick, 1955– . II. Jackson,
Robert H. (Robert Howard) III. Series.
BV2831.N47 1995
266'.28—dc20
94-43080
CIP

Contents

ROBERT H. JACKSON
Introduction, vii

DAVID SWEET
The Ibero-American Frontier Mission in Native American History, 1

ERICK LANGER
Missions and the Frontier Economy: The Case of the Franciscan Missions among the Chiriguanos, 1845–1930, 49

SUSAN M. DEEDS
Indigenous Responses to Mission Settlement in Nueva Vizcaya, 77

PAUL FARNSWORTH AND ROBERT H. JACKSON
Cultural, Economic, and Demographic Change in the Missions of Alta California: The Case of Nuestra Señora de la Soledad, 109

LANCE R. GRAHN
Guajiro Culture and Capuchin Evangelization: Missionary Failure on the Riohacha Frontier, 130

THOMAS WHIGHAM
Paraguay's *Pueblos de Indios:* Echoes of a Missionary Past, 157

ERICK LANGER
Conclusion, 189

The Contributors, 195

Index, 197

Robert H. Jackson

Introduction

Beginning in the late fifteenth and early sixteenth centuries, Castile and Portugal conquered and settled extensive territories in North and South America, initiating profound changes in the economy, social organization, culture and belief systems, and political structure of the native populations in the New World. The conquest of the Americas led to the demographic collapse and in some instances cultural and biological extinction of Indian groups. The impact in the core areas of Latin America (Mesoamerica, the Andean region, and the coastal sections of Brazil) of Spanish and Portuguese colonization and postindependence Latin American Indian policy has been thoroughly explored and documented by several generations of scholars. Paradoxically, however, with the exception of the region of colonial northern Mexico that now forms a part of the United States, the frontier in Latin America has received relatively little attention in comparison to the number and sophistication of historical studies of the core areas. In particular, the single most important frontier institution, the Catholic frontier mission, has in the last century been largely ignored by professional scholars.

Spain's frontiers in the Americas expanded in fits and starts, as miners, ranchers, and farmers followed or at times preceeded missionaries sent to evangelize and assimilate diverse Indian groups. In the core areas of Spanish America conquistadors subjugated sedentary hierarchical societies in many ways similar to Spain's own feudal society. Spanish frontier policy sought, in part, to modify the social and economic structure of semisedentary and nomadic native groups to conform more closely to that of the sedentary, town-dwelling agricultural communities that the Spanish successfully dominated and exploited in Mesoamerica and the Andean region.

At the heart of the mission program was the policy of *reducción* or *congregación*, the resettlement of Indians into compact villages. Population loss in the sixteenth century in the core areas of Spanish America led to efforts to form new villages from the remnants of older communities. In other regions, such as the Andean highlands, Spanish officials sought to concentrate Indians living dispersed in small farming hamlets. The formation of compact villages facilitated the collection of tribute, the organization of labor drafts, and evangelization. Along the frontiers of Spanish America, missionaries from the religious orders, generally supported by soldiers, congregated semisedentary and nomadic Indians into villages, where the Indians were to be converted to Catholicism and assimilated to Spanish colonial society and the new economic order.

Missions played a critical role in the colonization of frontier areas, which in many cases held little or no economic attraction for settlers or were still dominated by unsubjugated native groups that frequently enjoyed local military superiority over ill-equipped and poorly organized Spanish frontier troops. Missions were a cost-effective form of colonization: in exchange for a small annual stipend generally used to buy supplies for the mission, Franciscan, Dominican, Jesuit, and Mercedarian missionaries ran the evangelization and assimilation programs that pacified many frontier Indian groups and contributed to the economic development of frontier regions. Missions in frontier areas also solidified Spanish claims to disputed territory.

The role of the frontier missionary was very different from the role of the sixteenth-century missionaries who initiated the evangelization of the native peoples of Mesoamerica and the Andean region. Missionaries assigned to the frontier not only instructed natives in the rudiments of the new faith (which also was the primary function of the sixteenth-century missionary) but also exercised great control over the daily lives of the Indian converts. Converts living in the missions were defined as wards of the Spanish Crown, and the missionary was their legal guardian until they were legally emancipated. In some locations and during some time periods, the frontier missionary also controlled Indian labor and surplus communal production known as "temporalities." Sixteenth-century missionaries evangelized sedentary populations, whereas frontier missionaries first had to settle Indians in villages and change their way of life, which required greater control over the converts' activities.

Missions helped settle frontiers that were still dangerous because of raids by hostile Indians or rival European powers, or had little economic attraction for settlers. Spanish frontier advance by means of missions faced obstacles, however. In South America Portuguese expansion in Brazil stopped Spanish settlement, and at different times Portuguese groups raided Spanish missions. English settlement in the Carolinas beginning in the 1660s blocked an already anemic colonization effort in Florida. Nevertheless, in most frontier areas Indians who refused to accept sedentary life in the missions or who saw little gain from alliances with the Spaniards slowed or stopped expansion of the frontier: Apache, Comanche, and other groups in northern New Spain (Mexico); Cuna and other tribes in Panama; and Araucanians in Chile. The end of Spanish rule led to the end of the mission system throughout the frontier, although in some areas, such as southeastern Bolivia, republican governments resurrected missions to help control the frontier.

Only since the mid-1980s have scholars considered the missions a topic suitable for study, incorporating new methods and perspectives. Indian converts living in the missions are the focus of the new mission history, which combines social history, ethnohistory, and quantitative history in an effort to understand more fully the impact on Indian societies of the establishment of missions. The new mission history examines change in several areas: in the social and economic organization of Indian societies; in culture, including changes in the world view of the Indian groups brought into the missions; and in demographics.

Previously, the history of Catholic Indian missions on Latin American frontiers during both the colonial and republican periods, was the subject of studies by a small number of professional scholars and many avocational historians. Many of these studies, written by members of the religious orders that historically administered the missions, were one-sided. To a large degree, the older of such works are narrative church self-history with certain biases; the more recent examples are apologies for the activities of the different orders at an earlier date.

Traditional mission history emphasizes the role of the missionary, often presented in heroic or saintly terms, as the bringer of civilization to Indians, frequently depicted as barbarians with little culture of their own. These works assume that the civilizing role of the missionary is noble and correct, and they gloss over, trivialize, or ignore this role's negative aspects. The Indians who settled in the mission communities and provided the labor for constructing churches and other buildings, farming, tending the livestock, and other activities appear almost as one-dimensional shadows, as mere backdrops for the missionaries, who are the important actors in this history. Finally, church self-history of the missions presents the actions of the missionaries divorced from the context of colonial or republican government policy and from the socioeconomic and political relationships between Indians and non-Indians.

Numerous church self-histories of the missions were written in the last century for just about every region in Latin America where missions operated. Among scholars from the United States, studies of the missions in Florida and the southwestern states–Spanish/Mexican "borderlands" are best known. The Californias and Arizona are covered in the books published between 1899 and 1933 by the avocational historian Zephyrin Engelhardt, O.F.M.[1] Beginning in the late 1970s, the campaign to canonize Fray Junípero Serra, O.F.M., architect of the mission system in Alta California, has generated articles and books designed to enhance Serra's image and deflect adverse publicity from the canonization effort.[2] Four Jesuits, all trained historians with doctorates, documented the history of the Jesuit missions of northwestern Mexico and southern Arizona.[3] Marion Habig, O.F.M., published several studies of the Franciscan missions of Texas.[4] Finally, Maynard Geiger, O.F.M., contributed a short study of the Franciscans in Florida.[5] There are many examples of church self-history in other parts of Latin America.[6]

Until the 1950s only a handful of professional scholars studied frontier Indian policy and the missions. In many ways, however, the attitudes and biases of these professionals mirrored those of the authors of the church self-history described above. The best-known early professional scholars who studied frontier missions are the "Boltonians": the students of Herbert E. Bolton, who defined "borderlands" studies in the first decades of the present century. Two Jesuit historians, John Bannon, S.J., and Peter M. Dunne, S.J., were Boltonians. The Boltonians were hispanophiles who attempted to document Spain's positive contributions to the formation of America, contributions that had largely been ignored or denigrated by Protestant Anglo-Americans who dominated the history profession at the time. However, the Boltonians overcompensated for the strong hispanophobe tradition in early American historical studies. Bolton and many of his students wrote institutional history from the perspective of Spaniards. The way in which Bannon and Dunne depict the missions is characteristic of their academic generation and reflects the fact that they both were Jesuits defending the activities of their order.[7]

The writings of the Boltonians were in many respects similar to the pioneering studies of missions in central Mexico and the rest of Latin America. Robert Ricard and John Phelan for Mexico, Mathias Kiemen, O.F.M., and Alexander Marchant for Brazil, and Antonine Tibesar, O.F.M., for Peru all studied early missionary activities from the European point of view.[8] These works set the parameters of mission studies by describing the institutional setting and detailing the organization of the conversion campaigns and the ideology of the missionaries. The avocational and early professional studies of the missions established the basis for the reinterpretation of mission history from different perspectives: social history, cultural history, and ethnohistory.

A change in the writing of mission history began only in the 1980s.[9] A new generation of scholars has redefined the study of the missions, giving more attention to the Indian perspective of mission life, the larger political and economic context of colonial and republican missions, and the impact of mission life on converts.[10] Most scholars, however, work in relative isolation from colleagues with specializations in different geographical or temporal areas. A comparative approach would provide useful insights for a fuller understanding of the socio-cultural, economic, political, and demographic aspects of the mission programs, especially as they modified the lives of the Indian converts in the mission communities. Although many scholars today examine similar aspects of mission history, there is no common theoretical formulation that can be used to inform research.

This book brings together works of scholars in social history and ethnohistory on missions in different parts of Latin America. It describes the state of the art in the study of missions, provides the basis for a comparative discussion of mission programs in the colonial and republican periods, and points to areas for future research. The mission is presented not as a local phenomenon but as a continent-wide institution that deserves additional attention from scholars. Detailed case studies serve as correctives to the assumptions and interpretations of the older mission narrative histories. The study of historical missions is germane today, as Christian missionaries, both Catholic and Protestant, evangelize in Latin America and other parts of the non-Western world.

The objective of this volume is to present the ways in which native society, culture, economies, and political structures changed under the influence of mission programs: in other words, history from the bottom up. The chapters are organized around five themes.

The first chapter is an analysis of how mission history has been and continues to be explained at both the popular and academic level. David Sweet exposes the biases of some presentations of mission history and offers categories useful for future research. Sweet calls for a new mission history and suggests areas of work that will illuminate the impact of mission programs and a variety of native responses.

The second topic, the economy of the missions, is represented by Erick Langer's study of the effects of the republican Chiriguano missions in southeastern Bolivia on the development of the frontier economy. Langer shows that the Chiriguano missions had a significant role in the frontier economy, especially in providing labor for enterprises. At the same time, the Chiriguanos living in the missions had considerable freedom of movement, and thousands migrated from the missions to work in the sugar plantations of northern Argentina. Langer incorporates economic and social history to document Chiriguano accommodattion to the growth of the frontier economy in southeastern Bolivia.

The third and fourth chapters explore the social and cultural changes that occurred in the missions, as demonstrated by the reorientation of work habits to conform to the goal of reordering native societies along European lines, and subsequent Indian resistance. In a study of the northern frontier of Mexico (Chihuahua) Susan Deeds outlines sociocultural change, accommodation, and resistance in the missions. Using archaeological and documentary evidence, Paul Farnsworth and Robert Jackson establish the degree of cultural change at Soledad mission in Alta California, relating it to the economic objectives of the Franciscans. This chapter demonstrates the connections among demography, sociocultural change, and Spanish government policy.

The next chapter examines missions located on international

frontiers, frequently the scene of violent conflicts between European powers contending for control of territory and trade routes. Lance Grahn documents how the mission program among the Guajiro of northeastern Colombia failed, in part, because of trade between the Guajiro and the Dutch. In this case, the Guajiro were important actors in their own history.

Inevitably, pressures from settlers and the increasing secular orientation of the state forced mission closures throughout Latin America, especially in the late eighteenth century and in the years immediately following the independence of most Latin American nations. Thomas Whigham discusses changes in the Paraguayan *reducciones* after the expulsion of the Jesuits in the late 1760s. Local colonial officials placed the *reducciones* under the control of civil administrators, and Whigham reveals the fate of the resident Indians and the dissipation of the communities' accumulated wealth, primarily livestock.

The chapters in this volume use social history, ethnohistory, and other approaches to redefine the history of the missions, particularly to examine their effect on native societies. The importance of the mission is reevaluated: it is no longer the scene of the triumphs of the saintly missionary but rather the place where cultural, political, economic, and demographic changes occurred, dramatically modifying the lives of the Indian converts. The new mission history also recognizes Indians as important participants in shaping their own lives, not passive figures who had no influence on history.

Sources for Mission Studies

A variety of sources exist to reconstruct the life of the missions and the changes experienced by the Indians congregated there. Many are written by the missionaries or by government officials who oversaw the development of the missions and reported on their progress. An exception is the oral history of Indians who formerly lived in the missions, recorded in the mid- and late nineteenth century, and the oral memory of their descendants.

The missionaries left several classes of written records. The least reliable are the hagiographies of missionaries assigned to the frontier, generally written by other missionaries.[11] Though they contain details about the life and work of the missionary, hagiographies also stress the miraculous. More useful are the histories written by missionaries to document their activities, often to justify royal support for frontier mission programs. These histories generally focus on the missionaries' work and their trials and tribulations in bringing the gospel and European civilization to the Indians; such works are frequently self-congratulatory, exaggerating such items as the number of converts baptized and living in the mission communities. Nevertheless, histories written by missionaries previously stationed on the frontier often contain important ethnohistorical information about the Indians who lived in the missions.[12] In some instances officials from the religious orders assigned other members, who were never stationed in the frontier missions themselves, to write synthetic histories based on reports and letters sent by frontier missionaries.[13]

Various primary sources provide useful information on the missions and their native residents. The missionary order generally maintained its own archives at the regional and national level, depositing records such as letters and reports detailing the missions' material and spiritual progress. In a prestatistical era, reports on the population, numbers of livestock, and crop production were not kept regularly and were of uneven quality. In particular, population counts did not consistently record the same categories and at times did not even include young children. Accurate enumeration of the unstable mission populations was also difficult.[14]

By the end of the eighteenth century the Spanish government required missionaries to make periodic reports on the economic and spiritual development of the missions. The most complete data come from the collection of annual and biennial reports for the Alta California missions. Every year the Franciscan missionaries wrote detailed accounts, which were sent to the local father president of the missions, to the local governor, and to Mexico City. The father president in turn prepared statistical tables from the annual reports, copies of which were sent to Mexico City.

The most complete records were retained at each individual mission, including sacramental registers of baptisms, burials, and marriages; account books; and inventories prepared when one missionary replaced another. Although incomplete for many regions, sacramental registers provide basic demographic information on birth and death rates and patterns of congregation to the missions. Underregistration did occur in these records, such as incomplete registration of births and failure to record the deaths of converts who

Introduction xv

died away from the missions. Moreover, many missionaries, especially during the seventeenth and early eighteenth centuries, did not provide detailed information. Despite these deficiencies, sacramental registers are a valuable source for scholars.

Few account books survive from frontier missions, but those that do exist provide important insights into economic development. In addition to prices, account books record transactions with local settlers and the frontier military. They also contain information on the types of goods imported to the missions and the reliance of missions on these goods.[15] Mission inventories, infrequently used by scholars, also offer useful economic data, such as numbers of livestock, agricultural production, and the involvement of the missions in local and regional trade.[16]

Scholars writing the new mission history base their work on a solid foundation in the traditional accounts. The new historians also employ a range of sources of the types described above to illuminate the lives of the Indians congregated in the mission communities.[17]

Notes

1. For example, *Missions and Missionaries in California*, published in four volumes in 1908 and revised and republished in 1929–30 at Mission Santa Barbara.

2. See the articles by Francis Guest, O.F.M., in the *Southern California Quarterly*, a regional history journal edited by historian Doyce Nunis, who is also a supporter of Serra's canonization. An example is "An Examination of the Thesis of S. F. Cook on the Forced Conversion of Indians in the California Missions," *Southern California Quarterly* 61 (1979), 1–79; and "An Inquiry into the Role of Discipline in California Mission Life," *Southern California Quarterly* 71 (1989), 1–68. In the latter article Guest claims that in the Alta California missions the Spanish word *azote* was not associated with whipping but rather meant "spanking."

3. See Peter M. Dunne, S.J., *Pioneer Black Robes on the West Coast* (Berkeley and Los Angeles, 1940); *Pioneer Jesuits in Northern Mexico* (Berkeley and Los Angeles, 1944); *Early Jesuit Missions in Tarahumara* (Berkeley and Los Angeles, 1948); and *Black Robes in Lower California* (Berkeley and Los Angeles, 1952). Also see John Bannon, S.J., *The Mission Frontier in Sonora, 1620–1687* (New York, 1955); John Donahue, S.J., *After Kino: Jesuit Missions in Northwestern New Spain, 1711–1767* (Rome and St. Louis, 1969); and Charles Polzer, S.J., *Rules and Precepts of the Jesuit Missions of North-*

western New Spain (Tucson, 1976). Polzer analyzes the organization of the Jesuit missions and the rules laid out in documents drafted by high-ranking Jesuits, avoiding many of the negative aspects of earlier church self-history. Collections of documents have also been compiled compiled by Jesuits and ex-Jesuits. See, for example, Luis González R., *Etnología y misión en la Pimería Alta, 1715–1740* (Mexico City, 1977).

4. For example, *The Alamo Chain of Missions* (Chicago, 1968).

5. See "The Early Franciscans in Florida and Their Relation to Spain's Colonial Effort," in Curtis Wilgaus, editor, *Colonial Hispanic America* (Washington DC, 1936), pp. 538–50. Geiger later wrote on the Franciscans in Alta California and published a volume of biographies entitled *Franciscan Missionaries in Hispanic California, 1769–1848* (San Marino CA, 1969).

6. See P. P. Pastells, S.J., *Historia de la compañía de Jesús en la provincia del Paraguay*, 4 vols. (Madrid, 1912–23); Pablo Hernández, S.J., *Organización social de las doctrinas guaraníes*, 2 vols. (Barcelona, 1913); Guillermo Furlong Cardiff, *Misiones y sus pueblos de Guaraníes* (Buenos Aires, 1962); and Philip Caraman, *The Lost Paradise: The Jesuit Republic in South America* (New York, 1975).

7. James Saeger, "*The Mission* and Historical Missions: Film and the Writing of History," typescript.

8. See Robert Ricard, *The Spiritual Conquest of Mexico*, translated by Lesley B. Simpson (Berkeley and Los Angeles, 1966), originally published in French in 1933; John L. Phelan, *The Millennial Kingdom of the Franciscans in the New World* (Berkeley and Los Angeles, 1956); Antonine Tibesar, *Franciscan Beginnings in Colonial Peru* (Washington DC, 1949); Alexander Marchant, *From Barter to Slavery: The Economic Relations of Portuguese and Indians in the Settlement of Brazil, 1500–1580* (Baltimore, 1942); and Mathias Kieman, O.F.M., *The Indian Policy of Portugal in the Amazon Region, 1614–1693* (Washington DC, 1954).

9. While several generations of historians, especially the "borderlands" specialists trained by H. E. Bolton, presented a Spanish perspective on the history of the missions, scholars in related disciplines offered alternative views. Historical geographers presented more balanced interpretations of the missions, including discussions of the causes and manifestations of Indian demographic collapse and the use of corporal punishment. See, for example, Peveril Meigs III, *The Dominican Mission Frontier of Lower California* (Berkeley, 1935); and Homer Aschmann, *The Central Desert of Baja California: Demography and Ecology* (Berkeley and Los Angeles, 1959). Anthropologists have also examined the impact of missions on Indians. See, for example, Edward Spicer, *Cycles of Conquest: The Impact of Spain, Mexico, and the United States on the Indians of the Southwest, 1533–1960* (Tucson, 1962); and Edward Spicer, *The Yaquis: A Cultural History* (Tucson, 1980). Finally, physiologist-turned-historian Sherburne F. Cook wrote a series of studies be-

tween the 1930s and 1970s that pioneered the re-evaluation of the effect of the missions and Spanish colonialism on the Indians of the Californias, especially in the area of demographics. See, for example, *The Conflict between the California Indian and White Civilization* (reprint; Berkeley and Los Angeles, 1976), parts 1–2, 5; and *The Population of the California Indians, 1769–1970* (Berkeley and Los Angeles, 1976); and with Woodrow Borah, "Mission Registers as Sources of Vital Statistics: Eight Missions of Northern California," in *Essays in Population History* (Berkeley and Los Angeles, 1971–79), 3:177–311.

10. For examples, see James Schofield Saeger, "Another View of the Mission as a Frontier Institution: The Guaycuruan Reductions of Santa Fe, 1743–1810," *Hispanic American Historical Review* 65:3 (1985), 493–517; Erick Langer, "Franciscan Missions and Chiriguano Workers: Colonization, Acculturation, and Indian Labor in Southeastern Bolivia," *The Americas* 42 (1987), 305–22; Robert H. Jackson, "Patterns of Demographic Change in the Missions of Central Alta California," *Journal of California and Great Basin Anthropology* 9 (1987), 251–72; Robert H. Jackson, "Population, and the Economic Dimension of Colonization in Alta California: Four Mission Communities," *Journal of the Southwest* 33:3 (1991), 387–439; Robert H. Jackson, "The Changing Economic Structure of the Alta California Missions: A Reinterpretation," *Pacific Historical Review* 61 (1992), 387–415; Robert H. Jackson, "The Impact of Liberal Policy on Mexico's Northern Frontier: Mission Secularization and the Development of Alta California, 1812–1846," *Colonial Latin American Historical Review* 2 (1993), 195–225; Susan Deeds, "Rural Work in Nueva Vizcaya: Forms of Labor Coercion on the Periphery," *Hispanic American Historical Review* 69:3 (1989), 425–49; and Cynthia Radding, "The Function of the Market in Changing Economic Structures in the Mission Communities of Pimerá Alta, 1768–1821," *The Americas* 34 (1977), 155–69.

11. For an example, see Francisco Palou, O.F.M., *Relación histórica de la vida y apostólicas tareas del venerable Padre Fray Junípero Serra* (Mexico City, 1787).

12. For example, see Miguel del Barco, S.J., *Historia natural y crónica de la antigua California*, edited by Miguel León-Portilla (Mexico City, 1973). Del Barco worked for many years in the Baja California missions.

13. For example, Miguel Venegas, S.J., *Noticias de las Californias* (Madrid, 1757).

14. Daniel Reff, *Disease, Depopulation, and Culture Change in Northwestern New Spain, 1518–1764* (Salt Lake City, 1991), pp. 181–93, discusses the strengths and weaknesses of seventeenth- and eighteenth-century censuses.

15. For examples of recent studies that employ account books and similar

records, see Jackson, "Population and the Economic Dimension of Colonization"; and Jackson, "Changing Economic Structure."

16. See María Soledad Arbelaez, "The Sonoran Missions and Indian Raids of the Eighteenth Century," *Journal of the Southwest* 33:3 (1991), 366–86.

17. Unless otherwise noted, translations are by the chapter authors. Some quotations are taken from previously translated documents, cited in the notes.

The New Latin American Mission History

David Sweet

The Ibero-American Frontier Mission in Native American History

This chapter is primarily a product of research on the history of the Spanish and Portuguese Jesuit, Franciscan, Carmelite, and Mercedarian missions to the Amazon Valley during the seventeeth and eighteenth centuries. It draws as well on readings in the histories of missions to Paraguay, the Chiriguanía, the Orinoco Valley, and California in the same period. My purpose is to compare the experiences undergone by so-called savage hunter-gatherer and swidden horticulturalist native peoples in colonial Ibero-America as they underwent the processes of resettlement and reculturation in the frontier Roman Catholic mission. By so doing, I mean to suggest a reconsideration by scholars, Christian activists, and others of the role of that classic institution in Latin American history.

I have sought to shift the perspective from which the history of missions has customarily been studied—to view it not over the shoulders of the missionaries and government officials who left the documents from which this history is reconstructed but from the vantage point of the "missionized" Indians. This is not to presume that we are able to think as the colonized Native Americans did about their experiences in the missions. It is simply to recast the discussion of mission history in such a way as to make Indian experience rather than missionary experience its subject.

Research for this chapter was assisted by a grant from the Faculty Research Committee of the University of California at Santa Cruz. Rick Warner provided invaluable assistance by searching the literature of California mission history for material on the chapter's themes. Useful criticism of the manuscript was provided by Rick Warner, Guillermo Delgado, Frank Bardacke, Robert Jackson, Erick Langer, and Noel Q. King.

We are handicapped, of course, by the almost total absence of Indian testimonies in the documentary record, by the ethnocentrism and the self-serving character of most missionary reports, and by the universal missionary view of Indians as children barely capable of reason. All these factors have left deep marks on both scholarship and popular writing in this field since the beginning, and through them on the public memory. It is high time, I believe, that the old-fashioned missionary's view of Indian culture and history, like that of the other agents of colonialism, be left behind by thinking people who have rejected colonialism itself and who would reject as well a pre-Enlightenment view of human nature and of the role of religion in society. With the help of ethnohistorians, historical archaeologists, and others, it is possible at least to experiment with some Indian-centered generalizations about mission Indian history. As we do so, it behooves us to strain our ears to listen for such native voices as may still come to us faintly through the missionaries' documents and through the material remains and the dispersed yet still vital cultural heritage of the "mission Indian" societies themselves.

The canonical text for this discussion is the brilliant faculty research lecture on the "mission as a frontier institution" given by Professor Herbert Bolton at the University of California in 1917.[1] Bolton was a distinguished historian who wrote extensively on the history of what he called the "Spanish borderlands," from Florida to California. At Berkeley he trained or influenced a generation of graduate students (among them several Catholic clergymen), whose dissertations explored aspects of mission history in those regions. Late in life he helped launch the lamentable but so far successful campaign for the elevation to Roman Catholic sainthood of the pioneer California missionary Fray Junípero Serra. Acknowledging the extraordinary impact of this life's work, Charles Gibson wrote that "few persons have created and defined a historical field so successfully" as Bolton, noting that the work of his school was "weakest in social and economic history."[2]

Bolton and the Mission Frontier

Bolton invited his readers to move beyond the romantic hagiography and the Californian focus of the English-language mission histories of his day, to see the frontier mission as a key institution of Spanish colonialism throughout the Americas—one parallel in importance to the fur-trading post in French Canada or the homestead in English North America. That was the broad scope of his ideal type, although except for a fleeting reference to Paraguay, Bolton drew all his illustrative examples from the missions of New Spain's northern frontier. The importance and effectiveness of the frontier mission, he argued, was attested by the continuing vigor of Spain's language, culture, and religion in all the regions in which these missions had been established.

The central purpose of the frontier mission as Bolton described it was threefold: "to convert, to civilize" (elsewhere to "discipline" or "instruct"), and "to exploit" (p. 43) its Indian inhabitants in the service of the Spanish Crown. In classic liberal scholarly fashion, Bolton viewed the religious function as self-evident (or perhaps not susceptible to scrutiny); he had almost nothing to say, for example, about the character of religious instruction or the circumstances of baptism. The exploitative function he also apparently saw as unexceptional and therefore unworthy of critical examination. His own emphasis was on the "civilizing" function: missions served "not alone as a means of control, but as schools in self-control as well" (p. 44). Here he gave voice, perhaps unconsciously, to the prevailing North American educational philosophy of his day, one that looked to a formal and unapologetically Eurocentric system of public instruction, relying heavily on hands-on learning as well as discipline, to produce the mentally resourceful, mechanically skilled but politically uncritical, even obedient citizenry required by an emerging imperial capitalist regime.

To "civilize" had been the ostensible role of the *encomienda* in densely settled central Mexico, where the native peoples were "fairly docile, had a steady food supply and fixed homes, were accustomed to labor, and were worth exploiting" (p. 45). But the Indians the Spaniards found on the expanding frontier were less tractable; they "had few crops, were unused to labor, had no fixed villages, would not stand still to be exploited, and were hardly worth the candle," in Bolton's unfortunate phrase (p. 45). Subjecting them required a new approach, because the settlers in those regions simply refused to accept responsibility as *encomenderos* for the incorporation into colonial society of "wild tribes which were as uncomfortable burdens, sometimes, as cub-tigers in a sack" (p. 45).

The religious orders were therefore assigned to this important work. As they understood it, the tasks of converting, civilizing, and exploiting the frontier Indians were one. It could be accomplished, the orders decided, by congregating as many of the widely scattered barbarians as possible into a few new settlements under missionary administration. There the Indians would be instructed in the basic principles of Christian vassalhood, retrained for sedentary living and productive labor, and finally put to work in mission farms and workshops that would provide subsistence and self-sufficiency for the missionaries and for themselves. In this way the "unexploitable" savages might be transformed into a labor force useful to European enterprise. Missionaries were in principle to work with the newly "reduced" peoples for a decade or so, to confirm in them the new habits of mind and labor discipline; then the Indians were to be handed over to the administration of secular parish priests, and the missionaries would move on to new frontiers. In practice, "a longer period of tutelage was always found necessary" (p. 46), and the religious were obliged to expend a great deal of effort in defending their spiritual and temporal authority over their charges, at the same time protecting the Indians themselves against recruitment as slaves or forced laborers by enterprising settlers.

Frontier missionaries were supported financially by the colonial government, because in addition to ministering to the Indians, they served the state as scientific explorers, linguists, intelligence gatherers, map makers, and diplomatic agents in the cause of imperial expansion. Presidios, or frontier military garrisons, were built nearby the missions, with which they lived in an uncomfortable symbiosis; and the colonial treasury charged mission expenditures to its military budget. In return for their services to the king, the missionaries received startup funds to purchase bells, vestments, tools, and trade goods for each new mission establishment, as well as subsidies (irregularly paid) to help with their maintenance. These payments were an important supplement to regular income from pious donations, from the operation of the orders' agricultural estates in the colonial heartlands (worked by Indian peasants and African slaves), and from the productive efforts of the Indians settled in the missions themselves.

Bolton saw Spanish colonial policy as humanitarian, looking as it did to the "preservation of the natives, and to their elevation to at least a limited citizenship" (p. 52). Unable to conquer or settle the remote corners of its American empire, Spain sought to colonize the frontiers with natives who were gathered into missions and kept there by force if necessary, as long as was required for their reeducation. "The essence of the mission was the discipline—religious, moral, social, and industrial, which it afforded," and its physical layout was itself "determined with a view to discipline" (p. 53). A church and rectory were situated on a central plaza, around which the Indians' houses were arranged so that from the church door the missionary could survey all that transpired. Where Indians refused resettlement and there were not enough soldiers to oblige them, the system invariably failed to get itself established.

Discipline was typically enforced by one or two resident priests and a pair of soldiers. The armed men supervised the neophyte laborers as long as was necessary to retrain them, often administered physical punishments to the recalcitrant, and were sent out to round up the frequent runaways. Missionaries might complain about the soldiers' misbehavior (particularly their sexual liaisons with Indian women) but generally saw them as indispensable collaborators and protectors. Bolton cited a Franciscan's graphic observation that the ostensibly Christian mission Indians of the Sierra Gorda in Guanajuato were *"hijos del miedo"* (children of fear), more attentive to "the glistening of the sword" than to "the voice of five missionaries" (p. 54). Where obliged to work without military support, the frontier missionaries were indeed sometimes murdered by their charges, but "the principal business of the soldiers was to assist them in disciplining and civilizing the savages" (p. 54).

Bolton's mission was "a school for self-government" (p. 60), with legally appointed native civil and military officials and communally owned land. "Wisdom dictated that use should be made of the existing Indian organization, natives of prestige being given the important offices" (p. 60), perhaps with distinctive insignia and prominent pews in church. Other officials were appointed to a *cabildo*, or town council. "The Indians had their own jail, and inflicted minor punishments prescribed by the minister. Indian overseers kept the laborers at their work . . . indeed, much of the task of controlling the Indians was effected through Indian officers themselves" (p. 60). Bolton especially admired the mission's daily regimen, punctuated by the tolling of bells. The Indians were rounded up for sunrise mass; they worked, ate, and rested at prescribed times; they were gathered at sunset for group prayers. They played harps and violins for religious services, and both men and women sang in the choirs. On feast days they bore Christian religious images in their processions as devoutly as any Spaniard.

This very structured system of governance, insisted Bolton, was "not a farce" (p. 61). It could be compared with "student government in a primary school" (p. 61), and it worked, as was seen every time a few priests and soldiers succeeded in making "an orderly town out of two or three thousand savages recently assembled from diverse and sometimes mutually hostile tribes" (p. 61). The guiding model for these mission villages was the seminary, in which instruction was of a piece with discipline, "imparted by a definite routine, based on long experience, and administered with much practical sense and regard for local conditions" (p. 55). Instruction was in principle to be offered in the Indians' own languages, as had generally been the practice in the core areas of the Spanish empire. But faced with the bewildering linguistic diversity of northern New Spain, for example, most padres were persuaded that "just as the natives lacked the concepts, the Indian languages lacked the terms in which properly to convey the meaning of the Christian doctrine" (p. 55). In these circumstances the missionaries preferred to do their preaching in Spanish, with the help of interpreters.

Missionaries were not farmers, mechanics, or stock breeders by training, and it was Bolton's conviction that they had no desire to be "entangled in worldly business" (p. 57). But they had been charged by the king with making the missions productive economic units, and in their effort to do so they made each outpost a sort of "industrial school" (p. 57) that trained the Indians in the skills required by European-style agriculture, stock rearing and artisanry. This "not only made the neophytes self-supporting, but afforded them the discipline necessary for . . . civilized life" (p. 57). Women learned to "cook, sew, spin and weave"; men to "fell the forest, build, run the forge, tan leather, make ditches, tend cattle and shear sheep" (p. 57). The "erstwhile barbarians" thus became familiar with "almost every conceivable plant and animal of Europe" by working on "huge farms" and in the "various mechanical trades" (p. 58).

Bolton admired the frontier mission for having spread the faith and taught the Indians "good manners, the rudiments of European crafts, agriculture, and even self-government" (p. 61). It had preserved them, in sharp contrast to the wanton destruction characteristic of the Anglo-American frontier, "improving the natives for this life as well as for the next" (p. 61). If sometimes it failed to achieve its own objectives, its lasting glory was that it had introduced European civilization to the ancestors of millions of people alive in Bolton's day.

Reframing the Discussion

Bolton's picture of the mission was in some respects accurate as far as it went, faithful to its missionary sources and to the nineteenth-century, liberal-cum-Spanish colonialist perspective from which it was drawn. It was focused on the temperate zone rather than on the tropics, within which most of the Ibero-American frontier missions were found; it disregarded the severe epidemiological and demographic consequences of life in the missions on every frontier; and it did not even attempt to take Indian culture and know-how, Indian labor, or in general Indian "agency" into account as determining factors in mission history. But despite these severe limitations, its heuristic effect must be recognized in the lasting influence it has had on both scholarship and textbook writing.[3] Something akin to the Bolton view (because derived from the same sources, read with a similar ideological disposition) is to be found, moreover, in all the modern Spanish-language histories of the church in Latin America—including, surprisingly enough, the monumental *Historia general de la iglesia en América Latina*, written during the 1970s and 1980s and partially under the influence of the new "liberation theology."[4] The image of the mission as a benignly paternalistic educational institution has also been brought to the silver screen by the shameless fabricators of an apologetic film called *The Mission*.[5]

Historians both religious and secular, and their readers in every language, have clearly become attached to Bolton's (and the religious historian's) ideal typification of the frontier mission as a religious and educational institution and as a moral alternative within the tawdry chronicle of colonialism in the Americas. In the meticulously reconstructed mission museums of California, for example, one looks in vain for signs of the whipping post and stocks that were standard equipment in frontier missions everywhere, or of the *monjerías* in which young girls were locked away from family and friends for the protection of their virginity.[6] In these circumstances it is difficult for the modern student to learn to think critically about the mission as a frontier institution and as a context for the colonization of frontier peoples, or to develop an accurate impression of its role in the formation of Latin American societies.

The most serious problem with the conventional history of the mission in colonial Latin America is that its subject, however soberly and "objectively" represented, is always the missionary. Frontier missionaries were often enough men of strong character and fascinating personality, to be sure, men capable of extraordinary deeds. They were charged by the king with enormous responsibilities and did their best to carry them out; however, they represented only a small and a highly idiosyncratic segment of the population of the colonial Latin American frontier. They were for the most part lonely men working in extreme isolation; their relationship to their contemporaries was at best an artificial one, difficult to sustain; their vision of society and of human nature was severely cramped by orthodoxy and ethnocentrism. Their vast spiritual and socioeconomic projects and their mighty individual endeavors, admirable as they were in many respects, in the end came largely to naught.

The missionaries' indefatigable labors did, on the other hand, have a very great (if largely unintended) impact on the historical development of many peoples and vast territories.[7] The effect of the missions can be seen only in the experience of the peoples they were established to serve. It therefore seems reasonable to ask that mission history be concerned primarily with the consequences of that institution for the Indian inhabitants of missions, over both the short and the long terms, and that it concern itself only incidentally with the lives of the missionaries themselves. The traditions of the field leave us hard put to understand how much "conversion" actually took place in these institutions, what aspects of "civilization" were assimilated by their native residents, by what means and with what results "exploitation" was really practiced, with what impact on the lives of the exploited.

Mission history needs to be freed, therefore, of its obsession with missionaries and their affairs. This shift in perspective does not require that we deprecate or downgrade the good padres or their accomplishments, as has sometimes been done in angry response, for example, to the Serra canonization campaign. There is no need to demean the motives or debunk the remaining claims to fame of these stalwart servants of the state religion of colonialism. Their experiences are still worth recounting, if only as a contribution to the little-studied social history of the religious orders in colonial America.

But their story is not, as Bolton thought, that of the origins of modern Christian mestizo society in the frontier regions of Latin America. Those origins are to be found in the harder-to-get-at stories of the Indian followers, subjects, or "neophytes" who surrounded every missionary priest. To put mission history into balance, therefore, we must somehow gently remove the missionaries from the center of the stage. We must reread their accounts more critically than has sometimes been done, with an eye primarily to what they have to say about the dimly viewed Indian "other"; and we must learn to distinguish their high ideals and aspirations, the inflated claims of their fundraising appeals, and the well-meaning instructions regularly sent by their superiors from what we can reconstruct of their actual practice.

It is helpful to keep in mind a few a priori propositions that, though inoperative among traditional mission historians, seem self-evident today. The first is that real day-by-day Indian experience, though severely constrained by the missionary and in some crucial respects deeply informed by him, was never in fact lived out, guided, or defined —and certainly never fully understood—by any missionary. People lived their own lives, even in the mission. Another proposition is that adult Indians were never the children the missionaries imagined them to be, never clay in the missionary's hands. Not even Indian children could be indoctrinated more than partially, or persuaded more than partially to distrust and disregard their parents' wisdom and values, by the most zealous of missionary educators. The living mission community that existed around every missionary was a chronically resistant, only conditionally cooperative, decidedly restrictive context for his work (as is attested by the universal complaints of missionaries about recalcitrance and ungratefulness in their charges). The relationship of missionary to neophyte was, therefore, not simply an action but an *interaction*—not a "conversion," says a young historian of missions in another part of the world, but a "conversation."[8] These propositions, increasingly supported by the ethnohistories of once-missionized Indian peoples and others, [9] are essential tools for the reframing this subject requires.

Frontier missions were operated at one time or another between the late sixteenth and the early nineteenth centuries by most of the religious orders at work in Ibero-America. Franciscans and Jesuits had the greatest number over the widest area during the longest period of time; but Dominicans, Augustinians, Capuchins, Mercedarians, and Calced Carmelites also contributed substantially. The mission territories during that long period included the entire northern tier of New Spain, from California, Sonora, and Nayarit across to Tamaulipas and Florida; several regions of Central America, including the Petén, southern Honduras, and southern Costa Rica; the Orinoco Valley and much of the rest of modern Venezuela; the Colombian llanos; the eastern slopes of the Andes from Colombia to northwest Argentina; the entire Amazon Valley and most of the Paraguay-Paraná basin; the Chaco, much of coastal Brazil, the Argentine pampas, and southern Chile—at least half the entire geographical area of today's Latin America. These were the least populous and the least successfully colonized regions of the Spanish and Portuguese empires, by and large. Nevertheless, their total population at the beginning of the colonial era must have been somewhere between five and ten million people, divided among several hundreds of distinct societies. Millions of people died in the missions, and some regions are even less densely inhabited today than they were before the arrival of the Europeans, but in most of them some ex-mission peoples survive. These peoples everywhere practice Christianity in one form or another, just as they display a wide variety of other beliefs, behaviors, and artifacts that they appropriated and adapted from Europeans through the agency of the mission. The frontier mission therefore represents a significant episode in Native American history. What were some common features of the experience it provided for the missionized?

The following broad generalizations seem applicable to the histories of most indigenous communities under the influence of the frontier mission system in colonial Latin America. They are arranged according to an analytic distinction, crucial for Indian experience though little noticed by missionary chroniclers, between the elements of *constraint* in the mission environment (those that restricted the possibilities for autonomous action by Indian communities) and the elements of opportunity (those that expanded the possibilities for autonomous action). This exercise in regeneralization is intended to supplement if not correct Bolton's model of colonial mission history and by so doing to suggest some directions for research in the history of mission Indian societies. Like Bolton's, this characterization of the mission as a frontier institution transcends wide differences in time period, in geographical location, and in the organizational affiliation or nationality of missionaries. At this level of abstraction, indeed, the most important operative distinctions between mission systems as they influenced the histories of Indian societies appear to have been not those between Jesuit and Franciscan or between Spaniard and Portuguese, but those between the temperate zones and the tropics, between regions more and regions less accessible to penetration by European settlers, and between comparatively lax and comparatively rigorous regimes of missionary control.

This reframing of the history of Christian frontier missions is intended primarily as a contribution to the history of colonial Latin America. It will be of use to students of the histories of "missionized" peoples elsewhere, however, if it encourages them to put experiences already studied into a comparative perspective or if it suggests appropriate questions about experiences that have yet to be examined by historians. The history of missions to the frontier regions of colonial Latin America, for its part, is much in need of comparative study in the context of a world history of efforts by missionaries and others to incorporate the "primitive" peoples of all continents into the worldwide culture and economy, efforts that have been forged, at so terrible a cost to the world, by capitalism during the past five centuries.

Indian Life in the Frontier Missions: Elements of Constraint

Disease

The most common experience of frontier mission Indians was premature death. Most people who went to live in the missions died sooner than they would otherwise have done—often within a few months' time—as a direct result of having entered into intimate association with Europeans, their disease microorganisms, and their "civilizing" regime. The Indians of Baja California were all but obliterated while under missionary tutelage; those of Alta California declined in numbers by at least a third in only sixty-five years; and those of the Maynas region of the upper Amazon Valley were diminished by at least two-thirds during the two centuries before 1800.[10]

Population decline in many of the frontier missions was even more precipitous than these approximations suggest, given the low birth rate, the ease and frequency of desertion, and the chronic difficulty of recruitment in most mission locales. Generally speaking, where there was any growth in mission populations, it was due rather to recruitment and the rounding up of deserters than to natural increase. But whether inside the missions or outside them, the indigenous populations of all the frontier regions entered into rapid decline within a few years of the establishment of missions (or of any other permanent European presence) among them. Dozens of peoples brought into the mission regime ceased to exist altogether within a few decades' time. All the missionized peoples experienced severe decline in their numbers, and in demographic terms none of these peoples anywhere in the Americas has subsequently recovered.

This holocaust was primarily the result of repeated infection with the Old World's "acute crowd" epidemic diseases, to which New World peoples had no acquired genetic resistance: smallpox, measles, diphtheria, whooping cough, influenza, typhus, typhoid, malaria, yellow fever, the common cold. Syphilis also played a large part, in regions where mission Indians were in frequent interaction with European soldiers and settlers. The process of infection was accelerated by the congregation of previously dispersed peoples into mission villages, in which the Indians lived in greater numbers within confined spaces, and by the increased contact of these villages with the outside world. Epidemics were all the more devastating because they generally struck more sporadically on the sparsely settled frontiers than in the densely populated core regions of colonial America, where diseases tended to become endemic and where genetic resistance to them was increased sooner by the process of *mestizaje,* or race mixture with Europeans. High mortality in the missions was also often a function of cultural and nutritional change, an increased incidence of preconquest diseases such as intestinal parasitism, psychic discouragement, induced abortion, infanticide, suicide, and greater vulnerability to warfare—though all these factors are difficult to evaluate and impossible to quantify.

Deaths from the acute crowd infections tended to occur in periodic episodes of general devastation, in which a third or more of the entire settled population of a given locality would be lost within a few weeks. At such a time most households and the community as a whole would suffer severe, irreversible, and inexplicable trauma simultaneously, with a resulting general disorientation and despair.

The missionary, for his part, could do little to alleviate the people's sufferings. However inclined he might be to nurse the sick before comforting them with the last rites of the church, he did not know much about the causes of epidemic disease and was in addition apt to interpret such sufferings as a form of divine retribution for sinful behavior on the part of the Indians. In these circumstances the social consequences of each epidemic, and of a high rate of mortality over the long term, were indescribably great for each individual native community. Each lugubrious episode was a new holocaust, befalling a people already beset with tragedy; and its implications for family and community structure, for the subsistence quest, and for the survivors' self-conception and world view reached far beyond the mere diminishing of numbers.

A second, related dimension of mission life everywhere was chronic illness, both corporal and mental. Indians gathered into mission settlements were frequently and debilitatingly ill and prone to depression. The impact of chronic disease on the Indians' health, like that of the epidemics, was compounded by the decrease in public hygiene that resulted from the totally foreign experience of concentrated settlement, from the obligatory use of clothing even in damp tropical environments, and from the missionaries' discouragement of bathing. (Native Americans in hot countries had thought the daily bath indispensable, and in cold countries they had often been given to taking thermal baths; missionaries generally saw bathing as both immodest and unhealthy.) Peoples who had once inhabited a village site for two or three years, until the exhaustion of the tropical forest soils obliged them to relocate, now lived in permanent settlements. Those who had burned and replaced reed-and-thatch houses when they became infested with vermin now lived in permanent adobe structures. Mission settlements were generally larger than indigenous ones, and human wastes accumulated in unprecedented quantities, contributing to contamination. Crowding encouraged the spread of respiratory infections; stagnant water bred mosquitoes. High rates of both mortality and morbidity were universal, then, in the frontier missions. This was true even where, as in Paraguay, the missions themselves were thought to prosper because of their efficient administration, their steady recruitment of neophytes, their success in keeping contacts with the outside world at a minimum, and their ability to produce goods for sale in a regional market.

Missionaries might be sometimes trained in the rudiments of the medical theory and practice of their day, and some took pride in offering assistance to the sick. A few were alert enough to tap into the Indians' vast knowledge of the locally available *materia medica*, though most were reluctant to learn anything from Indians at all. But the variety of deadly epidemic diseases that afflicted the frontier mission populations was great. Europeans knew little about their causes or cures and in any event had never seen them wreak such havoc as they did in Native America. All these diseases were new, moreover, to traditional Indian medical practitioners. In these circumstances Indian sweat baths, emetics, salves, and herbal remedies were probably as effective as European bleeding, purging, and chicken soup. The missionaries themselves sometimes conceded this point and in a few emergencies might even go so far as to encourage the native practitioners to do what they could. But neither, generally speaking, could contribute much toward restoring a mission population to health once it was faced with an outbreak of Euroasiatic disease; and the main work of both was confined largely to helping the broken and disoriented survivors heal their wounds and restoring insofar as possible the lives of battered families and communities.

Apathy, not surprisingly, seems often to have prevailed in the mission environment. A visitor to California observed that "after several months spent in the mission, they grow fretful and thin, and they constantly gaze with sadness at the mountains which they can see in the distance. . . . I have never seen one laugh. . . . They look as though they were interested in nothing."[11] Any such loss of enthusiasm for life must be seen as a sign of mental illness. The native peoples had shown no lack of intelligence or enthusiasm in the conduct of their own ways of life; early foreign visitors everywhere had been impressed by their vigor, vivacity, and resourcefulness. Yet Indian catechumens in the missions on every frontier seemed almost perversely slow-witted to their missionary teachers, as they stumbled distractedly through their efforts to learn new rules, new values, and the basic but esoteric truths of Christianity. Even where such behavior can be understood as a *conscious* refusal and introversion, the mode of resistance exemplified by José Arguedas's Andean *pongo*'s dream,[12] it must be acknowledged as a symptom of extreme social distress and resulting psychic disorder. "Puttin' on ol' Massa" in any colonial context was artful, to be sure, but it was no substitute for a healthy, open, and enthusiastic engagement of life.

Malnutrition

Another reason for the chronically poor physical and mental health of mission Indians was the general decline in the level of their nutrition brought about by the mission regime. Native American peoples had learned to eat everything that was edible in their environments. Food procurement was the central concern of every society, and it occupied both women and men, day by day, in their separate rounds of greatly diversified activity. Advanced techniques had been devised for these pursuits, which varied greatly according to the demands of each microenvironment: harpoons and highly maneuverable canoes for taking the giant *pirarucu* and manatee from the Amazon River, elaborate wiers and fish-stunning poisons for capturing fish in the smaller streams and backwaters, the catlike stalking of deer to get close enough to kill them with arrows, slings and blowguns that could bring down birds or small animals from considerable distances, the burning of chaparral and grasslands for purposes of land management in California, the manufacture of a food staple from the poisonous root of the manioc. People ate whatever they could; and given the relative difficulty of food preservation (especially in the tropics), they ate most of it within a few minutes or days of when they found or harvested it and saved only a small portion for the lean periods. There were no regular mealtimes, by and large; eating was not artificially segregated from the rest of society's relationship with nature, except perhaps in times of festivity.

Missionaries, for their part, deemed many traditional native foods unfit for human consumption, and to make things worse they imposed stringent requirements on the Indians' time, cutting deeply into the amount of time available for food procurement. They also concentrated the labor of the Indians on the production of a much narrower range of foods than they had been used to. From the missionaries' point of view, food procurement was necessary, of course, but it was not to be the central focus of life. Food, they thought, should be taken in regular (and often short) rations; there was no need to gobble it down all at once just because it was available. Food should be stored where possible and eaten as needed; it might even be given out as a reward for cooperation with the missionary's program.

The result of such policies was to diminish the variety and often the quantity of the foods eaten by mission Indians and only partially to compensate them for this loss through improvements in food preservation and storage and through an increase in the regularity of the supply of foods that the missionary now defined as staples. Carbohydrates predominated over proteins and fats in the mission diet. Canoe crews in Amazonia, for example, were often obliged to subsist on nothing but *farinha de mandioca* for weeks on end. Cook estimated that California mission Indians took in about two-thirds of the minimum number of calories deemed necessary by mid-twentieth-century nutritional science for human health and productivity.[13] Poor nutrition must necessarily have increased the mission Indians' apathy and "indolence," along with their susceptibility to all kinds of disease.

Mission Indians experienced widespread hunger for their own traditional foods, and missionary writers often noted that "their" people would abandon the missions at the appropriate times for one or another phase of the traditional food procurement cycle—sometimes in open defiance of the rules and even at the risk of physical punishment. Mission Indians, even after a generation or two, seem generally to have preferred their own diet to that of the Europeans. On the other hand, they often came to prefer the Europeans' distilled alcoholic beverages to their own traditional fermented ones, as a more efficient means of escaping from (or refusing to undergo wholeheartedly) the harsh realities of mission life.

Regimentation

Missionaries introduced Indians to a new conception of time. This time was not yet fully the "clock time" of the modern era, but it was a linear rather than a circular (or cyclical) notion of the movement of events, and one infused with Christian notions of teleology and eschatology that gave each lifetime an externally determined purpose. Natives and missionaries had been brought together for that purpose, as the padres saw it; it was their lot to pass time together for God's purpose, and God's purpose ought to inform their use of every bit of time. Time was not to be wasted; and it was also broken up by the missionaries, for reasons of calculation and allocation, in ways that Indians everywhere must have had great difficulty getting used to: hours and even minutes as distinct from the familiar days, marked off by the rising and setting of the sun; weeks and years as distinct from the familiar months and seasons, marked off by the recurring phases of the moon or the rhythms of plant and animal life. These new notions of time were essential to the mission's system for the regimentation of Indian life. Much regimentation was indeed aimed precisely at training the Indians to do their work and practice their ritual obligations "in time."

One of the mission's chief objectives was to introduce to frontier Indians the European idea and practice of "work," understood as disciplined and routinized productive activity for the benefit of others. This reinvention, or redefinition, was to have an impact almost as great as that of disease on the conditions of native existence. The European's idiosyncratic view of the labor process was of a piece with his ideas of property, exploitation, and profit: I now claim this land as mine and am powerful enough to defend that claim; you therefore exist for the purpose of working on it in a disciplined fashion, so as to produce wealth for me. All these concepts were alien to the thought-world of Indians in the frontier missions and elsewhere, who were used to economies of reciprocity, redistribution, and ecological adaptation. In practice, these ideas were also very difficult for most Indians to assimilate.

It was perhaps fortunate for the Indians of the far frontiers that this reeducation for their new role as unwaged rural proletarians took place in a peripheral region of the colonial world and in an economy of comparatively finite demand. Life was harsher for the forced laborers of the core areas, obliged as they were to produce without surcease in response to an infinite demand for the surplus needed to maintain a parasitical elite and the full apparatus of the colonial church and state. Mission Indians for the most part worked only to produce the limited amounts of surplus required to support themselves and their missionaries, at what was by comparison a very modest level of consumption. At most, they might also be expected to produce a bit more for barter to nearby settlers or to the soldiers of the frontier garrison.

This special circumstance provides a material basis for the frequent claim that the frontier missionaries "protected" their Indian charges against the worst abuses of colonial rule. Those abuses were present on the frontiers mostly in the form of Indian slavery and its successor systems of forced labor. Missionaries, by and large, did stand against these systems as practiced by their neighbors the European settlers—or at least sought to bring them under some form of government (or missionary) supervision. In the few cases (notably Paraguay and Pará) where the missionaries themselves sought to squeeze out production from their protegés on a larger scale and for a wider market, the emphasis in "evangelization" shifted necessarily from recruitment and reeducation to out-and-out exploitation. Where that happened, the conditions in which mission Indians labored grew more akin to those endured by the forced laborers in the mines and haciendas of the core areas or on the plantations of the fringe. But generally speaking and even in those cases, the involuntary labor regime of the missions seems to have been rather less demanding than that of the colonial system as a whole.

Missionaries on every frontier nevertheless undertook to bring about as rigorous a regimentation of the productive activities of their catechumens as they could. These were peoples whose traditional labors had been devoted to productive activities freely engaged in and had allowed for an infinitely varied, challenging, and even adventurous round of activity, day by day and season by season. Mission labor, on the other hand, was both routinized and compulsory, whether or not it was comparatively arduous by the standards of the core areas of empire. Mission Indians were by definition deprived of the freedom to live their lives and procure their subsistence as they saw fit. In the missions they were retrained for unfamiliar and often unsatisfactory kinds of work and then "put to work" under close missionary supervision. They were obliged to produce as much as they were able more or less easily to produce, rather than only as much as was needed by their immediate families.

Often, moreover, both men and women were hired out by the missionary to serve the nearby settlers or the frontier garrisons in menial capacities, and during those periods they might be subjected to the same privations as other forced laborers in the colonial system. More often than not their low wages were paid directly to the missionary. Mission Indians were punished for any failures to perform as expected under this regime, and they received only token material rewards for their cooperation. Once baptized and resettled in missions, or "reduced" to the "yoke" of the gospel, in the language of the day, Indians were viewed in both law and practice as vassals of the Spanish or Portuguese king. They were no longer free to leave their places of residence as they chose. They were forbidden to maintain any sort of unsupervised communication with nonmission Indians, even blood relatives or members of their same tribes. Every effort was made to discourage them from returning to what missionaries considered their savage, libertine, idle state of life in nature. Whether or not we view this regime as a comparatively benign one within the colonial social order, it must be acknowledged that there was nothing voluntary about it. In practice, the mission was more like the slave plantation or the highland hacienda than like the semi-independent *pueblo de indios* of the colonial core areas, and more like the prison/reform school or the military base than like any other modern social institution.

The mission regime involved a new sexual division of labor for most native people. Women, who had previously practiced a variety of skills in food procurement and horticulture, in addition to cooking and childrearing, were restricted to the home and the artisanal workshop. Men, who had usually cleared the garden plots and done the hunting, fishing, and warmaking, now did "women's work" in the mission's fields and gardens in addition to laboring mightily in transport and construction. There was disciplined, obligatory work for the mission's children as well, who were employed at weeding, running errands, scaring crows, or herding sheep and cattle—rather than being allowed simply to run free as they once had done, learning adult skills and responsibilities by accompanying their parents or family friends on their daily rounds.

A corollary to the idea of work as introduced in the missions was the idea of "laziness," defined by the missionary's concept of what an Indian worker ought to be willing or able to accomplish within any allotted period of time. Mission Indians seemed lazy to their pastors everywhere, especially as mission economies matured and their emphasis shifted toward production for the wider market. Implicit in such judgments was a comparison with the imagined productivity of European peasants or of New World African slaves. Often Europeans thought the Indians indolent by nature, despite the abundant evidence that traditional Native American construction, transportation, food procurement, and artisanry had required extraordinary exertions. Mission Indians worked hard but sporadically where they could; to the exasperation of missionaries, they preferred to lie about doing nothing in particular during slack times. But what was expected of them by the mission regime, after all, was that they work steadily to provide personal services to the missionary on a daily basis, year in and year out, at the same time laboring hard under pressure to produce a surplus with which to support the missionary's enterprises. This was an expectation that they work more, after a different fashion and for a different purpose, than most Indians of the frontiers could readily see the need to work. The idea of working for others without regard for one's own desires at any particular moment was itself hard to accept. Those who did accept it were obliged to undergo a critical emotional and intellectual adjustment to subservience in the process; those who did not accept it often paid a high price for their independent attitude.

The missionary himself, unlike the leader of any other small-scale native community, was exempted from every sort of manual labor by right of his status as a gentleman in European colonial society. Elaborate arrangements were made to protect him from having to exert himself physically, as is suggested by the frequently evoked image of the priest's being carried piggyback across a stream by an obedient Indian follower, so as not to get his feet wet. Colonialism saw obligatory manual labor by the conquered and the low-caste as both natural and indispensable to human society, and exemption from it for the European elite as a necessary symbol of domination. Missionaries therefore viewed labor by Indians as a virtue in itself. They undertook to teach their charges to work with their hands in a disciplined fashion, as a means of becoming "fully human" and by that token admissible to the hereafter. Yet the fact remained that the highest status in this new society, a society established with the explicit purpose of teaching people to worship God by working with their hands, was reserved precisely to those who did not themselves engage in manual labor of any kind.

Missionaries everywhere sought to prepare the Indians under their administration for a peculiar sort of self-reliance in dependence, to be exercised under strict missionary supervision and within the constraints established by colonial society. In practice, the consequence of this training program was to transform most Indians into hewers of wood and drawers of water—into domestic servants and ranch hands rather than skilled workers—first under the missionaries and then, once the mission system was disbanded or secularized under the onslaught of enlightened despotism and nineteenth-century liberalism, under the European and mestizo settlers of the frontiers. No matter how far-reaching the program of "civilization," of reeducation for colonial citizenship, may have been, there appears to be no single instance in which an ex-mission Indian frontier population succeeded in retaining its local economic and administrative autonomy for more than a few years after the secularization of missions and the departure of their missionary managers.

Discipline and Punishment

The constraint most widely discussed by critics of the missionary regime, then as now, was its universal practice of physical punishment. The most common procedures were public flogging, clapping in irons for extended periods of incarceration or forced labor, and placing in the stocks for public humiliation. Defenders of this feature point to the facts that flogging in particular was a normal feature of European labor discipline as well as of childrearing in the period, and that self-flagellation as a sign of humility before God was a discipline commonly practiced by the missionaries themselves (notably by Padre Serra, who is said to have performed it before his Indian followers in exemplary self-denial). A modern apologist writes that "the punishment system was relatively moderate (whip and gaol but no death sentence), and reminiscent of the world of childhood."[14]

This analogy with childrearing, revealing as it is of a persistent Euroamerican attitude toward adult Native Americans and their cultures, serves to hide from view the painful truth that however customary the practice of flogging may have been, its purpose and result in any context were to affirm authority over the flogged and to achieve discipline by breaking his or her spirit. The inappropriateness of the analogy in the present case is only heightened by the frequent references in missionary writing to Indians as "brutes" and "wild animals" and by the widespread use of the verb *domar* (to tame, break, or domesticate, as with wild horses or with Shakespeare's willful woman) in describing interactions with them. These usages and practices were direct and explicit contradictions of the messages of love and equality in the eyes of God, which were central to Christian teaching. For the missionary to flog the Indian "convert" was violently to break the bond of fellowship with him in Christ, and to assert not parenthood or pastorhood but a harsh social inequality that was incompatible with any such notion of fellowship. On the other hand, to become accustomed to being flogged by a missionary or by anyone else was in effect to be broken in spirit. It was to be forced to accept one's permanently low status in an unjust and hierarchically organized social order. This was the more palpably true for the Indians who were caught up in the mission system, since an absolute exemption from physical punishment or public humiliation (corollary to the exemption from manual labor) was the prerogative of missionary priests and other gentlefolk in the social order of colonial Christendom.

Missionaries and other colonial functionaries nevertheless saw flogging as a normal, necessary, and desirable feature of life in a properly administered Christian society (though some shared with contemporary critics the view that the other missionaries' use of it might sometimes be excessive). Indians, for their part, must have found physical punishment nearly as hard to understand as it was to justify or to accept, unless perhaps they associated it with their own sometimes painful traditional rites of passage into adulthood. The frequent claim that mission Indians, once "reduced" to the status of Christian vassals, actually came to expect physical punishment and to undergo it willingly as penance for their "sins," is very difficult to accept nowadays. Flogging in the missions would seem to have replaced a traditionally retributive Indian sense of justice with an abstract European sense of justice, one severely skewed in practice by social hierarchy. Around this white man's Christian justice, whose principles legitimized flogging, it is inconceivable that any real consensus can have been achieved within mission Indian communities.

Whatever they may have thought of it, mission Indians grew quite familiar with the pain and humiliation of harsh physical punishments, administered regularly to both men and women by an alien authority. Every mission had its whipping post, its jail cell, its set of iron shackles, its stocks. All these instruments of control embodied concepts and practices that were new to Indian culture. Physical punishment was ordered not only for theft, for open sacrilege, for concubinage and other departures from a newly imposed sexual morality, or for inflicting bodily harm on a fellow Christian (as might perhaps be expected in a community organized on biblical principles), but also for desertion, for slacking in the workplace, sometimes for the mere neglect of pious duties. As Jean François de la Pérouse observed in California, "many faults which in Europe are wholly left to divine justice are here punished with irons or the stocks."[15]

Deculturation

The mission, as Bolton noted without using the term, was an institution designed to bring about the systematic deculturation of Indians. More often than not, it was a multiethnic community constructed without regard for ethnicity. Most neophytes lived among strangers, with many of whom they could not communicate until both had learned a new language. The authorities were not familiar with or respectful of the details of the various Indian cultures of their followers, nor were they eloquent in expounding the intricacies of their own culture for native audiences. Their concern was to cajole, prod, guide, or if necessary force their charges into what might be called a "mindless" conformity with the mission's rules for individual and community behavior, leaving cultural adaptation to occur haphazardly.

The language employed in missionary instruction, and in the administration of the mission labor force, was sometimes Spanish or Portuguese; more often it was an Indian lingua franca such as Nahuatl, Quechua, Guaraní or the neo-Tupian *lingua geral* of Brazil. This was a language that the missionaries had learned from Indians and then reworked and codified for the purposes of "evangelization." They taught it to all newly recruited Indians, of whatever linguistic background, as they came into the mission's fold. The principle here was that any Indian language was more suitable than a European language for communicating with Indians. In addition, it was recognized that the use of such a language was one means of maintaining a desirable isolation of the mission community from nearby secular European outposts. But whatever language was employed in the mission, it can have been learned only partially and with great difficulty by any new recruits. Given the artificiality of the introduction and dissemination of these languages on the mission frontiers, moreover, it seems likely that they were severely limited and even restrictive vehicles for interpersonal communication, whether between the missionaries and the Indians or among the Indians themselves. Communications within the mission environment must for the most part have been reduced to standardized forms, conveyed with forceful simplicity. For frontier mission Indians, unlike those of the *doctrinas* of the Andean and Mesoamerican core areas, then, the experience of conversion, civilization, and exploitation required learning or accommodating one's self to a new language as well as to a new culture—and doing so in circumstances that were as restrictive of the possibilities for the exercise of a free intelligence as they were to one's freedom of movement. Missionaries on the Latin American frontiers seem generally to have found nothing in indigenous culture worthy of retaining, though in practice they were obliged to learn to live with most of the beliefs and practices they encountered, while working hard to replace as many as they could with elements of their own contrivance. Few sought to distinguish those components of Indian culture that were not actually incompatible with Christian teachings, so as actively to embrace them and encourage their followers to retain them within the neo-Indian mission way of life. Here there was no parallel to the "rites controversy" that arose when Jesuit missionaries to "civilized" Asia during the same period strove to accommodate or "inculturate" the gospel to the values and expectations of their potential converts. The strategy for the American frontiers was tacitly to declare war on Indian culture as a whole, putting up with most of it as a practical necessity over an extended period while hammering away at those features that particularly outraged the Christian moralist. The objective over the long run was to subject Indian culture to a permanent stress and thereby to overwhelm it with a peculiar, specialized missionary's decoction of European culture, one whose superiority to anything Indian was taken for granted and was seldom seriously questioned by any contemporary observer.

Missionaries learned quickly, however, that the spiritual conquest they sought was virtually impossible to achieve with fully socialized adults and could be accomplished only by dint of patient and systematic effort among mission Indian children. The reeducation in the principles of Christian vassalhood even of a receptive Indian community, and one with a comparatively stable population, was a task the missionaries might hope to complete, at least superficially, within perhaps three generations. This work required confronting steadily and contradicting relentlessly the most basic cultural patterns, beliefs, and behaviors of the missionized Indians. It required interrupting the normal process of children's socialization by parents and family friends, replacing it insofar as possible with formal instruction by the missionary himself. But even where this program was carried out most zealously, uniform results were impossible to achieve. As Friar Senan wrote from California, "the son counts eighteen years as a Christian, but the father is an obstinate savage still enamored of his brutal liberty and perpetual idleness. The granddaughter is a Christian but the grandmother is a pagan. Two brothers may be Christian but the sister stays in the mountains."[16]

One sign of the missionaries' hostile attitude toward Indian culture is the general absence in their accounts of Indian society of any appreciation for the healing skills or the oratory, dance, music, or the plastic or graphic art through which all Native American peoples expressed their aspirations for beauty and holiness. This is true even of those accounts that wax eloquent in their praise for the handsomeness, the manual dexterity, the physical endurance, and the cheerfulness of Indians, qualities Europeans viewed as desirable in an emerging caste of manual laborers. Another sign of enduring hostility is the persistent doubt registered by missionary writers with regard to the very humanity of their native charges. The temptation to interpret spiritual and ideological opposition to colonial rule as savagery or bestiality was one that the educated European colonialist, whether clergy or layman, found hard to resist.[17]

A central feature of the mission's deculturation program was the complete overhauling of the generally open attitude of Indian societies toward the body and sexuality. Missionaries abhorred nudity and required the use of clothing by their neophytes, even in the humid tropics. They fulminated against what they viewed as polygamy, fornication, adultery, incest, sodomy, and bestiality, and often enough against the sexual practices of Indians within the bonds of matrimony. All these behaviors had been regarded as functional and respectable, or at least tolerable, in many indigenous societies before the establishment of the mission regime, or they had been punishable according to traditionally established norms. But the Indian rules governing sexual expression were drastically altered everywhere the mission regime was established. On the other hand, resistance against prohibitions in the realm of sexual behavior, and against the punishments with which missionaries attempted to enforce them, was a key factor in rebellion on many frontiers. Often enough it led to the wholesale abandonment of missions by their Indian inhabitants. The missionaries nevertheless continued to experiment with such practices as the residential segregation of young women and men for the protection of virginity; they intervened actively in the choice of marriage partners; they raged at the functional but un-Christian practices of abortion and infanticide against deformed babies; in general, they supervised insofar as they were able, and worked hard to subvert, the normal conduct of Indian family life. They seem to have acted in this way even while functioning themselves, as was frequently or perhaps even usually the case among missionaries other than Jesuits and conventually trained Franciscans, as the sexual partners of Indian women and de facto heads of their families!

Missionary interventionism was especially active in the area of childrearing, which the padres tended to view as excessively lax among Indians everywhere and in which despite their many handicaps for such work they sought to take the largest role possible. Here the long-term objective was nothing less than the destruction of traditional Indian family and community life and their reconstruction on a semblance of European Christian principles—admittedly, a doubtful and probably unfeasible undertaking in any circumstances. It is notable that such intervention seemed to the missionaries to work best with the peoples whose processes of social and cultural disintegration were most advanced when they came to the missions. The evidence is strong, moreover, that the Indian peoples who offered most resistance to the missionaries' program—and who survived the mission period most nearly intact (having adopted such elements as they could use from European Christian culture in the process)—were precisely those such as the Tarahumara and Yaqui of northern Mexico, or the Campa and Cocama of the Peruvian Amazon, who held on most tenaciously to their own cultures and social arrangements (or took charge most firmly of the process of their own cultural transformation), throughout their missionization period.

Finally, and in ways closely related to their attitude toward human sexuality in general, missionaries expressed the misogyny that was both common to their profession and explicit in their doctrinal tradition. By demeaning, deemphasizing, and discouraging the previously critical role of women in Indian society, they sought by precept to deprive native women of their traditional spiritual and moral authority and their key economic functions. Missionaries viewed and treated women as childbearers, as domestic and artisanal workers, as irrational persons, and as congenital sources of trouble within societies that without their presence (the padres seem to have thought) might have been free to evolve as rationally ordered, patriarchal theocracies. No one stood lower on the scale of human worth operative among the Spanish and Portuguese colonial Christian priesthood than a "savage" Indian woman; and generally speaking, missionary writers were reluctant to acknowledge virtue, intelligence, or any useful contribution to mission society in even the most faithfully Christian of their female followers. This twisted feature of mission culture surely heightens the historic drama of the later emergence of poor women, and ex–frontier mission Indian women among them, as principal sustainers of the life of the church in contemporary Latin America.

Infantilization

In a social context such as the frontier mission, it was virtually impossible for adult Indians who "converted" to Christianity, or who accepted any of the other elements of European culture, to do so with dignity as adults. The mission was a context for the virtual infantilization of adult Indians and for the raising of Indian children to remain childlike as adults. Where its program was most effective in controlling people's lives—in cutting off people's access to their own cultural traditions and to the opportunities these traditions provided for achieving excellence, success, and esteem in the eyes of their neighbors—there the discouragement was greatest and self-confidence was least. The Jesuits of Paraguay, always viewed as the most successful missionaries of all, referred habitually to the Guaraní as children: "The missionary has to be like the father of a family; for the Indian, whatever his age, is like a child in needing to be trained and punished for his own good."[18] Secular commentators on the sad fate of the missionized Guaraní after the Jesuit expulsion of 1768 follow the Jesuit writers in comparing the rapid dissolution of mission society with that of a family that has lost its parents. Adult European Christians had somehow persuaded themselves during the preceding centuries that their notions of God as omnipotent father, and of priestly "father" as God's authoritarian representative in the human community, were compatible with the human dignity of the faithful. Among the Christians of colonial Latin American society, and especially of its "savage" frontiers, these notions functioned primarily as instruments of domination.

The mission system made it a practical impossibility for any Indian to become sufficiently familiar with European Christian culture so that he or she might consciously adopt it and thereby become a morally self-sufficient person capable of independent action in accordance with European Christian principles. Given the refusal of missionaries to provide Indians with direct access to the Christian scriptures or to any training in the rational principles and propositions of Christian thought and praxis, it was literally impossible for their catechumens to become informed, believing Christians with fully functioning consciences—or even to understand the thinking of such persons when they met them. Learning by emulation was severely handicapped by the social distance that was carefully maintained between the neophyte and his or her missionary teacher. Indeed, one sign that these limitations were intentional is the fact that nowhere in the frontier missions could an Indian be taught Latin or be recruited to or trained for the priesthood, no matter how complete his "conversion," how sharp his intelligence, or how burning his vocation. Herein lay one of the more decisive internal contradictions of the mission system. Not even in class-ridden, monarchical late medieval Spain and Portugal were ordinary Christian men of low station thought to be ineligible for religious instruction and even ordination to the priesthood, if they showed an exceptional inclination and aptitude for such studies and were fortunate enough to catch the eye of a teacherly clergyman.

Indians, like children, were expected to memorize and recite formulae they did not understand, to engage unthinkingly in behaviors that their "betters" thought were beneficial to them. They were expected to learn to be follower Christians, not leader Christians; to be members of a childlike caste of Christian manual laborers. One deep irony in this arrangement, and in the missionaries' insistence on the childlike character of the Indians was that, whereas children anywhere were dependent on working adults for food, shelter, and protection as well as guidance, in this case it was up to the "dependent" mission Indians to do all the productive work in their communities and to provide their very pastors with food, shelter, and protection—even during their own most desperate sicknesses and deprivations.

The oft-cited docility, as well as the rebelliousness, the sullenness, the stupidity in learning lessons, even the loyalty of Indians to their pastors in the mission system, all these were childlike characteristics that resulted *from* the mission regime rather than having determined its character. The mission was in this respect an intrinsically self-defeating institution: the Indian convert who sought to attain or maintain the full dignity of Christian adulthood within it was obliged to defy the missionary's program. To cooperate fully with that program was to forgo one's right to the full enjoyment of adult status in one's own community, and it is therefore not surprising that missionary accounts leave the general impression that most people cooperated only partially or externally with the program and that they resisted the process of infantilization in every feasible way.

Alienation from Nature

A final constraining feature of the mission regime was that it sought to undermine and replace the Indians' vital sense that the self and the community existed and acquired meaning through their intimate relationship with nature. In exchange for this awareness the mission offered a sense of self and community as existing primarily in relation to human institutions—and to the God who served to legitimate those institutions. Along with this message went the Christian colonialist's ignorant, sterile, and dysfunctional view of nature (including most of humanity) as a storehouse of resources disposed by the same God for Europeans to exploit. Indian hunter-gatherers and horticulturalists, for their part, had generally experienced nature in a more dynamic, interactive, participatory, and at the same time fearful way. They needed urgently to know how things functioned around them and why, so as somehow to subsist among the creatures and forces of nature and avoid being hurt by them. Sometimes this respectful attitude had led Native American peoples to devise small ways of helping to keep nature going and to prevent its depletion. Sometimes through miscalculation they had hunted or gathered or cultivated too intensively, with harsh consequences for themselves. Never, it seems, had they sought by design to control, measure, own, or exploit to the point of exhaustion any of the bounties of nature.

The mission reeducation program, on the other hand, included lessons on how to organize the systematic exploitation of nature and its products for commercial purposes and with the greatest possible efficiency. This project was, of course, not immediately destructive of nature on a large scale during the seventeenth and eighteenth centuries, given the small number of missions, the primitive character of colonial technology, and the low initial demand of the world economy for the products of the mission frontier. But the first visible signs of environmental destruction were not long in coming, as when the population of the great edible river turtles of the Amazon went into precipitous decline once the commercial production of turtle-egg oil was launched from missions in the early eighteenth century and became a key feature of the regional economy.

Indians must often have seen missionaries as shamans from an alien tribe, men who possessed a few remarkable artifacts and powers but who were notably lacking in wisdom about the requirements of life within American nature. These unapologetic interlopers offered their followers some crude elements of a mechanically mediated technology, along with their greatly simplified and even foolish-sounding cosmology and their senseless routinization of the procedures of worship. All these innovations contributed to diminishing rather than enhancing the fearful respect (or the awe?) with which Native American people had always beheld all-powerful nature. As witch doctors, the missionaries proved unable even to heal the terrible plagues that they had themselves introduced. Their authority over their followers was imposed and maintained by force rather than earned, as was customary in Native America, through bravery, virtue, generosity, or eloquence. The missionaries strove, moreover, to make this authority as nearly and unnaturally absolute as possible, instead of contenting themselves with the more tentative, partial, conditional, natural, and realistic authority with which their Indian followers were familiar.

The intellectual and spiritual activity of Indians had always focused on nature, and one role of their spiritual leaders had been to lead them in reflection on their oneness with nature. Missionary priests, for their part, were concerned only incidentally and instrumentally with nature. Borne along on the unnatural experience of conquest and domination—and at the same time condemned to living unnaturally alone among strangers in an unfamiliar land—the missionaries insisted on the centrality of power to spirituality. The pretension to power over nature was a corollary to the pretension to power over humanity. Their religious discourse was concerned above all with the reinforcement of authority, with the reiteration and imposition of Christian rules of conduct, with the punishments of a vividly imagined hell, and with the promise of heaven for those who subjected themselves willingly to the powerful of this world. Spiritual life as they understood it was confined to the church and mediated by its priesthood. Data of a useful sort might reasonably be collected about the natural productions of any region, but nature itself was not, to most of them, a suitable subject for permanent observation, reverence, or communion.

To the extent that mission Indians accepted this comparatively sterile view of themselves in the world, they lost their sense of membership in nature and became small-time, generally not very successful exploiters of nature. They learned to hunt and fish and harvest more than they needed to feed their families, to waste that which they could neither use nor sell. They learned to plant in rows, to chop down all the trees when clearing a field rather than planting around the stumps of a few. As an especially eloquent testimony to their alienation from nature, they learned to tend herds of livestock in some places and to plant a single "cash" crop in others. They learned to peel off the whole bark of the "clove" tree, rather than cut just a strip that would shortly heal over, or to pick the green cacao beans along with the ripe—all in order that they might fill up their collection canoes with more lucrative cargoes in record periods of time. They learned to render tens of thousands of pots of oil from turtles' eggs each season, for use in the colonists' lamps and frying pans. In time, of course, they came to threaten the species that had once fed them, to destroy the forests, to provoke the erosion and hardening of the soil itself by altering landscapes to conform to ill-conceived human designs. They removed themselves physically from nature, settling in artificial towns, and they were often enough found pining there for the life of the forests they had left behind. Perhaps this was the real "conversion" that occurred among every missionized indigenous people within a few years' time: from a spirituality of participation to a monotheism of powerlessness and exploitation. The mission's idea of work and of time and property, Europe's idea of the subject person, colonialist Christianity itself—all these were exercises in alienation from the real world that continued to exist around every native community in America.

Indian Life in the Frontier Missions: Elements of Opportunity

From an Indian point of view, the frontier mission experience on balance was surely a catastrophe. Positive or mitigating features do emerge from the record, however, and it is important that they be kept in mind as we study this history. Without them it is impossible to understand why the native peoples of the Latin American frontiers, rational beings who generally acted in pursuit of their own interests as they saw them, ever had anything to do with the missions. The truth is, of course, that though many resisted the mission system, most of the Indians who managed to survive its epidemics and its disciplines ended up in an attitude of acquiescence to missionary rule. To speak of the opportunities that existed for Indian communities in the frontier mission, therefore, is not to whitewash the institution. It is not to enter into the discussion of whether it was essentially benign or whether the services it performed for the colonial state were real services to the Indian population as well. Rather, it is to acknowledge the material and social aspects of mission life that were genuinely appealing to Indians, the spaces for autonomous action, and the limits that always existed on the mission's ability to constrain day-by-day Indian existence.

Survival

The principal opportunity, and the one that drew most Indians into frontier missions in the first place, was the generally chimerical possibility of mere physical survival. Indians for the most part settled in missions only after having been badly battered by disease, famine, enslavement, the intensification of intertribal war brought about by contact with the Europeans, war with the conquerors themselves, or some combination of these pressures. They came to the missions hungry and frightened, in search of subsistence and protection. Missionaries to the central California coast reported that recruitment increased substantially during the drought years, when the harvest of acorns, the Indians' staple food, grew scarce. *Descimentos* (voluntary settlements) to the Amazon missions were most easily arranged with the chiefs of tribes being victimized by the Indian slave trade. In the mission settlement there was usually a steady supply of food, a resident European advocate, and perhaps a certain reassurance in numbers. Finally, the well-organized mission, with its small garrison and its force of armed Indian auxiliaries, could sometimes provide military protection when needed from both Indian and European enemies.

Most Indians who settled in missions did not, it must be remembered, usually survive. But some groups seem to have made good use of the institution for this purpose, at least in the short run. Those who survived best or most fully over the longest period were generally those who arrived in large numbers and managed to retain a high degree of cultural and linguistic homogeneity within the mission community, as in the case of the Guaraní speakers of the Paraguayan reductions. Another conditioner of survival was the Indians' willingness on occasion to risk armed resistance against the missionaries themselves (examples include the Tarahumara, the Campa, the Chiriguano, and the Yaqui). Other favorable factors were a previous experience of sedentary agriculture and town life (as with the Pueblo and Zuñi), a measure of continuing self-sufficiency and of connection to nature under the mission regime (Tarahumara and Campa), and the discovery of special means of being useful to the Europeans (as with the Mundurucu and Opata in their capacity as allies against the Mura and Apache). Survival might also be achieved by abandoning the missions altogether and withdrawing to remote places where the people could only with great difficulty be found by future missionaries or their retainers, as was done by the Mayoruna of the Peruvian Amazon in disillusionment with mission life, after being struck by a deadly epidemic in the 1650s.[19] A final strategy, the most frequently followed of all, was for the surviving individual members of a once-missionized people to abandon ethnicity and simply join with, or lose themselves among, the emerging racially mixed laboring population of the frontiers, as was done by the Guaraní of Paraguay after the Jesuit expulsion and by the multiethnic "domestic Indians" of Pará.

A general feature of survival seems to have been that those who managed it best achieved a gradual rather than an abrupt process of adaptation to European ways, under their own leadership and on partially Indian terms. Florence Shipek notes that of the California mission Indians only the Luiseño of the San Diego hinterland survived as an ethnic group; her explanation is that instead of destroying their sociopolitical structure, the founder of that mission "apparently used it (whether knowingly or unknowingly) to develop" the mission. Generally speaking, however, every strategy of adaptation that was conducive to Indian survival was viewed with suspicion by the missionary, and these strategies were the hardest for people to retain in the mission environment.

New Tools, Cultigens, and Techniques

A second critical area of opportunity for Indians in the missions was the acquisition of knowledge and equipment that could be used to increase the efficiency of their continuing quest for subsistence. Alfred Métraux wrote of a "revolution of the ax" through which tropical forest horticulturalists, peoples accustomed to hacking away at giant tree trunks with tools of shell or bone as they labored to clear their garden plots, were introduced as by a miracle to the Europeans' cutting tools, which could sever such trunks with comparative ease. These peoples quickly became utterly dependent on those who could supply them with the priceless new tools and were willing to go to great lengths to obtain them (for example, making war on their neighbors with the purpose of capturing prisoners who could be sold as slaves in exchange for axes, knives, and machetes). Sometimes they would even settle in a mission station with this exclusive purpose; always it was a major incentive for them to do so.[20] Missionaries' accounts are quite consistent in acknowledging that iron tools for gift giving were indispensable to their work and that in the absence of an ample supply of such goods many Indian peoples would have nothing to do with the mission.

The frontier missionaries also introduced a variety of (at least ostensibly) valuable new cultigens into the lives of Indian peoples, especially in the temperate zones: fruit trees, melons, grapevines, European vegetables, and grains. Even more significant in some localities was European livestock—pigs, chickens, cattle, sheep, goats, and especially horses—wherever it was thought that such animals might survive. Where any of these innovations took hold, they carried with them a potential for feeding more people with less labor, at the same time subtly changing Indians' perceptions of the relationship between productive activity and power. (The Indians of the Americas were, of course, making similar contributions to the demographic growth of Europe, Africa, and Asia during this period, as their maize, manioc, beans, potatoes, yams, ground nuts, squashes, peppers, tomatoes, avocado, and many other useful plants were spreading around the world.) Alongside these important European introductions came startling new technologies for cultivating the soil, for manufacturing cloth, for cooking and preserving food, for transporting merchandise, for killing one another, and for lighting up the night. Each was compelling in its own way, with its own implications for the transformation of life in society.

Finally, and perhaps most significant or most ominous over the long run, the missionaries introduced the Old World distillation process and its products. This was a particularly seductive innovation among peoples who had previously consumed only fermented alcoholic beverages, mostly for ritual purposes. "Demon rum" as an item for festival use, and eventually for daily consumption, seemed at first to help people escape for a time from the harsh realities of a rapidly deteriorating social and ecological order. Only later, when the addiction had grown widespread, did it appear to Indians to be a problem in its own right. By that time the production and distribution of alcoholic beverages to Indian communities had become a key feature of colonial frontier economies and sometimes a major source of revenue to the religious orders. Indians everywhere had come to depend on it for distraction and solace. In time hard liquor worked its devastating impact on virtually every Indian community in America.

The success of these innovations in increasing the efficiency or diminishing the hardships of the subsistence quest, and thereby contributing to the well-being of Indian communities, was greatest where the Indians managed to adapt them on their own terms. This required that they remain in their own villages, visiting and trading with the Europeans only occasionally; and it was evident everywhere in the adaptation of the ax, the knife, the machete, the fishhook, even the firearm for hunting. Success was least where the Indians had to allow themselves to be incorporated into the white men's life-destroying new social order, whether in its mission or its secular sector, in order to enjoy the benefits of the new devices. Indians, generally speaking, preferred their own lifeways to those of any Europeans. Even after several generations of contact with European institutions, native peoples generally surprised outsiders with this predilection. But Indian communities could always find uses for new tools, weapons, sources of nutrition, or entertainments.

The missionaries' own very limited successes depended in large measure, on the other hand, on their ability to bring about an increase in the Indians' material standard of living through the introduction of new tools, food crops, and livestock. The missions also made substantial improvements in food preservation and storage (notably in the smoking, dehydration, and salting of meat; in the making of sausage, cheese, and wine; and in the storage of these products in bottles and barrels). These techniques, together with grain storage and warehousing, went a long way toward ensuring the regularity (though not the nutritional quality) of the food supply for those Indian peoples who adapted them. A modern Jesuit historian sums up these material aspects of the mission's appeal, and their limitations, when he acknowledges that most missionaries were able to see clearly,

> though the conclusion was painful, that initially the appeal of Christianity was rarely its religious or moral excellence, but rather the fact that the mission Indian usually enjoyed certain material advantages.... The prospective mission Indian was faced with a major personal decision in the practical order: was material advantage, namely, a reasonably assured food supply and the personal security promised, worth the sacrifice of freedom and the rejection of traditional beliefs and long-cherished values?[21]

With regard to the introduction of new tools and cultigens through the frontier mission, an important distinction must be made between the temperate and the tropical zones of the Americas. In the tropics European tools and some artisanal techniques became very important, whereas new cultigens and stockrearing practices were not so easily adapted and generally had little impact. In the missions to the tropics, by and large, the Indians taught the missionaries what to eat; mission Indians continued for a long time to procure most of the missionaries' food from the wild, using Indian techniques modified only slightly by European influence (as when manatee were harpooned with the help of a steel point). In the temperate zones, including Paraguay, the Chiriguanía, and California, on the other hand, both the Europeans' cultigens and their livestock were probably as important as European tools in conditioning the long-term process of social change. Here, so to speak, the missionaries eventually (and with great difficulty) taught the Indians what to eat and for the most part how to produce it. The far-reaching implications of this crucial distinction should be explored in comparative studies of mission Indian history. In general, it may be observed that the record of survival was marginally better among mission Indians in the tropics.

New Forms of Community

Once the full impact of the European presence had been felt, Indian communities found their old arrangements destroyed and "traditional" life rendered impossible. Missionaries urged and guided or co-opted the creation of new structures of community and of communal authority, which would prove influential in the organization and subsequent evolution of every mission Indian society. As Bolton suggested, the mission community was often administered in day-by-day matters by native officials, closely supervised by the missionary. These officials, like the European gentlemen of their day, employed visible symbols of authority such as articles of luxury clothing or ceremonial staffs. This represented an element of opportunity for a few individuals in every mission society. They were exempted by the new status from physical punishment (though not from manual labor), and that symbolic privilege and enhanced status was sufficient to co-opt them. Sometimes it served to corrupt them as well, by encouraging petty abuses of authority. It seems likely that some measure of similarity between the new political arrangements of the mission community and those that had been traditional in each Indian society was an important factor in enabling that society's survival within the mission system.

Seen from another angle, the mission was a context for the forging of new communal ties and structures, not so much by the missionary as by those who came to live under his tutelage. The story of how the Indians responded to this challenge is a large part of the still unwritten history of nearly every missionized people. For the mission system to function at all, people had to devise means of living and working together in the new context on some sort of an amiable and sustainable basis. Trust had to be established; patterns of ritual and recreation had to be reconstituted. Some of the forms for this reconstruction were laid down by the missionary, for example when he decreed that people must attend daily prayers or that there should be an annual celebration of the festival of a patron saint. Within these forms, however, the implementation fell necessarily to the Indians, and they worked best under the guidance of their own leaders. The appointment of leaders by the missionary was not sufficient to this purpose, because the most effective authority was the "natural" authority of leaders who were respected because they knew the ways of their people and the ways of nature, as well as having accommodated themselves to European domination. This authority had somehow to be restored and continually reaffirmed by the community, in the face of the "unnatural," imposed, and alien hierarchy culminating in the missionary. A reauthenticated Indian authority was more palatable and ultimately more real than that of the missionary, and as such it was indispensable to a viable community life. On the other hand, native authority was structurally constrained, actively undermined, and occasionally even humiliated by its submission to the authority of the missionary.

The mission lingua franca, destructive as it was of particular cultures and limited as a vehicle for communication, seems at the same time to have helped build wider community among the surviving mission Indians of the frontiers. It did this at least for the Guaraní speakers of all the Jesuit missions of Paraguay and for those who spoke the *lingua geral* from one end of Portuguese Amazonia to the other. A Spanish-speaking Indian ranch hand was able to find employment and people to talk to, for example, anywhere in mid-nineteenth-century California. Traders who spoke the lingua franca could travel widely through a mission territory, confident that people would understand them wherever they went. An auditive bilingualism must have expanded the range of partial communication in mission territories far beyond the limits of actual fluency in the mission language. Much research remains to be done, however, concerning the practical implications of these mission languages, with all their limitations and associations, for the process of the recreation of community in the mission context.

All mission Indians had maintained viable community structures before the arrival of the Europeans and then had largely lost them in the ensuing holocaust. The mission was an institution designed to fill that void, within which the surviving Indians might learn to function in community once more and thereby equip themselves in some measure for coping with the growing pressures of the interconnected colonial and modern capitalist world. But this process was fraught with dangers. In Paraguay an indigenous Guaraní communalism, which had recognized no private ownership and expected each community to share its food equitably, was replaced by the Jesuits with a theocratic "communism." The mission Guaraní enjoyed the usufruct of their houses and fields on the mission's land; the products of their labors were stored in common warehouses controlled by the missionaries and redistributed as the padres deemed appropriate. The missionaries also managed a limited and strictly controlled trade with the outside world, ostensibly on the Indians' behalf. The Indians underwent military training; their daily lives were tightly regimented; their clothing itself was a kind of uniform and symbol of disciplined community. The construction of this neo-Indian community under Jesuit guidance, like that of the Franciscan missions in California a century later, occurred to some extent in defiance of the interests of the state, and just as capitalism was setting about its worldwide promotion of individualism and greed at the expense of community. These countervailing forces led in both cases to the expulsion of missionaries and to the secularization and absorption of mission communities by settler societies within a few decades. In such circumstances, few of the communal forms forged by mission Indians were destined to last. But among such groups as the Yaqui, Tarahumara, and Campa, where they have survived down to the twentieth century, they show a vigor comparable to that of the institutions of the "closed corporate peasant community" of the Andean and Mesoamerican cores.

Appropriation of Christianity

That the teaching of religion was difficult to accomplish in the frontier mission is abundantly attested in missionary memoirs. The cultural distance between missionary and neophyte was too great; communications were too limited; participation in the life of the mission community was too involuntary. Ignorant as they therefore were of the conceptual basis for the sacrament of baptism, most mission Indians probably did not experience it as a radical change in their personal outlook. Many presumably underwent it in a spirit of complete mystification and did so primarily to please (or to allay the wrath of) the missionary. For others, given the epidemiology of missions, it was an augury of early death. The gospel stories the Indians were told and the theological notions the missionaries boiled down for them must in practice at best have supplemented rather than replaced their own notions of origins and divinity, and have been worked into their own cosmologies. What quickly did become clear to every missionized Indian was that once a person was confined in the mission, he or she was expected to follow the regulations closely and could be punished for any transgressions against them.

There was, then, a fundamental difference in the ways missionaries and Indians understood the Indians' relationship to the new faith. This difference was the source of much frustration to missionaries, but it also gave the "praying" Indians of every frontier a certain comparatively safe space within which to maneuver culturally and ideologically. Inside that space they could hold on to whatever traditional beliefs were still persuasive to them, dissembling when necessary to keep both private and communal beliefs and practices from the missionary's view; at the same time, they could work at adapting and developing their practices as obedient Christians.

Religious "acculturation" in the mission context may perhaps best be understood as a selective appropriation and reinterpretation by native communities of Christian stories, practices, and ideas. Indian societies came to the mission experience with their own notions of a creator deity presiding over many spirits, their own millennial dreams, their own understandings of the shaman/priest as healer, intermediary with the spirit world, and presider over ceremonies. These beliefs must sometimes have made aspects of the mission religion easier to accept. Regular attendance at mass, participation in Catholic religious festivals and processions, and indoctrination in the rudiments of Christianity all had considerable impact on the Indians' traditional religious views. The Europeans' religious art and biblical homilies, the stories of their saints, and their practice of intercessionary prayer made an impression, as did the enforcement by missionaries of a new morality with regard to clothing and sexual behavior. Mission Indians grew familiar with these ideas, images, and practices; they understood, readapted, and made use of them as they were able and saw fit.

The mission was unquestionably a repressive cultural environment, but it was also a space within which Indians could get a head start, so to speak, in understanding the Europeans and their ways and in figuring out what might be worth taking hold of and retaining. Among the aspects of mission culture most susceptible to appropriation were the visible elements of religious practice, the missionary's stories of a covenanted people and their justice-seeking but punishing God, and above all his stories of the life and ministry among poor people, the rejection of temporal and priestly authority, and the death and miraculous resurrection of Jesus Christ. These stories, though heavily interpreted for the Indians by a colonialist priesthood deeply compromised by its association with the exploitative earthly structures of power, seem often to have been taken up and used as their own by mission Indians, just as they have been appropriated by colonized peoples elsewhere and used for their own purposes. Once owned and retold time and again by Indians, they would sometimes come to function as powerful myths for liberation from European oppression.[22]

The European view of religion as a separate and superior realm of human experience must have seemed to any recently missionized

Indian a weak and disappointing substitute for the spirituality of his previous full participation in nature, and in the mission context religion was perhaps as stultifying to the spirit and as it was to the intellect. But the separateness of the religious realm does seem to have helped it to function among the colonized as a space for creative self-expression and for the reimagining of justice, as "missionary religion" became "folk religion" by a process that largely remains to be studied. This is most clearly evident so far in the history of the Yaqui, but the surviving mission peoples all seem to have managed, at least to some degree, to take advantage of the opportunities provided by the mission to reaffirm themselves culturally in this way.

Resistance

To see native resistance as an opportunity provided by the mission system is to remind ourselves that the constraints of that system were never absolute, that missionary control was only relative, and that the constraints themselves could on occasion be catalysts of mobilization. Those Indians who survived it biologically found plenty of space in the mission regime for both active and passive resistance and for a continuing reaffirmation of selfhood and self-valorization. The essential form of resistance, here as elsewhere, was the insistence of individual Indians precisely on being themselves, on thinking and behaving as nearly as possible as they chose to think and behave (in the face of the mission's tremendous pressures for conformity), and on teaching their own experience and their own understandings to their children. The missionary chronicles frequently express exasperation with this type of resistance, complaining of "inconstancy," of the widespread unwillingness of Indians to follow through on the commitments that missionaries (but not Indians) considered inherent in the acceptance of the sacrament of baptism.

Resistance might take the form of a stubborn maintenance of language and symbols or of the traditions of shamanic ritual and herbal medicine within the mission community itself. Despite the missionary's efforts to extirpate such "evils," the possessors of traditional wisdom often managed to keep them alive in themselves, to practice them in consultations with their neighbors, and to pass them down through apprentices, sometimes for generations, under the missionary's watchful eye. Other signs of this cultural resistance were the persistence of a "superstitious" belief in the significance of the Indians' own dreams and the almost universal refusal to stop propitiating and otherwise communicating with the spirits that were known to inhabit the immediate environments around mission communities. Such resistance seems to have been greatest among the least sedentary and least "political" of the missionized peoples, as in California. These groups in turn received the sternest treatment in the missions, fled from them most, were most effectively broken by them, and in the long run were least likely to survive them. But cultural resistance was present everywhere, most visibly where the punishments seemed exceptionally unjust, where millenarian expectations took hold (often nourished by the missionary's apocalyptic oratory), where interventions in the Indians' private and family lives got out of hand, or where people simply tired of the oppressive mission work regime.

Desertion was another major form of resistance, practiced wherever feasible and whenever the rigors of the mission regime seemed to outweigh its advantages. Often, however, it was not easy to abandon the mission community. The soldiers were there to round them up, and the Indians' home territories might be too far away to be easily reached or their tribes of origin might no longer exist. Many mission Indians in fact had nowhere else to go, and life alone in the wilds was presumably not appealing to most of them. But the call of the old environments and the old subsistence cycle was nevertheless strong in those who remembered it, and even in long-established mission settlements there were frequent comments on the Indians' preference for the "wandering life."

Finally, of course, the annals of the frontier mission contain hundreds of examples of armed uprisings in which the missionaries might be wounded or killed (in European parlance, "martyred," regardless of the circumstances or provocation). On these occasions the padres' houses and church buildings might be destroyed and every sign of the European presence obliterated—save always the precious metal tools, which rebels seem never to have wanted to leave behind.

Resistance of whatever sort, however manifested, was a reaffirmation of self or community that gave people a purpose and served to limit the effectiveness of the colonial mission as a system for the conversion, civilization, and exploitation of Indian society. More often than not, it came too late or was too small in scope or too soon repressed to ensure the physical survival of the resisters. Sometimes, however, it was the means by which a people actually succeeded in preventing its own destruction or disintegration, whether in the short term or the long. In all these cases, it was the mission as space, and as new context for organization, that enabled the resistance itself to be attempted.

Impassioned denigrators of the frontier mission enterprise sometimes confuse genocide with ethnocide when appraising its disastrous consequences for Native American history, but such incendiary argumentation casts more heat than light on our subject. Missionaries sought to exterminate Indian culture, not Indian people. Their policy toward the Indians themselves was one of stern but "paternalistic," systematic reeducation. Yet in the mission environment, appallingly, the people proved even more vulnerable than their cultures, and cultural resistance was itself greatly undermined by demographic decline. Those who died in the missions succumbed for the most part to biological and socioeconomic forces operating beyond the missionary's control and understanding, a situation that led one mission historian to characterize the wholesale destruction of humanity within this system as "inexcusable but not intentional."[23]

One curious and lamentable feature of the genocide school of criticism is that in effect it perpetuates Bolton's perspective on the history of the frontier missions by reaffirming the primary agency of the missionaries in mission Indian history. But the Indians of mission history, like other historical peoples, were always more actors than acted on. They constructed their own histories, though they did so within exceptionally severe constraints. The constraints were erected by missionaries, by the political economy of colonialism, and by the Euroasiatic disease microorganisms, working in unintended collaboration. It is therefore a waste of ammunition to attack the missionaries for the genuine and unprecedented demographic and cultural catastrophe that was mission history on every frontier. In recent years the historical demography of mission territories has gone a long way, at least in the Californias, toward rectifying both the whitewashed romantic and the more political Boltonian version of mission history; more important, it has contributed in significant ways to laying the foundation and raising some key questions for future reconstructions of the social and cultural histories of missionized peoples. This groundwork remains to be laid for most of the other mission territories of colonial America. But over the long run, what historians and others will be interested in is less when and why or in exactly what numbers so many people died, but what those who had not yet died did with the system, what their survivors did with what was left to them of their forebears' culture and patrimony, and what that history has to say to people alive today.

When the history of Native Americans in the mission system is written from an Indian perspective, employing categories derived from the reconstruction of Indian experience, it will presumably become even clearer than it is today that the system's constraints on the autonomous activity of Indians vastly outweighed the opportunities it provided them. This is the opposite of what Bolton, focusing his thought on the missionary himself, on the mission as a constructive and rational enterprise, and on the interests of the Spanish colonial state, concluded. Bolton and subsequent historians have for the most part taken the language and the conceptual frameworks for their discussions of mission history from the missionaries themselves. A sign of this approach is the curious persistence in the writings on the colonial mission, even of liberal secular historians, of terms such as "conversion," the "saving" of "souls," and "protection."

"Conversion" cannot be done to people. It is undergone voluntarily by rational adults who have learned something new that makes sense to them and that seems so important as to cause them to want to adjust the rest of their thinking and behavior to it. It is an active and not a passive experience. Children may be separated from their families, taken to boarding schools where they are taught by missionary teachers to hold beliefs different from those of their parents, and thereby raised as believing Christians (something that was seldom feasible on the frontiers of colonial America). But no one could "be converted" through an act of another's will, no matter how artful or kindly. "Conversion," then, is not an accurate term for the real transformations that took place among Indians in the frontier missions. The missionary record makes it clear that Indians were frequently persuaded or even required, at least as a survival strategy, to accept the Catholic rite of baptism. It reveals that those who outlived the disease and hardships that followed incorporation into the mission regime, and who found reasons to continue to endure it, also generally managed to accommodate themselves to the mission's conventlike regimen, including frequent attendance at Catholic rituals and the daily recitation of Catholic prayers. On the other hand, the record provides little evidence that adult Indians in the missions ever stopped believing what their previous lives and their parents and respected leaders had taught them, in order to begin believing what the missionaries had taught them instead.

If "conversion" has little to do with what transpired in missions, what about the "salvation" of the "soul"? Whatever one understands souls to be, to attribute their salvation to missionary labors in the present context requires a leap of faith that few secular historians today, if examined closely on the point, would probably be willing to make. Similarly, "protection" was in practice usually a euphemism for hegemonic control. The conventional language of mission history is therefore a serious handicap to understanding. It reifies an archaic notion of Christian spirituality and praxis, and it dehumanizes, infantilizes, and "otherizes" the Indian just as did the missionary enterprise itself. Yet so prevalent is this language that it is difficult even to talk about the colonial frontier mission without making use of it. The social history of missions needs to be freed from this mission historian's language and from the anti-Indian bias and perspective it embodies. Nothing about the mission enterprise is self-evident, and in view of its terrible consequences for the native populations it was designed in principle to benefit, nothing about it should any longer be taken for granted or at face value by serious historians.

Seen from the perspective of Indian experience, the frontier mission appears to have been an institution within which religious "conversion" was all but impossible, in which the "civilization" process was rather more forbidding than inviting, and in which "exploitation" itself was severely handicapped by Indian resistance and demographic decline. Its major features, on the other hand, were sickness, death, forced labor, flogging, deculturation, infantilization, and alienation from nature. It was therefore scarcely a benign context for the assimilation of intractable natives into the colonial socioeconomic order or into the process of the construction of new mestizo cultures and nationalities. Few people survived it long enough or in good enough health to flourish and multiply within that order; for most, it was a bitter disappointment, a dead end, and an early grave. These features were intrinsic to the mission regime, and they may be attributed to its ideology, ecology, and political economy as well as its epidemiology. They were little affected by the character and practice of individual missionaries, no matter how high-minded or saintly.

At the same time, the mission regime offered survival to a limited number of the beleaguered Indian inhabitants of the colonial frontiers. For survivors, it provided access to, and a prolonged period of exposure in which to assimilate, some of the more valuable aspects of European culture: superior tools, some useful domestic plants and animals, some usable notions of community and of production for exchange in the world market, some biblical visions of justice and loving community. The mission was at its best a context for the appropriation of these cultural features on the surviving and half-re-educated mission Indians' own terms, with lingering results for themselves and their mestizo descendants. These results survived and transcended the mission regime itself.

© 1994 University of Nebraska Press

Notes

1. Herbert E. Bolton, "The Mission as a Frontier Institution in the Spanish-American Colonies," *American Historical Review* 23 (1917), 42–61; subsequent quotations from this work are cited directly in the text. See also John F. Bannon, editor, *Bolton and the Spanish Borderlands* (Norman OK, 1964); John F. Bannon, "The Mission as a Frontier Institution: Sixty Years of Interest and Research," *Western Historical Quarterly* 10 (1979), 303–22; Lewis Hanke, editor, *Do the Americas Have a Common History?* (New York, 1964); James A. Sandos, "Junipero Serra's Canonization and the Historical Record," *American Historical Review* 93:5 (1988), 1253–69; and James A. Sandos, "Junipero Serra: Canonization and the California Indian Controversy," *Journal of Religious History* 15:3 (1989), 311–29.

2. Charles Gibson, *Spain in America* (New York, 1966), p. 231.

3. For example, Bailey W. Diffie, *Latin American Civilization: Colonial Period* (Harrisburg PA, 1945), pp. 577–87; C. H. Haring, *The Spanish Empire in America* (New York: 1963), pp. 182–88; and Gibson, *Spain*, pp. 80–83, 185–89. Mark A. Burkholder and Lyman L. Johnson, *Colonial Latin America* (New York, 1990), pp. 897–98, pay scant attention to the institution; only James Lockhart and Stuart B. Schwartz, *Early Latin America* (Cambridge, 1983), provide a context for understanding the frontier mission phenomenon in their imaginative chapter entitled "The Fringes." Cf. J. Fred Rippy and Jean Thomas Nelson, *Crusaders of the Jungle* (Chapel Hill NC, 1936); Alistaire Hennessy, *The Frontier in Latin American History* (Albuquerque, 1978), especially pp. 54–60; and brief references in the chapters on church history by

Eduardo Hoornaert and Josep Barnadas in Leslie Bethell, editor, *Cambridge History of Latin America*, vol. 1 (Cambridge, 1984), pp. 511–56, 616–23.

4. Enrique Dussel, editor, *Historia general de la iglesia en América Latina* (Salamanca, 1965–). See, for example, the treatment of the Jesuit Orinoco mission by P. José del Rey Fajardo, 7:96–121.

5. For a revealing memoir of the making of this film, see Daniel Berrigan, S.J., *The Mission: A Film Journal* (San Francisco, 1986).

6. Maynard Geiger, O.F.M., *Indians of Mission Santa Barbara in Paganism and Christianity* (Santa Barbara CA, 1968), p. 27.

7. For a reasoned discussion of such an impact, see James Schofield Saeger, "Another View of the Mission as a Frontier Institution: The Guaycuruan Reductions of Santa Fe, 1743–1810," *Hispanic American Historical Review* 65:3 (1985), 493–517.

8. Vincent Diaz, personal communication, 1990. Diaz is a doctoral candidate in the History of Consciousness program at the University of California, Santa Cruz, whose research is focused on the seventeenth-century Spanish Jesuit mission to Guam and the twentieth-century campaign for the canonization of its founder, P. Diego Luis de Sanvitores.

9. An especially good example is the history of the Yaqui of northwestern Mexico, studied by Edward Spicer in *The Yaquis: A Cultural History* (Tucson, 1980) and many other works; by Evelyn Hu-DeHart in *Missionaries, Miners, and Indians: Spanish Contact with the Yaqui Nation of Northwestern New Spain, 1533–1820* (Tucson, 1981) and others; and by José Velasco Toro in *Los yaquis: Historia de una activa resistencia* (Xalapa, Mexico, 1988). Cf. the following for some very different themes in book-length historical studies of other frontier peoples: Florence Shipek, "A Strategy for Change: The Luiseño of Southern California" (Ph.D. dissertation, University of Hawaii, 1977); Mary W. Helms, *Asang: Adaptations and Culture Contact in a Miskito Community* (Gainesville FL, 1971); Nancy C. Morey, "Ethnohistory of the Colombian and Venezuelan Llanos" (Ph.D. dissertation, University of Utah, 1975); Stefano Verese, *La sal de los cerros (una aproximación al mundo Campa)* (Lima, 1973); Robin Wright, "The History and Religion of the Baniwa Peoples of the Upper Rio Negro Valley" (Ph.D. dissertation, Stanford University, 1981); Branislava Susnik, *El indio colonial del Paraguay*, 3 vols. (Asunción, Paraguay, 1965–71); Branislava Susnik, *Los aborígenes del Paraguay*, 8 vols. (Asunción, Paraguay, 1978–87); Juan Friede, *Los andaki, 1538–1947: Historia de la aculturación de una tribu selvática* (Mexico City, 1953); Neil L. Whitehead, *Lords of the Tiger Spirit: A History of the Caribs in Colonial Venezuela and Guyana, 1498–1820* (Dordrecht, 1988); and Jean Marcel Hurault, *Français et indiens en Guyane, 1604–1972* (Paris, 1972).

10. Homer Aschmann, *The Central Desert of Baja California: Demography and Ecology*, Ibero-Americana 42 (Berkeley, 1959); Sherburne F. Cook, *The Indian vs. the Spanish Mission*, Ibero-Americana 21 (Berkeley, 1943);

48 David Sweet

and reprinted in *The Conflict between the California Indian and White Civilization* (Berkeley and Los Angeles, 1976); David G. Sweet, "The Population of the Upper Amazon Valley, Seventeenth and Eighteenth Centuries" (master's thesis, University of Wisconsin, 1967). The most detailed and suggestive reconstruction since Cook's of demographic decline in a frontier mission population is to be found in the series of articles by Robert H. Jackson on Alta and Baja California in the *Journal of California and Great Basin Anthropology* 3, 4, 5, 6, and 9 (1981–87), *Southern California Quarterly* 63 (1981), and *The Americas* 44 (1985). Work of this kind is notably absent for frontier mission populations elsewhere in colonial America.

11. Ann Lacy Stodder, *Mechanisms and Trends in the Decline of the Costanoan Indian Population of Central California: Nutrition and Health in Pre-Contact California and Mission Period Environments* (Salinas CA, 1986), p. 39, citing visitor Louis Choris, *Louis Choris in San Francisco 100 Years Ago* (San Francisco, 1913).

12. José María Arguedas, *El sueño del pongo y canciones quechuas tradicionales* (Santiago de Chile, 1969).

13. Cook, *The Indian*, pp. 47–48.

14. Michel Clevenot, "The Kingdom of God on Earth? The Jesuit Reductions of Paraguay," *Concilium* 187 (Oct. 1986), 72.

15. Jean François de la Pérouse, *Monterey in 1786: The Journals of Jean François de la Pérouse* (Berkeley, 1989), p. 82.

16. Maynard Geiger, O.F.M., and Clement W. Meighan, translators and editors, *As the Padres Saw Them: California Indian Life and Customs as Reported by the Franciscan Missionaries, 1813–1815* (Santa Barbara CA, 1976), p. 48.

17. See David G. Sweet, "Misioneros jesuitas e indios 'recalcitrantes' en la amazona colonial," in Jorge Klor de Alva, Miguel León-Portilla, Manuel Marzahl, and Gutiérrez Estevez, editors, *De palabra y obra en el Nuevo Mundo*, vol. 1, *Imágenes interétnicas* (Madrid, 1992), pp. 265–292.

18. Clevenot, "Kingdom of God," citing Jesuit Superior General Aguilar of the Paraguay missions, p. 73.

19. Francisco Figueroa, *Relación de las misiones de la Compañía de Jesús en el país de los Maynas* (Madrid, 1904), p. 123.

20. Alfred Métraux, "The Revolution of the Ax," *Diogenes* 25 (Spring 1959), 28–40.

21. Bannon, "The Mission," 315.

22. For a rare insight into the dynamics of an Indian appropriation from missionaries of elements of Christian thought in a later period, see Gonzalo Castillo-Cardenas, *Liberation Theology from Below: The Life and Thought of Manuel Quintin Lame* (Maryknoll NY, 1987).

23. Robert Archibald, *The Economic Aspect of the Hispanic California Missions* (Washington DC, 1978), p. 184.

Erick Langer

Missions and the Frontier Economy: The Case of the Franciscan Missions among the Chiriguanos, 1845–1930

The image of the Latin American mission conjures up ideal communities where friars kept the Indians working in the mission fields, tried to protect their charges from the nefarious influences of outsiders, and strove to maintain the mission as a self-sufficient religious, social, and economic unit. Much of the early historiography on this institution, with its emphasis on the mission founders' spiritual goals in the sixteenth century, reinforced this image. Two of the most influential writers were Robert Ricard and John L. Phelan. Ricard's classic study on the early efforts of the mendicant orders in central Mexico heavily stressed the ideals and enthusiasm of the friars without worrying much about the economic changes that the congregation of natives entailed. Phelan's study, *The Millennial Kingdom of the Franciscans in the New World*, reiterated in numerous ways the isolation the Franciscans endeavored to impose on the Indians in an attempt to keep the corruption of their countrymen from spreading among their charges. Even François Chevalier's seminal article on the founding of Puebla, in which he showed the difficulties the clerics had in creating an ideal society, counterpoised the ideals of a perfect Christian community with the ugly realities of colonial exploitation.[1]

A more recent current of mission history has tried to counteract

---

Research for this chapter was funded through the Fulbright-Hays Program (CIES), Maurice Falk Semester Leave Program (Carnegie Mellon University), the American Philosophical Society, and the American Historical Association, through its Albert J. Beveridge Research Award Program. This work benefited from the comments of Guillermo Madrazo, Heraclio Bonilla, and Robert Jackson.

the overwhelmingly apologetic historiography by examining old evidence more critically and proposing new ways to get at the realities of the mission experience. Rather than describe the motives of the missionaries or their views of the mission populations, the revisionists have concentrated on the effects the missions had on the Indians. Relying heavily on demographic data found in parish records, the new mission historians have emphasized exploitation and rapid depopulation due to epidemic diseases. These scholars have seen the mission essentially as arms of the European state, with horrifyingly high costs to the indigenous peoples.[2] According to this view, Indians were often forced to work and constituted the economic support in terms of both labor supply and food production for the settlers and the soldiers of the frontier forts.

Though much more sensitive to economic issues than the traditional and apologetic approach, the new mission history's economic arguments have played a subsidiary role in a framework that emphasizes the destructive relations between missions and indigenous peoples. This emphasis is probably related to the higher levels of coercion that existed in colonial missions than in the republican period.[3] Since most historians continue to focus on the missions during the period of Hispanic domination, the stress on coercion is an important corrective to earlier, often self-interested versions of mission history. Nevertheless, the debate over the relative benevolence of the mission system prevents an explicit comparative discussion of other important issues, such as the economic importance of the missions in the frontier economy. We must go back all the way to Herbert E. Bolton's path-breaking article, written in the early twentieth century and in many ways also very Eurocentric, to get a sense of how the mission was an essential part of the Hispanic frontier.[4]

How do we take into account the economic importance of the mission in Latin America? Was it a hindrance or an asset to the economic development of the frontier? How do we include, as social history and ethnohistory have rightfully rejoined, not only the European side but also that of the Indians? For such an approach, we must examine some closely related issues. First of all, what intensity of economic interaction did missions foster? Did missions aim at self-sufficiency or did they represent important economic enterprises that had repercussions within the frontier region? What level of exploitation of the indigenous population did the missions permit? How was this related to the survival of the mission population and the way in which the Indians were integrated into the European economy? And last, how were missions similar to and different from other frontier institutions, such as haciendas and military posts? Addressing these complex issues requires the study of specific cases to provide a basis for comparison. In this chapter I examine the Franciscan missions among the Chiriguano Indians of southeastern Bolivia during the republican period. These missions were founded in Tarija, Chuquisaca, and Santa Cruz departments by Italian Franciscans based in Tarija and Potosí. The Tarija missionaries founded Itau (1845), Chimeo (1849), Aguairenda (1851), Tarairí (1854), San Francisco del Pilcomayo (1860), San Antonio del Pilcomayo (1866), Macharetí (1869), and Tiguipa (1872).[5] From Potosí the friars established Boicovo (1875), Santa Rosa de Cuevo (1887), Ivo (1893), San Antonio del Parapeti (1901), and San Francisco del Parapeti (1903). The ideas developed here might serve as a model, or at least a point of dispute, for the examination of other missions, particularly during the republican era. Here I break the economy of the mission into its constituent parts, namely, the mission as a labor resource, as a developer of infrastructure, as a place of production, and as a market for goods. Then I compare the mission's efficacy with that of other frontier institutions. Since the mission's interactions in the frontier economy in each rubric depended to a large extent on the particular point in the mission life cycle, a brief discussion of this concept is in order.

The Mission Life Cycle and Economic Interaction

Most studies fail to differentiate the development of the mission after its establishment other than noting such events as the rise of political opposition to the mission regime. Historians have noted three periods in the life of the mission—establishment, mature functioning, and eventual secularization—but have tended to concentrate on only one aspect. This approach distorts the history of the mission, as events in different time periods and different stages of the mission are lumped together or actions in one phase are seen as typical over the life of the mission. Usually, historians have focused on the actions taken in the early phases of the mission life cycle, such as resistance to missionary influence or, conversely, the initial heroic efforts of the missionaries to get a mission running. The day-to-day life of the mature mission has often been ignored, especially outside the spiritual realm.

Only the new demographic historians have been sensitive to a differentiation during the period after the mission's establishment. For example, in the case of Alta California, the ethnic composition of the mission population changed as the mission aged, because as the original population died, the friars gathered new ethnic groups from farther afield to keep the mission afloat.[6] The concept that the missions changed over their lives in many aspects, in addition to demographic factors, helps considerably in understanding the economic significance of the missions on the frontier. I argue that this significance changes dramatically over time.

Two major factos are involved in the changing economic importance of the missions. First, the mission itself matures. Among other things, those indigenous peoples who survive adapt to their new circumstances, profoundly influenced by European models. They tend to speak European languages, adopt some imported customs (though often in creative ways), dress differently, and follow a new daily routine. The Indian population decreases usually, while members of other ethnic groups move in. Converts increase, their world view is at least partially modified.

Second, the frontier itself changes as non-Indian settlers arrive. The frontier becomes more secure for the Europeans, the economic basis of the region changes, and the state asserts more of its power. Clearly, both factors are related to the economic activities of the missions, where it is possible to discern significant changes. Thus, a sophisticated analysis of the missions' economic impact must take into account these changes over time. In this chapter I concentrate on three issues: labor demands, mission production, and the mission as a market for goods.

The Mission as a Source of Labor

The issue of labor usage of the mission population has been frequently examined, for it fits into the debate over the demographic impact of the mission in Latin America. Moreover, settlers often saw the missions primarily as a source of labor (at least at a certain point in the life of a mission), and much documentation has survived on the numerous disputes over labor among settlers, missionaries, and the government. Thus, many of the classic mission histories make mention of this issue, although it is usually treated by emphasizing the fight between missionaries and settlers over this resource.[7]

Labor demands and the mission's ability to add to the settlers' labor resources depended heavily on, among other things, the particular point in the mission's life cycle. Labor demands for work within the mission, for example, tended to be higher in the initial period after establishment, because Indian men were used both to build the various structures contained within the missions and to protect the mission from attacks by neighboring groups opposed to the mission's existence. This was the case in Santa Rosa de Cuevo. Two years after the foundation of the mission the Franciscans boasted of a town with two plazas (one for the neophytes and the other for the heathen) with neat rows of houses for all the families. In addition, the Indians had built a parish house, with "a spacious parlor, two comfortable apartments, two hallways on each side, and four rooms," plus a separate kitchen, pantry, and toolshed. The new mission church, thirty meters long and eight wide, was already half built by that time. The Indians had also constructed a school for the girls with two large classrooms with hallways, measuring twenty by six meters and seventeen by six meters, as well as two rooms for the female teachers. Only in 1892, five years after the founding of the mission, was the church completed.[8] The establishment of the mission thus represented a major outlay in native labor. The missionaries did pay the Indians for their work, but probably only minimal sums. Usually only after the Indians fulfilled the labor demands inherent in setting up the mission did they begin to work outside their new settlement with any regularity.

Important changes in the indigenous labor economy also occurred after the mission's establishment. The overall labor demands for male workers almost certainly went up. In the case of the Chiriguanos, women did most of the agricultural work; men were responsible only for clearing, sowing, and weeding the fields. In the missions, however, men also harvested the fields.[9] Building construction, for which the missionaries used exclusively male labor, was a new activity, which meant that Indian men had less leisure time than before. It is important not to overemphasize this point, for even before the establishment of the missions, the Chiriguano men worked in agricultural tasks, such as harvesting corn and other products, on the settlers' haciendas. Apparently, they did not do this type of work in their own villages, where it was considered women's work. Whether men found harvest labor on haciendas demeaning is not known. It is clear, however, that these labor demands outside the village economy and non-traditional labor for men existed before the establishment of the republican mission system. In fact, many of the Chiriguano groups asked for missions, because, among other problems, the settlers demanded excessive labor from the native villages. Once the mission was established, invariably the indigenous population had to defend itself from incursions by neighboring groups that considered the mission a threat. Thus, the men also engaged in the first few years in much warfare until the mission was, if not accepted, at least tolerated by those who refused to join. The process of acceptance was often a long one and depended on the relative strength of those opposed to the missions. The first missions established in the republican period, in the middle of the nineteenth century, suffered through more warfare and attacks by other groups than later ones. Thus the men were frequently fighting and away from the mission; until the 1860s the missionaries and frontier authorities had no choice but to permit the mission Indians to conduct their own raids on their enemies. Such was the case with the Tarairí Indians, who received permission in 1858 from the military commander of Salinas to make war on the Toba Indians, another ethnic group from the Chaco that traditionally preyed on both settlers and Chiriguanos.[10] Warfare was a traditional activity among the Chiriguano men and in that sense did not interrupt previous patterns.

The rhythm of warfare changed, however, once a Chiriguano group allowed the establishment of a mission. Before they were incorporated into a mission, Chiriguano settlements allied themselves with various groups (European, Chiriguano, or another ethnic group), often breaking their alliances when it was in their best interest. This tactic proved impossible once a mission was established, for then they effectively entered into a permanent alliance with the settlers. As a result, the manpower requirements for warfare shot up dramatically, because the government saw the mission Indians (*neófitos*) as a permanent source of auxiliaries for exploratory expeditions and the many campaigns against other indigenous groups. As early as 1832 the Bolivian army dragooned 180 Indians from Mission Itau to combat an invasion of Argentine troops.[11] The Daniel Campos expedition of 1883, which explored the Pilcomayo River to find a route to Paraguay, was also notorious (and caused much ill will among the missionaries and their charges) for its constant requisitions of men. Although Campos paid the Chiriguanos who worked as sappers, transporters of cargo, and cowhands, the hundreds of individuals he requested severely strained mission resources. Some *neófitos* died or sickened under the dangerous conditions and heavy workload; the continuous requests for more laborers during the planting season created problems as well. During this period the subprefect even required the Indians of Mission Aguairenda to hunt down ten deserters from the militia of a frontier batallion.[12] The conflict between Bolivian forces and autonomous indigenous groups was waged largely by Indians on both sides; the "national" frontier forces were primarily composed of mission Indians.[13]

After the initial phases of the mission life cycle, labor demands and work patterns changed significantly. As a new generation grew up in the mission and the demands of war lessened somewhat, the Indians began to use new agricultural techniques learned from the missionaries, and some became specialized in some nonagricultural skills. The mission Indians abandoned the digging stick for planting corn and successfully adopted European technology such as the use of teams of oxen and the plow. According to Bernardino de Nino, this change had occurred by the early twentieth century on the missions run by the Franciscans from Potosí, where the *neófitos* "are competitive with and even outperform many mestizo workers."[14] The mission Indians also cultivated European plant species. By the late nineteenth century a visitor to Mission Tarairí, for example, found that the Chiriguanos had their own groves of banana, lime, fig, and orange trees, as well as fields of sugarcane, rice, and cotton.[15]

New agricultural practices were only one facet of the changing work patterns on the mission. Erland Nordenskiöld, a Swedish adventurer and pioneering anthropologist, at the turn of the century decried the loss of old skills, such as designing pots and making traditional clothing.[16] Instead, the missionaries from the Tarija monastery taught the boys "tailoring, hat-making, carpentry, weaving, masonry, leather-working, ranching, mule-driving, pottery, [and] saddlery" in school, although the vast majority practiced only agriculture and ranching.[17] In Santa Rosa de Cuevo, under the jurisdiction of the Potosí Franciscans, in 1901 some young Chiriguanos were working as shoemakers, tailors, and leatherworkers.[18] The girls in the mission schools also learned European arts, such as "embroidery, trimming, weaving, and other tasks suited to their sex," which, as one missionary boasted, "can compete with those of the schools in the cities."[19] The girls apparently did not use their newly acquired skills once they left the mission schools, however. According to

Nordenskiöld, the Chiriguano girls found the flowers and other European patterns "too strange for their fancy" and so never wore the ornaments they had learned to embroider.[20] Possibly, the mission school experience led to a net diminution in traditional women's skills, such as pottery making, toolmaking, and herbal lore. These skills were passed on from mother to daughter; since the girls spent most of their time in school, they might not have had the opportunity to learn from their mothers.

The frontier also changed as the missions provided security to the ever-increasing numbers of settlers. More settlers meant more labor demands on the indigenous population. Though Indian men learned certain new skills beyond hunting and traditional agriculture and used them in the mission, the settlers near the missions were interested primarily in securing agricultural laborers. After the Indians defended the missions (and the settlers nearby) during the mission's early days, the use of *neófito* labor was of paramount economic importance to the Bolivian landlords on the frontier. In the case of the Chiriguanos, the need was particularly acute because the Indians tended to retreat from areas newly overrun by the colonists, leaving them with too few workers for agriculture. Thus, by the late nineteenth century the hacendados perceived the missions primarily as labor pools, to be used when cash advances and coercion proved insufficient for recruiting enough peons.

Unfortunately, the account books detailing how many mission Indians went to work on neighboring haciendas and at what wage rates, if they ever existed, have not been found. It is therefore impossible to provide statistics on numeric or relative importance in terms of workers or the time they spent there, although this type of work appears to have been quite common. Some evidence remains, indicating the significance of *neófito* labor. For example, in 1883 an expeditionary leader to the Chaco requested two hundred men from the Aguairenda mission. The friar could not fill this order, since "many found themselves occupied by Mr. Arce and J. Abenabar and by other Christians [i.e., landlords]." A few written requests for mission labor also survive, documenting the demand for Chiriguano labor. In some even the wage rates are specified, as in 1883, when the hacendado was willing to pay three Indians three *reales* and food to build a house and three others to excavate earth for the foundation, paying them two *reales* and food for a term of four or five days.[21]

The Franciscans regulated, apparently quite successfully, wage rates and prevented abuses to their charges.²² This involvement led to numerous conflicts between missionaries and settlers and much ambivalence from the latter over this issue. The hacendados on the one hand wanted unrestricted power over the Indians but on the other hand saw the necessity of keeping the missions in order to have access to enough workers. Since the Franciscans controlled 25 to 40 percent of the total Chiriguano population when the labor crisis became acute in the late nineteenth and early twentieth centuries, the missions' contribution to frontier agriculture must have been considerable.²³ Most of the land had been divided into huge estates, and few mestizo frontiersmen (and even fewer landlords) were willing to get off their horses and work the land with their own hands. Moreover, the other ethnic groups of the region, the Tobas, Matacos, and Choretes, were hunters and gatherers and made poor agricultural workers. As one Franciscan asserted, throughout the frontier region "the only *jornalero* [i.e., agricultural day laborer] . . . is the Chiriguano."²⁴

The only problem with this arrangement, from the European viewpoint, was that the Franciscans of republican Bolivia were not inclined to use the same amount of physical coercion that many of their brethren had employed during the colonial period. Initially, at least, the missionaries had to rule through the traditional chiefs. Only after many years did the Franciscans have a large enough number of converted Indians (most adults never converted) to assert much authority over labor recruitment. Even then, the friars did not permit any forced labor. Unfortunately for the missionaries and the settlers, it was precisely then that the Indians began to emigrate in large numbers to neighboring Argentina to work in the sugar cane plantations of Jujuy. *Neófitos* as well as heathen were prone to leave; in fact, it appeared that the young men of the mission schools, the future population of the mission, were most willing to go. Since the Franciscans possessed no means to keep their charges from leaving, the region lost many of its prime Indian workers. According to one source, by the early twentieth century the migrants averaged about 20 percent of the able-bodied male population. Although much of the migration was seasonal, many workers after a while simply remained in Argentina, exacerbating the already severe labor problems in southeastern Bolivia and seriously depleting the mission populations. Underscoring the importance of Chiriguano labor to the regional economy, by the early twentieth century the government defined the missions' primary function as keeping valuable Chiriguano workers in Bolivia. The missionaries, however, found themselves powerless to implement this goal, not least because the largely anticlerical Liberal party that came to power at the turn of the century slowly but surely undermined the Franciscans' authority in the missions.[25]

Production

The establishment of a mission brought about a change in production patterns as well. In the case of southeastern Bolivia, the trend of diminishing agriculture was reversed in favor of the expansion of the cattle economy. Bratislava Susnik has characterized the conflict between Chiriguanos and settlers as a struggle between corn and cattle.[26] Although this observation is more applicable to certain periods than others, especially in the nineteenth century much of the frontier expansion took place when cowhands drove their cattle herds onto the Indians' cornfields. As the Franciscans themselves recognized, the Chiriguanos requested missions not because of the presumed benefits of Christianity (as mentioned earlier, few adults ever converted) but because the missions permitted the Indians to escape the exploitation of the settlers and get their cattle off the cornfields.[27]

When the Franciscans founded a mission, they also reasserted the Indians' rights to their land and thus made it possible for the Chiriguanos to cultivate their corn unmolested. The missionaries aggressively rounded up cattle on mission lands and forced their owners to take their animals elsewhere.[28] After the establishment of a mission one of the first concerns was to make it self-sufficient in food production, and so agriculture was undoubtedly encouraged. It is difficult to estimate either food production or the amount of land given over to agriculture. In the only figures of land under production, for the Tarija missions for 1883, it appears that approximately seventy-two acres were cultivated in the entire mission system.[29] This amount of land was clearly incapable of sustaining the more than ten thousand Indians who lived in the seven missions. Presumably, the figures refer only to the land cultivated for the personal needs of the Franciscans or for distribution to widows and orphans and do not take into account the much more numerous private plots that each Indian family farmed.

The *visita* of Manuel O. Jofré of 1893 provides a more detailed picture of the extent of agricultural production in the missions. Jofré implies that the Indians cultivated lands apart from the fields that benefited the mission as a whole. In the case of Aguairenda, according to Jofré, the vast majority of the cultivated land was in the hands of the Chiriguanos: "Other than the three small kitchen gardens of the mission the Indians have thirty banana plantations, thirty-four sugarcane fields, and thirty-six orange orchards, other than plantings of less consideration, and their plantings of corn."[30] Although we have no useful information on types of agricultural production in the Indian villages before the founding of the missions (other than a list of "traditional" crops—but did the Chiriguanos also cultivate "nontraditional" plant species?), it is nevertheless logical to assume that the mission Indians cultivated certain European crops, such as sugarcane, more intensively once the missions were established.

Information on the extent of mission lands under cultivation should shed light on production. Unfortunately, land use data are too scattered to indicate with any accuracy changes over time. On the missions of Tarairí, Tiguipa, and Aguairenda, cultivated land varied between one-fifth and one-sixth of the total area, with the rest used as pasture. Because Machareti's land was not suitable for agriculture, only a few fields "of little consideration" existed. In all, on the three missions where figures are available, it can be estimated that in 1893 the missions and the Indians cultivated approximately 1,290 hectares, or 3,680 acres, a substantial amount in the largely cattle economy of the frontier. This extent of land had to feed the 3,344 mission inhabitants.[31]

Whether agricultural production expanded once the missions were established is a difficult question to answer precisely, given the dearth of reliable information. It is likely that initially agricultural production was emphasized, since the mission had to be self-sufficient in food and all missions among the Chiriguanos were founded on the sites of already existing villages. One might assume that as the missions began to lose population because of disease and emigration (the latter being more serious in terms of the labor supply, given the fact that able-bodied males tended to predominate among migrants), agricultural production decreased. That was not the case. Cadastral surveys provide spotty and somewhat unreliable, but nevertheless suggestive, information. In 1900 on Mission Santa Rosa de Cuevo the population of approximately two thousand worked 336 out of 50,625 hectares and produced 6,000 *cargas* of corn. In the same year on San Buenaventura de Ivo approximately one thousand inhabitants worked 225 out of 40,000 hectares and produced 1,600 cargas. For 1906, we unfortunately do not have production figures, but the proportion of population to acreage under cultivation is suggestive. Although the population on Santa Rosa dropped by a quarter, to fifteen hundred, the acreage under production increased by almost 18 percent, to 395 hectares. On Ivo a similar pattern can be discerned. In the same year, the population had been reduced by more than a quarter, to about seven hundred Indians, while the area under cultivation increased by one hectare, to 225.[32] The increase in productivity in the face of population decline (if area under cultivation can in this case be assumed to indicate productivity, given the lack of production data for 1906) was probably due primarily to the growing use of the plow and draft animals in place of the traditional digging stick.

It is not clear how much of the harvest was sold to outsiders and how much was consumed in the mission itself. We have few production figures for agricultural products (in contrast to the yearly livestock inventories), and those that exist are inadequate (for example, what else and how much did the Santa Rosa and Ivo missions produce in 1900 besides corn?). At best, Jofré's unusually detailed description of the Tarija missions asserts, for example, for the mission at Aguairenda that "one sees that the principal sources of income for the mission are the sale of some cattle, hides, animal fat, cheeses, and fruits, such as oranges and bananas."[33] This statement, frustratingly, ignores the mission Indians' participation in the agricultural market. Depending on the efficiency and productivity of agriculture (about which we have no quantitative data), there was probably a substantial surplus that was sold to sustain the rest of the region. Clearly, as the cadastral data show, the missions farmed much vaster areas than any other properties along the frontier. Since most of the mission fields were farmed by the families living there, to dispose as they saw fit, it is likely that the mission Indians helped feed much of the frontier population.

As is clear from the Franciscan records, cattle was not banished from mission lands; on the contrary, the missions maintained their own herds and other livestock as well. The few extant mission account books show that, outside clerical fees, the sale of cattle was by far the largest source of mission income. Unfortunately, the account books' notation system, in which the name of the buyer rather than the product sold is most commonly given, makes it impossible to provide accurate statistics on the sale of cattle. The only concrete numbers on the sale of mission cattle are available for the years 1877 to 1885, in which the Tarija missions sold a total of 2,801 head. Internal consumption used another 1,114 head, while theft and natural death took a toll of 1,563. In the late 1920s, after some of the missions had been secularized, one expert estimated that the missions sold more than 3,000 head of cattle a year; the primary source of livestock was Machareti.[34]

In view of the importance of this source of income, it is surprising that, unlike in agriculture, the Franciscans apparently did nothing either to improve the breeding stock of the animals that roamed the mission lands or to introduce more efficient ranching methods. The missionaries' numerous complaints about cattle rustling, committed first primarily by unconquered Chaco tribes and later by the mission Indians themselves or settlers, attest to the fact that there was little control over the herds. Losses sometimes mounted into the hundreds, but the missionaries felt powerless to stop this theft.[35]

The *neófitos* maintained their own cattle, independent of that of the missions, although they collectively owned fewer animals than the mission. According to the Jofré report, the Chiriguanos owned about half as many head as the mission herd; for example, on Tarairí the mission herd numbered 1,007 head, whereas the Indians owned only 660. Even at Mission Machareti, where there was little agriculture, the Franciscans controlled almost 2,000 head, while the Indians collectively possessed 705. Overall, in the four active Chiriguano missions of the Tarija convent, the mission owned 4,509 head of cattle; the Indians, 1,715. Typically, however, the Chiriguanos had more horses than the Franciscans, 626 versus 136. The relatively small numbers and the predominance of stallions suggest that horses were bred primarily not for sale but to provide animal power for agricultural tasks and, above all, transportation for their owners.[36] Mission animals and those owned by the resident families were about equally vulnerable to theft.

It is important to note that the cattle herds tended to increase on mission lands from the late nineteenth to the early twentieth century, paralleling the upward trend in cattle raising throughout the region.[37] The figures are suggestive: in the Tarija missions, cattle increased from 2,819 in 1883 to 3,997 only two years later, although some of this growth probably resulted from more systematic cattle roundups (*rodeos*). In 1893, despite severe problems with cattle rustling, the herds in the Tarija missions nevertheless increased to 5,897 head.[38] The missions founded by the Potosí Franciscans beginning in 1887 exhibited the same trend. In 1893 mission lands held only 1,405 head of cattle, which after four years increased to more than 2,000 head. By 1909 the mission herds had multiplied to 4,093 head.[39]

Apparently, this increase in cattle did not come at the expense of agriculture, although one might assume that as the population at the missions declined, the remaining inhabitants substituted agriculture for cattle ranching, a much less labor-intensive activity. Instead, productive activity appears to have intensified throughout the missions, offsetting the loss of workers, at least at the missions themselves. No wonder the settlers were more vociferous in complaining about the emigration of Chiriguanos to Argentina than the Franciscans, as the former suffered much more severely than the latter, at least in economic terms.

As noted earlier, the missions also trained the Chiriguano children in artisanal crafts, thus changing indigenous labor patterns but also introducing greater specialization (and so presumably greater productivity for the national market) among the Indian population. It is not possible to quantify the effects of this artisanal activity on the frontier economy, because of the lack of sufficiently detailed information. For example, virtually all missions made roof tiles, but the records suggest that the entire production was used for covering the Indian families' houses and the other mission buildings. Likewise, it is not clear whether the boys were competent enough or willing to use the skills in carpentry, shoe repair, tailoring, and the like that the Franciscans boasted they taught in the mission schools. Since what the frontier landowners (and for that matter the sugar planters in Argentina) wanted most from the Chiriguano men was work in the fields, most mission Indians probably did not use the skills acquired on the missions extensively.

Only two principal types of production found a ready market outside the missions, although both were secondary to the sale of cattle as the main source of mission income. These were distilling sugarcane to make brandy (*aguardiente*) and weaving. The former employed exclusively boys and was primarily exercised at Mission Tarairí. It is not clear when the distillery was established, but the Jofré report mentions it as an income source in 1893. Apparently, other Tarija missions also began distilling sugarcane but ceased doing so in 1905, when the Tarija convent authorities forbade it "to silence the grumblings against the Missionaries for the retailing of liquors." Only the distillery in Tarairí was permitted to function, and in 1908 new machinery was inaugurated. In 1912 the distillery was repaired again; in 1913 the sugarcane fields yielded one thousand Bolivianos (Bs) (presumably in the form of *aguardiente*).[40]

Information on the sale of weavings manufactured in the girls' mission schools is even more dispersed and difficult to quantify. In all missions the sale of these items is mentioned occasionally in the reports as a source of income for the mission itself. Given the skill level needed to create these weavings, it is likely that only the schools (and therefore the missions) that had been established for some time could produce a significant number. There were many girls available to do this work, but information is lacking on the ages of the school girls and the age at which they made weavings. In 1901, at the height of the missions among the Chiriguanos, for example, the Franciscans had 1,037 girls in their schools.[41] Even if only a third were capable of weaving, there would be a significant number of weavers. Since this activity remained very much on an artisanal level, however, with no attempts to systematize the weaving process, production was probably very low compared to that of the *obrajes* of the Andean highlands.

One way to measure the frontier missions' economic impact is to look at their incomes and expenditures. Unlike the Jesuits during the colonial period, the Franciscans did not attempt to create commercial enterprises out of their missions; instead, they aimed at subsistence. Their reports reflect this goal, although they did not take into account the economic activity of the mission Indians, which, as we have seen, was probably substantial. Thus the figures represent only a portion of the total circulation of money at the mission. As the mission reached maturity, the relative importance of its accounts in the total mission economy probably shrank, since the contribution of the mission Indians in all likelihood increased as they participated in greater numbers in the monetary economy. In any case, especially when the mission was established, the injection of money into the frontier economy as a result of the mission's organization was substantial. Unfortunately, the account books for the Tarija missions, founded earlier in the nineteenth century when the frontier area was much larger (and the economic impact of the missions more important), are not extant. The oldest records come from the Mission San Pascual de Boicovo (established 1875), where the Potosí Franciscans in the first twelve years spent 53,634 Bs and earned 54,009 Bs.[42]

One might hypothesize that as the missions matured, income increased, reflecting greater efficiency and the socialization of the mission Indians into European work patterns, while expenses decreased, since costs for infrastructure presumably went down. This hypothesis is not borne out by the figures. Because the Franciscans attempted to sell only an amount sufficient to cover their costs, their income and expenditures (both total amounts and per capita) fluctuated widely without any discernible pattern. Mission Santa Rosa de Cuevo presents a typical case study (table 1). Expenses and income were thus not directly related to how long the mission was established, the educational levels achieved by the younger generations, or the gradual loss of population.

The table is difficult to interpret, for mission expenditures and income appear to be largely immune to agricultural crises, inflation, or other economic or climatic changes. For example, during the last years of the nineteenth century and early years of the twentieth, when a series of droughts caused great hardship in southeastern Bolivia, per capita expenditures did not go up consistently. Perhaps the high expenditures of 1904–5 were related to this drought, but by then a normal crop year had improved conditions substantially. Likewise, there is little accounting for inflation, which was relatively high in the early twentieth century, for the friars had reached similarly high levels of expenditures and income in the last years of the nineteenth century, as they did during the subsequent period when inflation began to be a problem elsewhere in Bolivia.

The only trend that can be seen in these mission accounts was that as the population declined, it became more difficult to provide for a small surplus. Even this trend is not clear, however: for example, between 1907 and 1909 the friars were still able to earn almost 23,000 Bs —a huge sum for the area—despite the drastic population loss in the first years of the twentieth century. This suggests that the Franciscans maintained a large reserve of resources on the mission, to be used when necessary. It also helps explain the relative lack of concern over the theft of livestock. Since the mission possessed much more cattle than the friars would sell in any year, the theft was

Table 1
Population, Income, and Expeditures at Mission Santa Rosa de Cuevo, 1887–1912

Year	Population	Annual Income (Bs)	Annual Income per Capita (Bs)	Annual Expenditures (Bs)	Annual Expenditures per Capita (Bs)
1887–89	2,027	3,188.96	0.79	3,018.96	0.74
1889–92	2,137	8,450.50	1.32	6,550.20	1.02
1892–93	1,905	5,833.09	3.06	5,154.17	2.71
1893–94	1,908	2,003.65	1.05	2,041.90	1.07
1894–95	2,050	4,365.75	2.13	2,556.65	1.25
1895–97	1,984	12,911.05	3.25	9,479.75	2.38
1897–98	1,917	10,267.55	5.36	4,334.35	2.26
1898–1901	2,065	23,578.35	3.81	20,076.10	3.24
1901–3	1,614	8,485.30	2.62	8,617.90	2.67
1903–4	1,467	4,052.25	2.76	5,955.65	4.06
1904–5	1,589	12,200.70	7.68	16,072.24	10.11
1905–7	1,503	10,262.42	3.41	8,801.83	2.93
1907–9	1,225	22,852.70	9.33	21,561.04	8.80
1909–10	1,218	2,034.70	1.67	2,274.05	1.87
1910–12	1,416	10,147.91	3.58	9,191.44	3.25

Source: Santa Rosa de Cuevo, "Santa visita, 1889–1912," AFP.

Bs = bolivianos

not an important issue. Only in the twentieth century, when mission resources were dwindling, did the missionaries begin to complain more consistently about losses from their herds.

The theft of livestock might have been related to the increasing number of outsiders in the missions as they matured. The missionaries rented land to neighboring landowners and landless mestizos beginning in the 1920s, when the population decline left some mission lands underused. Since the missions controlled not only large numbers of workers but also some of the few sources of water, the rental of mission property was very advantageous to the tenants. However, according to the generally anticlerical Gran Chaco national delegates, the region's highest political authorities, the Franciscans did not promote this type of activity and by 1927 stopped the practice. By this time the government saw the missions as hindering the economic and social progress of the region.[43] To a certain extent that was true, for, unlike the Jesuits during the colonial era, the Franciscans in republican-era southeastern Bolivia never tried to make efficient economic units of their missions or provide much more than for the subsistence of their charges.

The Mission as a Market

As with most studies on Latin American institutions in the countryside, we know more about production than we do about the consumption of goods not produced by the economic unit, in this case the missions. I have suggested elsewhere that the Chiriguanos in the missions were important consumers and that because of their market participation the seasonal fairs of the Azero region thrived in the second half of the nineteenth century.[44] The evidence for this argument is unfortunately only circumstantial. The fairs increased in importance when the missions were established and declined when the missions lost their population because of emigration to Argentina. Coca, a stimulant grown on the eastern foothills farther north, was a significant trade item at these fairs. Chiriguanos today are known to be avid consumers of these leaves, and it is reasonable to assume that these consumption patterns were established during the period under question.[45] Unfortunately, we do not have any records from the petty merchants who lived near the missions. Cuevo, next door to the important Mission Santa Rosa, had twenty-nine merchants, according to the census of 1900. In Ñancaroinza, a tiny settlement on the eastern limits of the Chaco frontier but close to the mission at Machareti, there were twelve merchants. Carandaití, another frontier outpost, had nine merchants.[46]

What we do know is that the Franciscans spent considerable sums clothing the children in the mission schools in European dress. In Mission Boicovo alone the annual cost of providing clothes in the 1890s for the two hundred children was one thousand *bolivianos*.[47] Apparently, the efforts to change the clothing styles were successful, for the photographs of the missions at different stages of their life cycle show the Indians increasingly in Western dress.[48] This was part of the campaign to "civilize" the neophytes. As one friar from the Potosí missions explained: "It is necessary that the [Indian] forgets all that had to do with their savage and superstitious state.... With this goal in mind, it has been determined to have all the school boys and girls adopt the clothing of the Christians: the boys wear shirt, pants, poncho, and hat, and the girls use blouses, skirts, and *mantillas* just like the Christians of those regions."[49]

Moreover, the Chiriguanos were not at all averse to purchasing Western clothing when they left for the sugarcane harvest in northern Argentina. The missionaries complained frequently that those who returned to the missions had spent all their hard-earned money on new clothes and had also acquired some unsavory habits, such as a propensity for hard liquor, wife beating, and knife fights.[50]

The use of Western clothing was common by the early twentieth century among all Chiriguano men; according to Erland Nordenskiöld, "the Chiriguano and Chané men of the present day wear European clothes which they buy at the stores, get at the missions, or more often still, when working at the sugar factories in northern Argentina."[51] It is highly likely that the mission experience helped create the demand for ready-made clothing among the Chiriguanos, although the seasonal migration to Argentina, where the Indians received part of their payment in goods such as clothes, must also have been important. In any case, the missions presented the largest market (at least in terms of the numbers of customers) for clothing along the frontier. It is clear that by the twentieth century the Franciscans believed that the promise of clothing was a powerful incentive for remaining at the mission. In 1908 the missionaries used the distribution of coveted Western clothes to induce children to attend school; for example, the missionary in Tarairí promised that after Easter he would give "one pair of pants and one shirt to those who frequent the school daily."[52]

Clearly, the Chiriguanos at the missions became important consumers of goods from the national and international markets, particularly clothing and coca. This phenomenon was not confined to those who converted; in most missions throughout the republican period the unconverted outnumbered the converted. It is likely, however, that converts, usually raised in the mission schools, were the most avid consumers of Western goods. As the mission system matured, more and more Indians began to participate in the market as consumers of these types of products.

The missionaries, however, opposed what they considered an excessive and corrupting consumerism among their charges. Moreover, the friars saw that the Chiriguano culture mitigated against the accumulation of goods in a capitalistic manner. Chiriguano culture laid great importance on the sharing of goods, for in this way the gift giver received added prestige. Thus, when Chiriguanos returned from Argentina with goods such as clothes, horses, and donkeys, these items were often shared.[53] The Franciscans admired this cultural trait and did nothing to change it. The mission Indians often quickly spent whatever money they had accumulated but soon did not have much to show for it in material possessions.

Comparisons with Other Frontier Institutions

In most ways the missions had more economic importance than any other frontier institutions, including the newly founded haciendas and the villages that surrounded the small forts (*fortines*) scattered throughout the region. Only the haciendas, with their focus on cattle ranching, provided a significant economic impetus. How important were the ranch herds compared to those of the missions? Unfortunately, little information is available on cattle production along the frontier outside the missions; many landowners could not read or write, and most did not bother to keep records or such records were lost because of the climate or the unsettled conditions of the frontier. The few inventories found for this period suggest that ranchers practiced an extensive style of ranching in which the land was worth little in comparison to the cattle on it, a common pattern throughout Latin America and elsewhere in the world. A thousand or more head per ranch was probably not unusual, as in the case of Ranch Partiñanca close to Yacuiba, inventoried in 1899 and numbering 1,225 head of cattle.[54] The cadastral data for the same time period notoriously underestimated the number of cattle but are still suggestive. In 1906, for example, the cadastre for Yacuiba canton (where Partiñanca was located) counted only 893 head of cattle. The cadastres of 1906 for the provinces where the missions were located estimated a total of 61,406 head of cattle. Clearly, if the mission counts were accurate while the cadastral surveys were very low estimates (as is likely), the missions owned a relatively insignificant number of the total cattle in the region, especially when considered on a per capita basis.[55]

Other than in this respect, the ranches in many ways held back the frontier economy. Land grant documents indicate that petitioners attempted to gain legal possession over land that included Indian villages, which could be forced to provide labor for the new landowner. Settlers often greatly exploited the hapless Indians who remained on these tracts and refused to pay them adequate wages. This practice, of course, encouraged out-migration from the region altogether, to Argentina or elsewhere. The settlers therefore had to take much of the blame for the labor shortage. Instead of paying higher wages, the landowners resorted to getting the Indians into debt, providing legal grounds for the retrieval of any peons who tried to flee. In the poorly controlled conditions of the frontier more coercion was simply not an effective method in the long run. Moreover, the Indians who became hacienda peons could not afford the higher consumption patterns of the missions, for the landowners permitted them to maintain only a few plots to meet bare subsistence needs. Settlers rightly feared that if they allowed any more than that, their peons might buy themselves out of their debts and leave to work in better conditions.[56]

The *fortines* were not much better. In the early 1840s Manuel Rodríguez Magariños, the dynamic prefect of Tarija, had established some small forts along the Pilcomayo River. Presumably, the forts would be staffed temporarily by soldiers and later, when the area had been colonized, turned over to the local settlers. Events turned out rather differently, however. The soldiers refused to work as laborers in the small fields next to their fortifications and began killing Indians in an indiscriminate manner.[57] Other than a few exceptions, the forts were abandoned within a short period. Even in the 1880s, when the state could afford to maintain the forts more consistently, they proved ineffective in promoting much economic activity. The soldiers were chronically underpaid, often went hungry, and, as a result, deserted frequently. Out of thirty troops in Crevaux, for example, in 1893 almost half had deserted their posts.[58]

The only effective *fortines* were those established in the 1860s in the Ingre-Iguembe area and in the 1870s near Cuevo. Colonists had built these forts, and they contained no regular soldiers. The forts served only as refuges for the settlers during periods of warfare with the Chiriguanos, such as in 1874–78. Later traders and some ranchers settled next to the forts of Ingre and Iguembe and formed small towns known by the same names. Similarly, the grandiosely named forts of Bolívar and Sucre became the centers around which Cuevo was formed. A short period of town growth occurred once the frontier had been secured. In the late nineteenth century these towns briefly became important trading entrepôts in the commerce between Argentina and eastern Bolivia.

Soon thereafter, however, the push out into the Chaco depleted the towns of population. When overgrazing destroyed the pastures surrounding the towns, the settlers moved eastward. Thus, most of these towns did not have the same long-term economic impact as the missions. None became as large as the most important missions, rarely exceeding even for a short time a population of one thousand. Even then these towns often relied on the labor of neighboring missions. That was the case with Huacaya, next to Mission Boicovo; with Cuevo, a few miles north of Santa Rosa; and Camatindi, sandwiched between the missions at Tiguipa and Tarairí.[59] In sum, the towns had some economic significance as centers of commerce and as places of extension of creole influence. They were also vital parts of the frontier hinterland, for they represented permanent links to the national government and the national economy. Nevertheless, they depended to a large degree on the missions, as sources of both labor and consumers to buy the town traders' merchandise.

What then was the economic importance of the mission in the frontier economy? What does the specific case of the Chiriguanos reveal about mission systems in general? Clearly, the missions were integral parts of the frontier economy while the non-Indian population remained sparse. Two conclusions are readily apparent. One deals with the life cycle of the mission and the other with the importance of mission Indian labor.

First, the role of the mission in the frontier economy changed as the mission matured and the frontier moved farther outward. Initially, the mission was crucial in permitting the establishment of colonists' settlements. The mission Indians were essential auxiliaries in the fight against unconquered groups, as reflected in the colonists' settlements, most of which clustered as closely to the mission grounds as possible. In the beginning the Indians were occupied in establishing the mission economy—in other words, constructing often imposing buildings that made up the mission's physical plant, cultivating communal fields, and caring for mission cattle, as well as reorganizing their own production once the threat of land usurpation diminished. Thus relatively little labor was available for the settlers.

Once the mission was firmly established and the military threat from other indigenous groups had faded somewhat, the missionaries were able to fulfill some of the labor demands of the surrounding haciendas as well as devote their charges' time to the development of infrastructure such as forts and roads. Moreover, they trained a whole generation of workers in the mission schools; for the most part these workers were relatively highly skilled (possibly more so than most of the settlers) and were beginning to value the acquisition of Western goods. Nevertheless, many Chiriguano traits, such as the emphasis on sharing to gain prestige and the disregard for accumulating material goods, persisted.

As the mission matured and the frontier area was integrated more fully into the national economy, certain restrictions precluded the full development of the mission's economic potential. These restrictions, noticeable in the spheres of labor, production, and consumption, were inherent in the mission's purpose and eventually created serious frictions with settlers and local government officials. First of all, the missionaries mediated the relationship between workers and hacendados and so prevented the wholesale exploitation of the Indians at the hands of the settlers. The colonists objected to this intervention, especially because the missions represented the largest pool of indigenous labor in the region. Second, the missionaries did not foster much production beyond subsistence. The mission account books are eloquent testimony to this phenomenon, although they capture only one aspect of the mission economy. The mission kept out of circulation a large part of its resources and did not require the Indians to participate fully in the national economy. Although evidence suggests that the Indians themselves began to produce for the market, such production was not done systematically. Third, the mission did not become a free market for any and all traders, despite the large number of people assembled there (larger than any mestizo settlement). The Franciscans abhorred the crass materialism of the traders, mostly located in adjacent towns, and tried to shield their charges from many of the worst abuses. Thus, the role of the mission was a type of refuge for the frontier indigenous population, although it probably kept many more Indians in the area than if there had been no missions, in the long term also prevented the full use (and severe exploitation) of the indigenous population that otherwise might have occurred.

Like virtually all mission systems in the history of Latin America, as the Chiriguano missions matured, their populations decreased. In the Chiriguano case, this decline was related largely to out-migration rather than to extremely high mortality. The missions grew in importance as the Indian population dwindled, because they represented the last labor reserves in an area that was losing most of its indigenous workers. This situation created even greater problems for the missionaries. The settlers became more vociferous against the missions because the Franciscans refused to relinquish their protective role. The missionaries, acutely aware of and demoralized by the population drop, became even more recalcitrant against the exploitation of their charges.

Thus, on the whole the missions played a crucial role, especially at the beginning of the colonization process, by altering radically the indigenous economy and, after the first few years, making a much larger number of indigenous workers available to the settlers. Once the frontier had moved past the missions, the importance of Indian labor increased, but the restrictions put on it as well as subsistence-oriented production and low consumption severely limited the economic usefulness of the missions. As both the colonial and later national governments throughout Latin America recognized (in perhaps a less systematic manner), there came a point when the missions had outgrown their usefulness and the role of the missionary as the protector of the Indians was impeding the region's economic development. It is a tribute to the political skill of the Franciscan missionaries in the twentieth century and their dedication to the protection of the Chiriguanos that most of the missions in southeastern Bolivia were effectively secularized only after 1932, when the Chaco War brought about their physical destruction.

Notes

1. Robert Ricard, *The Spiritual Conquest of Mexico*, translated by Lesley Byrd Simpson (Berkeley, 1966); John L. Phelan, *The Millennial Kingdom of the Franciscans in the New World*, 2d rev. ed. (Berkeley, 1970); François Chevalier, "Signification sociale de la fondation de Puebla de los Angeles," *Revista de Historia de America* 23 (June 1947), 105–30.

2. The new historiography on the missions was inspired in large part by the demographic studies of Woodrow Borah and Sherburne F. Cook. See especially Cook and Borah, *Essays in Population History* (Berkeley, 1971–79), various volumes. This perspective is not completely new, of course, at least for Brazil. See, for example, Alexander Marchant, *From Barter to Slavery: The Economic Relations of Portuguese and Indians in the Settlement of Brazil, 1500–1580* (Baltimore, 1942). Much of the new mission history has focused on California, where an important debate over the canonization of Fr. Junípero Serra has brought the demographic question into the limelight. See, for example, James A. Sandos, "Junipero Serra's Canonization and the Historical Record," *American Historical Review* 93:5 (1988), 1253–69; Robert H. Jackson, "Patterns of Demographic Change in the Missions of Central Alta

California," *Journal of California and Great Basin Anthropology*, 9 (1987), 251–72.

3. Erick D. Langer and Robert H. Jackson, "Colonial and Republican Missions Compared: The Cases of Alta California and Southeastern Bolivia," *Comparative Studies in Society and History* 30:2 (1988), 286–311. James S. Saeger, however, has found relatively low levels of coercion in the colonial Chaco missions, where the Indians remained much more powerful in relation to Spanish society. See his "Eighteenth-Century Guaycuruan Missions in Paraguay," in *Indian-Religious Relations in Colonial Spanish America*, edited by Susan E. Ramirez (Syracuse NY, 1989), pp. 55–86.

4. Herbert E. Bolton, "The Mission as a Frontier Institution in the Spanish-American Colonies," *American Historical Review* 23 (Oct. 1917), 42–61. This is not to say that others, such as Marchant, have not taken the economic aspect into account. These authors have simply not made the missions' economic role their primary focus. The notable exceptions are the works on the Jesuits, in particular those of Nicholas Cushner in his trilogy on the Jesuits. See, for example, *Lords of the Land: Sugar, Wine, and Jesuit Estates of Coastal Peru, 1600–1767* (Albany NY, 1980).

5. The San Francisco and particularly the San Antonio missions had only a small proportion of Chiriguanos. These missions were dedicated primarily to settling the Tobas and Matacos, two hunting and gathering ethnic groups from the Chaco region proper.

6. Langer and Jackson, "Colonial and Republican Missions Compared."

7. This aspect has been developed especially for colonial Brazil. See, for example, Marchant, *From Barter to Slavery*, as well as Mathias Kiemen, O.F.M., *The Indian Policy of Portugal in the Amazon Region, 1614–1693* (Washington DC, 1954). This is also the central theme in Chevalier, "Significatlon suciale," although it is not strictly a mission history.

8. "Santas visitas, 1889–1912," pp. 2–3, 6, Archivo Franciscano de Potosí (hereinafter AFP).

9. Bernardino de Nino, *Etnografía chiriguana* (La Paz, Bolivia, 1912), pp. 207–9.

10. Erick D. Langer and Zulema Bass Werner de Ruiz, editors, *Historia de Tarija (Corpus documental)* (hereinafter HT) (Tarija, Bolivia, 1988), 5:224–25.

11. Cited in HT, pp. 264–66. Francisco Burdett O'Connor, however, claims in his memoirs that only eighty-four men were inducted into his Third Battalion. See Francisco Burdett O'Connor, *Un irlandés con Bolívar*, 3d ed. (Caracas, 1977), p. 234.

12. The correspondence between Aguairenda mission and the command center in Caiza is copious. See especially Archivo Franciscano de Tarija (hereinafter AFT), Gaveta 8. The order to capture deserters is contained in Eulojio Raña to Fr. D. Giannecchini, Caiza, 3 Aug. 1883, "Libro 20 Copia, Notas de la

Prefectura de las Misiones Franciscanas del Colegio de Nra Sra de los Angeles de Tarija que comienza el dia 7 de Abril de 1883–1890," AFT.

13. See Erick D. Langer, "Las 'guerras chiriguanas': Resistencia y adaptación en la frontera surboliviana (siglo XIX)" (paper presented at the Primer Congreso Internacional de Etnohistoria, Buenos Aires, 17–21 July 1989.

14. De Nino, *Etnografía chiriguana*, p. 241. Since the Potosí missions were founded in 1875, 1887, 1893, 1901, and 1903, the change from indigenous to European methods occurred within one or two generations. Again, it is difficult to measure if and whether exposure to European agricultural methods before missionization made the transition easier or if this transition had occurred in Chiriguano villages before missions were allowed to be established.

15. Manuel Jofré O. (hijo), *Colonias y misiones* (Tarija, Bolivia, 1895), p. 51.

16. Erland Nordenskiöld, *The Changes in the Material Culture of Two Indian Tribes under the Influence of New Surroundings* (1920; reprint New York, 1979), p. 201.

17. HT, p. 349.

18. "Santas visitas," p. 24, AFP.

19. HT, p. 373.

20. Nordenskiöld, *Changes in the Material Culture*, p. 178.

21. Quoted in Doroteo Giannecchini to Eulogio Raña, Aguairenda, 16 Aug. 1883, "Libro 20 Copia," p. 32, AFT. For labor requests, see Eulogio Raña to R.P. Fr. Doroteo Giannecchini, Caiza, 12 Aug. 1883, Gaveta 3, AFT. Also see Ignacio Estenssoro to R.P. Sebastian Pifferi, Caiza, 26 Oct. 1885, Gaveta 3; and Andrés Rivas to R.P. Fr. Bernardo, Caiza, Feb. 1886, Gaveta 8, all AFT.

22. Angelico Martarelli, *El colegio franciscano de Potosí y sus misiones*, 2d ed. (La Paz, Bolivia, 1918), pp. 210, 219.

23. See Erick D. Langer, "Franciscan Missions and Chiriguano Workers: Colonization, Acculturation, and Indian Labor in Southeastern Bolivia," *The Americas* 42:1 (1987), 310.

24. De Nino, *Etnografía chiriguana*, p. 237.

25. For Chiriguano migration to northern Argentina, see Langer, "Franciscan Missions," pp. 319–21, and Erick D. Langer, *Economic Change and Rural Resistance in Southern Bolivia, 1880–1930* (Stanford, 1989), pp. 142–46.

26. Bratislava Susnik, *Chiriguanos* (Asunción, Paraguay, 1968), 1:60, 214–16.

27. Langer, "Franciscan Missions," pp. 311, 316; Langer, *Economic Change*, pp. 127–8.

28. See, for example, Fr. Marino Mariani to R.P. Conversor de Tarairí, 16 Aug. 1876, "Libro en que se transcriven las Notas mandadas y recibidas . . . Fr. Marino Mariani, 1876," Gaveta 13, AFT.

29. "Libro 20 Copia" pp. 7–14, AFT.

30. Jofré, *Colonias y misiones*, p. 26. On p. 23 Jofré asserts that in all missions, the mission and the families living there have separate plots.

31. Jofré, *Colonias y misiones*.

32. Population figures are taken from "Santas visitas," 1901, 1907, AFP; production and acreage from "Rectificación del catastro de la Provincia del Azero. Libro registro. Año 1900," and "Libro de declaraciones (1900)," Cuevo, 49–55; "Registro de la rectificación del Azero. Año 1906," and "Libro de declaraciones (1906)," Cuevo 47, 48; all in Tesoro Departamental, Fondo Prefectural, Centro Bibliográfico Documental Histórico, Universidad San Francisco Xavier de Chuquisaca (Sucre, Bolivia). A *carga* equals about one hundred kilograms.

33. Jofré, *Colonias y misiones*, p. 28.

34. "Memoria que en ocación de las elecciones capitulares del Colegio de Tarija el Prefecto de sus Misiones de Infieles Fray Doroteo Giannecchini presenta," fs. 28, 29, AFT. Manuel Mendieta S., *Tierra rica, pueblo pobre: Por nuestras fronteras* (Sucre, Bolivia, 1928), pp. 40, 48.

35. See, for example, Documents no. 102, 103, 106 in "Varios documentos, 1866–1921, relacionados con las Misiones," Gaveta 8, AFT. Among the largest thefts, in 1878 Tobas stole one hundred fifty head of cattle from Tarairí and the following year two hundred fifty more. The situation did not improve; see Fr. Gabriel Tommasini to Fr. Santiago Romano, Tarairí, 1 Feb. 1907, p. 4, Gaveta 15, AFT.

36. Jofré, *Colonias y misiones*, pp. 26, 52, 59, 67.

37. For an analysis of cattle ranching on the frontier, see Langer, *Economic Change*, pp. 123–42.

38. HT, pp. 349–53, 386; Jofré, *Colonias y misiones*.

39. "Santa visita, 1889–1912," AFP

40. Jofré, *Colonias y misiones*, p. 52; Ven. Discretorio to Prefecto de Misiones, Tarija, 7 Oct. 1905, no. 7, Gaveta 15; "Libro de visitas, 1900–1912," pp. 215, 222, 224; both AFT.

41. "Santas visitas," 1901, AFP.

42. "Santas visitas," 1901, Boicobo, p. 2, AFP.

43. Julio A. Gutiérrez, *Delegación del Gran Chaco* (Santa Cruz, Bolivia, 1980), pp. 28, 69–70.

44. Langer, "Franciscan Missions," pp. 307–8.

45. William E. Carter, personal communication. For a more general discussion of coca consumption patterns in the Chaco area, see William E. Carter, Mauricio Mariani, José V. Morales, and Philip Parkerson, *Coca in Bolivia* (La Paz, Bolivia, 1980), pp. 67, 77. Carter et al. also reported that much of this coca is acquired through barter; apparently, the ranchers pay their workers partially in coca. Such payment corresponded to one quarter of the Chiriguanos' total consumption (p. 77).

46. Oficina Nacional de Inmigración y Propaganda Geográfica, *Censo general de la población de la República de Bolivia según el empadrona-*

miento de 10 de Septiembre de 1900, 2d ed. (Cochabamba, Bolivia, 1973), pp. 12–13.

47. Martarelli, *El colegio franciscano*, p. 221.

48. Volumes of photographs are preserved at both the Archivo Nacional de Bolivia and the AFT.

49. Martarelli, *El colegio franciscano*, pp. 209–10.

50. See, for example, de Nino, *Etnografía chiriguana*, p. 305.

51. Nordenskiöld, *Changes in the Material Culture*, p. 59.

52. Fr. Fernando Ambrosini to Santiago Romano, Tarairí, 28 Mar. 1908, p. 2, Gaveta 15, AFT.

53. De Nino, *Etnografía chiriguana*, pp. 79 n. 1, 125.

54. HT, p. 273.

55. "Libro 60, Comisión Catastral de Salinas, 1906, " Ct T68; "Libro de cuadros estadísticos de la rectificación del catastro del Gran Chaco, Año 1906," Ct T48, both in Tribunal Nacional de Cuentas, Archivo Nacional de Bolivia.

56. Langer, *Economic Change*, pp. 134–35, 146–55.

57. HT, pp. 282–83, 285–86.

58. Domingo Paz, *Informe que eleva al Supremo Gobierno el Prefecto y Comandante General de Tarija sobre la administración del departamento* (Tarija, Bolivia, 1893), pp. 25–26.

59. For the growth of towns and trade, see Mendieta, *Tierra rica*, pp. 39–40, 57–71; and Langer, *Economic Change*, pp. 138–42.

Susan M. Deeds

Indigenous Responses to Mission Settlement in Nueva Vizcaya

"These Indians are vagabonds and layabouts, with even worse vices that, taken together, make them vain, sneaky, faithless, cheating thieves and drunks." So wrote the missionary at Santiago Papasquiaro in 1731, more than one hundred years after the Jesuits initiated their conversion efforts among the Tepehuan Indians of northern Durango.¹ This pronouncement was echoed in 1793 by Viceroy Conde de Revillagigedo, who characterized northern mission Indians as "feeble, cowardly, vengeful, lazy, thieving and without ambition."²

Far different were the judgments of the early Jesuits who, on the threshold of their great labor in the north, forgave the Indians for what the missionaries saw as immorality and vices and even discerned virtue in their state of nature. "There was peace and concord . . . and freedom from deceit, fraud or trickery which is still so common in the more enlightened countries of the world." Such optimism often characterized the initial views of dedicated missionaries in the era of the Catholic Reformation.³

The pessimism of the eighteenth-century remarks indicates that the missionaries did not live up to their own expectations in imposing new cultural criteria on what they perceived to be a religious tabula rasa. It also suggests that the Indians had succeeded, to some degree, in thwarting the Spaniards' program. Nonetheless, there is little doubt that the mission regime brought considerable upheaval,

---

I thank the following persons who commented on various drafts of this chapter: Harry Crosby, Victoria Enders, and Karen Powers. I also acknowledge the support of a Northern Arizona University summer research grant for this project.

corrosion, and reconstruction to northern Mexican Indian societies. In this chapter I examine these processes in Jesuit and Franciscan areas of Nueva Vizcaya, chiefly among the Tepehuan, Tarahumara, and Concho Indians of northern Durango and Chihuahua. Although the mission system cannot be totally divorced from its ties to civil institutions and society, especially in the ways the latter made Indians and their resources more accessible to Spaniards, I do not focus primarily on issues of labor appropriation, land tenure, and demography, which I have treated elsewhere.[4] Instead, I consider the political interactions and power relationships that evolved within the missions themselves, in an attempt to analyze indigenous strategies for refashioning collective structures and identities in novel circumstances. This is a story not of a simple dichotomy between destruction and survival but of complex and diverse processes of subversion, accommodation, appropriation, invention, and obfuscation.

Although no single progression of responses to the mission regime can be applied to all groups, a general pattern is evident. Initially, Indians tended to allow missionaries to get a foot in the door. Often that was followed within a generation or two by rebellion intended to expel priests and civilians alike. When the futility of this tactic had been established, less aggressive types of resistance were combined with certain accommodations to the new regime. Scholars are increasingly exploring these patterns of "resistant adaptation" and "weapons of the weak" among native peoples and peasants responding to invasive colonial situations in other parts of the world.[5]

When Spanish miners and other settlers moved into northern Durango and southern Chihuahua in the last half of the sixteenth century, they found the area inhabited by several Indian groups (map 1). Among them were the Tepehuan Indians, who lived in the valleys and mountains of the Sierra Madre Occidental and its central plateau in northern Durango and southernmost Chihuahua.[6] To the north and west, Tarahumara Indians inhabited the plains, valleys, and canyons of central and western Chihuahua.[7] East and north of the Tarahumaras were the Conchos, scattered along the river valleys and in the deserts of eastern Chihuahua.[8] Of these groups, a significant number of Tarahumaras and a smaller group of Tepehuanes still survive as distinct indigenous cultures. The Conchos were assimilated by the nineteenth century. Other indigenous groups, such as the Acaxees, Xiximes, Humes, Guazapares, Chinipas, and Tubares,

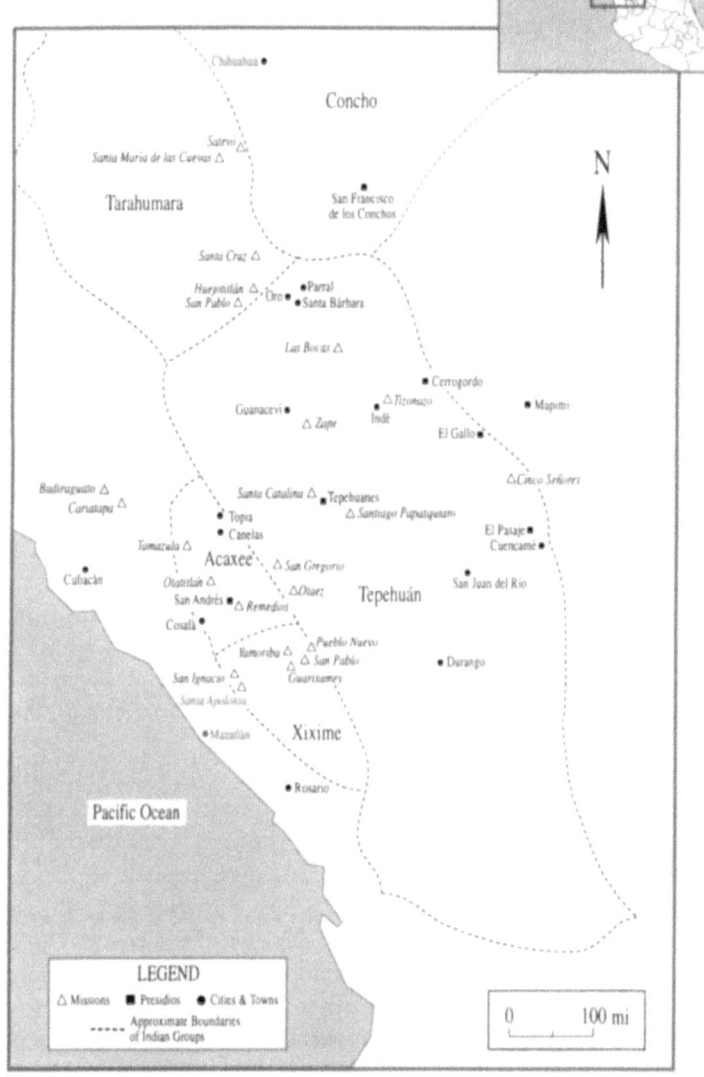

Map 1. Seventeenth- and Eighteenth-Century Jesuit Missions in Southern Nueva Vizcaya.

lived in the western escarpment of the Sierra Madre and eventually disappeared as separate cultural entities.[9]

What we know about the Tepehuanes, Tarahumaras, and Conchos comes largely from Spanish accounts and sparse archaeological evidence. From these sources, we can try to imagine a "pristine" moment in Indian history, on the eve of conquest. This moment must be seen not as static but as a point at which an ever-changing culture is captured and described. The Tepehuanes and Tarahumaras shared certain cultural and material features, although the Tepehuanes may have had more Mesoamerican affinities.[10] Both groups lived in *rancherías*, dispersed settlements consisting of contiguous households. Tarahumara *rancherías* tended to be smaller and farther apart than those of the Tepehuanes. *Rancherías* were located at irregular intervals, usually along a water source where the Indians practiced flood farming, cultivating maize, beans, and squash with digging sticks. Because these Indians were also hunters and gatherers, they found it necessary to change *ranchería* locations in accordance with seasonal cycles and weather conditions.

Most anthropologists assert that political organization was atomistic, with a headman and elders directing the affairs of each *ranchería*. These men have been characterized as moral authorities rather than political chiefs with executive powers. They were expected to promote the well-being of the community by inspiring consensus and exhorting their fellows to proper and wise behavior in public speeches, called *platicas* and *sermones* by the missionaries.[11] Ceremonial ties may have linked several *rancherías* informally, but only in warfare did supra-*ranchería* leadership emerge.

A divergent view holds that political organization among northwestern Mexican groups, especially in Sinaloa and Sonora, was more hierarchical and centralized, at least in the early sixteenth century, but that waves of epidemic disease, reaching the area before sustained Spanish penetration, caused these structures to collapse, leaving Indians disorganized and, in the eyes of the earliest chroniclers, very decentralized.[12] This hypothesis may have more validity for the Tepehuanes than for the other two groups considered here. Warfare was probably frequent, especially between the neighboring Tarahumaras and Tepehuanes; the latter were characterized by all early chroniclers as more warlike. There is evidence that the Tepehuanes had expanded their boundaries in the late fifteenth century, pushing west into Acaxee territory and northward into the Tarahumara. Tarahumaras expressed fear of Tepehuan warriors.[13]

War leaders were distinct from the moral/religious authorities who guided the community in peacetime. They earned their leadership positions by demonstrations of bravery and through magical shamanistic powers. Warfare served several functions, providing the opportunity to acquire supernatural power necessary for group welfare, material possessions, and female slaves. The Tepehuanes were known to demand slaves, along with corn and other commodities, from the Acaxees.[14]

Common cosmological features included belief in various stages or levels of creation, a flood myth, and dual supernaturals in opposition to each other.[15] Supernatural forces were associated with sun, moon, and rain. Idols representing these and other forces such as sickness and fertility were often found among Tepehuanes and only occasionally mentioned in the case of the Tarahumaras.[16] Dreams were a source of knowledge and power. Ceremonial life linked to agriculture and warfare incorporated the use of intoxicants as well as singing and dancing rituals. Ritual cannibalism was associated with Tepehuan warfare, and consuming parts of the enemy was thought to impart qualities of bravery. It is not clear whether the Tarahumaras and the Conchos shared this practice, although they used enemy scalps in purification ceremonies during wartime in a manner that resembled Tepehuanes' dances with the severed heads of their victims. Individual shamans had curing and prophesying powers. The dead were feared and thought to pressure the living to join them. Religious beliefs were inextricably linked with material survival, and supernatural forces demanded reciprocity in the form of sacrifices of food and even human life in some cases.[17]

Kinship organization was bilateral and centered in the cooperative economic activities of the extended family. Tarahumaras often lived in caves in kin groups; each head of household within this *parentela* had a discrete room in the cave.[18] Children were valued productive members of these cooperative nuclei and rarely needed to be disciplined by their elders.[19] Polygyny and serial monogamy were practiced, and leaders (*principales*) were more likely to have more than one wife.[20] Agricultural and gathering tasks were performed by both men and women, although hunting with bow and arrow and the collection of *mescal* were the preserves of males. Women were considered weaker and expected to be subservient. Men thought to be cowardly were referred to as wives and women.[21]

Archaeological evidence concerning the Conchos is more scanty. Although they were mainly described by Spaniards as bands of twenty to fifty persons (with scores of different names), there is some evidence that the Conchos were not solely nomadic but rather practiced limited agriculture. There were kinship and raiding ties across bands. Conchos also conformed to many of the cultural characteristics recorded for the Tepehuanes and Tarahumaras but were more loosely organized with even less sense of tribal identity than the Tarahumaras. The headmen of Concho bands tended to exert more coercive than moral leadership.[22]

The first contacts between the indigenous groups and Europeans occurred well before missions began to be established in the late sixteenth century, first by the Franciscans among the Conchos and then by the Jesuits in Tepehuan and Tarahumara country. In most cases, the early contacts were violent. Conchos and Tepehuanes were taken as slaves or assigned forcibly to *encomiendas*. Some Indians, including Tarahumaras, traded corn directly to Spaniards and even went to work voluntarily for brief periods in the mines of Guanaceví, Indé, or Santa Bárbara or on haciendas proliferating in the Valle de San Bartolomé.[23]

The haphazard appropriation of Indian labor was eventually supplanted by the creation of missions, or *reducciones*, that congregated Indians of several bands or *rancherías* in villages near water sources. This reorganization of space and land use was intended to facilitate production of an agricultural surplus that could be marketed to surrounding mines as well as to introduce Indians to Spanish norms of civilized life. The new pattern conflicted with indigenous emphasis on the importance of *monte* (wilderness) for hunting and gathering and threatened this locus of myth and supernatural power. According to the Jesuits, both the Tepehuanes and the Tarahumaras believed that when a person died, his or her soul went to the wilderness, where a beast (*fiera*) waited to take away those who had been bad and allowed the good souls to pass to a better place. The emphasis on the accumulation of surpluses clashed with indigenous custom, which, while not eschewing petty trade, embraced more immediate uses for agricultural production in consumption, gift giving, and supernatural offerings.[24]

Generally speaking, the missionaries' introduction of a set of governing officials disrupted a less hierarchically differentiated social structure and introduced new parameters for social and economic divisions within Indian communities. A note of caution is in order here. Recently, ethnohistorians and anthropologists have suggested that the widespread application of the concept of egalitarianism to indigenous communities should be reevaluated with a view to considering whether *principales* have manipulated it as an ideology to obfuscate the inequalities underlying their power.[25] Although we cannot be sure to what extent reciprocity, balance, and consensus characterized the indigenous extended kinship systems, the imposition of a new system by outsiders at the least encouraged new patterns of favoritism and uneven individual accumulation. Furthermore, the moral/religious authority of elders was called into question by the missionary, who chose assistants to aid him in religious matters (*fiscales* and *temastianes*) and influenced the selection of governing officials. The offices of governor, lieutenant governor, captain, and *alcalde* required selected Indians to exercise more coercive power.

Even when Spaniards chose these officers from among the chief elders, the latter were not accustomed to the roles required of them. Consider this description of the Tarahumaras in 1686: "The governors and *principales*, who are usually the most ladino in buying and selling in the name of others, are more like brokers or captains. In most cases, they simply make suggestions, and everyone does what he wants. Thus it is not enough to reduce the *principales*, but rather each individual in particular.... When the governor orders them to undertake any task, only love, not fear or punishment, will make them do it."[26] Many Indian officials were simply unable to reconcile the old and the new—especially when they could still call on support that derived from their previous prestige—and were replaced by more pliant individuals. These substitutions were often accompanied by the public shaming of those who had fallen into disfavor. Such acts as flogging or head-shaving were excruciatingly humiliating.[27]

Missionary attempts to eliminate warfare between traditionally hostile groups stripped entire male groups of their source of power and prestige, leading many of them to argue that "they would be better off to die like men, defending themselves in battle, rather than quietly accepting their fate like women." Christian virtues of kindness and mercy were perceived as emanating from fear and cowardice.[28]

Missionary emphasis on the sanctity of marriage and the nuclear family unit along with taboos regarding sexuality challenged existing male-female ties, reproductive patterns, kinship arrangements, and a social order based on reciprocal work relationships. Several missionaries commented on the sometimes violent reaction to attempts to eliminate incest and perceptively noted that prestige accrued not from material possessions but rather from the size of the kin group. Furthermore, by singling out children as more malleable converts, missionaries upset generational relations.[29]

The Christian concepts of sin and salvation required a greater emphasis on the individual than existed in societies whose religion and economy were based on the cooperative efforts of extended families. When Indians believed aspects of Catholicism were not inimical, they sometimes included them within their own polytheistic, encompassing views. They had more trouble with the priests' efforts to end ceremonial practices that reinforced social networks and allowed them to offer gifts to supernatural powers. All these groups engaged in drinking parties (called *tesguinadas* by the Tarahumaras today), consuming alcohol fermented from corn or agave.[30] Often these parties, or debauches (*borracheras*), as the missionaries called them, occurred at the coming together of *ranchería* groups to cooperate in work or to transact business. They also complemented ritual activities that centered on ensuring good harvests, promoting health, and honoring the dead. Missionaries were intent on ending what they perceived as displays of the devil's power and the sexual promiscuity, incest, and violence that often accompanied them. Among these missionaries, Father Joséph Neumann, compared by a later-day Jesuit to "a wrathful Moses discovering the golden calf," was particularly dogged in employing trickery and brazen intervention to destroy jugs of corn liquor and end clandestine late-night celebrations.[31]

Given all the potential for clash, why did Indians so often invite the missionaries to enter their territories? One of the answers lies in a demographic argument. In Nueva Vizcaya, contacts with missionaries always followed the arrival of other Europeans years before. This meant that epidemic diseases had begun to take their toll before the priests arrived, perhaps even before any Europeans, having been carried along pre-Columbian trade routes. One anthropologist has argued that what attracted Indians to the Jesuits was the latter's ability to cope with the terrible suffering brought by disease. Smallpox, measles, typhus, and other epidemics produced rates of Indian demographic decline similar to those in other areas of the New World, often reducing the population by as much as 95 percent within a hundred years after contact. Therefore, both the material and spiritual comforts offered by missionaries were enticing to groups whose socioeconomic and religious fabric was being ripped apart. According to this argument, the Jesuits filled a void and helped reconstitute native adaptive strategies in a period of immense stress.[32] The thousands of baptisms performed by missionaries in the early contact period at least indicate that Indians may have incorporated this act into their ritual systems as a possible protection against disease.

The demographic argument downplays some of the other reasons advanced to explain early peaceful acceptances of missionaries in Nueva Vizcaya. These center on the Indians' desire for the material benefits that would accrue from new farming and irrigation techniques, an expanded diet, and other material artifacts introduced by the Spanish. Furthermore, there was a relative absence of coercion on the part of missionaries in the beginning. Many Jesuits and Franciscans began their labors intending to teach by example, bringing in other paid laborers to dig irrigation ditches, plant fields, and build churches. These workers included not only local Indians but also Tlaxcalans and Tarascans from central Mexico: "Mexican Indians living among the Tepehuanes are of great importance in instructing them in proper conduct and in appreciation of and reverence for things of the church; this is because example [rather than reason] is more persuasive among barbarians."[33]

Although presidios were eventually established in Tepehuan, Tarahumara, and Concho country, in the early years soldiers did not constitute an effective coercive force over large areas. Only in the areas of earliest Spanish settlement around Topia and Santa Bárbara did settlers and soldiers wield sufficient power to begin assigning Acaxee, Xixime, and Concho Indians in *encomiendas* to work in mining and agriculture. In these cases, missions were perceived as an alternative or a means of protection from civil and military authorities. Military officers and missionaries often conspired to manipulate this impression by staging situations in which priests intervened to stop soldiers about to administer whippings and more severe punishments.[34] Protection from traditional enemies was another factor; the Jesuits reported that the southern Tarahumaras saw that missions could provide a haven from the Tepehuanes. Certainly, some individuals within Indian groups were willing to make greater accommodations in order to reap larger rewards, and all were attracted by the promise of a more secure food supply.[35] In the early period of contact, missionaries were usually more disposed and able to employ greater resources in gift giving and festive occasions.

Finally, one is struck when reading Jesuit accounts of conversions by the zeal with which missionaries threw themselves into combat with the devil, who took the human form of Indian *hechiceros*.[36] Jesuits contrived quite deliberately to show that the magic and miracles they could work were far more powerful than those of shamans. Their reports are replete with accounts of daily battles intended to upstage these *hechiceros*.[37] Judging from the number of reported successes from prayers bringing rain in times of drought, causing torrential rains to stop in times of flood, and striking witches dead, missionaries either were especially lucky in enlisting the cooperation of the elements or failed to mention the occasions when divine power did not heed their call.

In the beginning Jesuits also capitalized on Indian perceptions that conversion might protect them from illness. Smallpox and other diseases continued to take their toll indiscriminately among the newly baptized and the unconverted, however, and over time the association of conversion with death was strengthened by the Jesuits' zeal to baptize and confess those who were dying.[38] Although missionaries could construe death by disease as God's vehicle for selecting the most devoted converts for heaven, Indian shamans explicitly tried to use the correlation between baptism and death in inciting rebellion, averring that "the fathers had brought them pestilence and death with baptism because after they are baptized, they fall ill and die."[39] Jesuit and Indian perceptions found little common ground in another arena as well. Although they had been cautious about the use of force in the beginning, the fathers increasingly elected to punish backsliders by flogging.[40] Their targets had difficulty appreciating that this painful and humiliating experience was intended to save them from a worse fate of eternal damnation.

Whatever the reasons for the initial acceptance of missionaries, within twenty to forty years after resettlement (*congregación*) all the Nueva Vizcayan Indian groups participated in what might be called first-wave or first-generation revolts. The Acaxee and Xixime of the eastern Sierra Madre rebelled in 1601 and 1610 after a generation of mining *encomiendas* and mission establishments in Topia.⁴¹ In the most serious of these revolts the Tepehuanes rebelled in 1616, attracting Acaxees, Xiximes, Conchos, and Tarahumaras to their side. Before the rebellion was crushed in 1620, nearly three hundred Spaniards (including eight missionaries) and more than a thousand Indians lost their lives.⁴² Conchos rebelled again in the 1640s. Tarahumara rebellions in 1648, 1650, 1652, and the 1690s followed the establishment of Jesuit missions first in the southern and eastern Tarahumara country (Tarahumara Baja) in the 1630s and later (1670s) in the more rugged mountainous terrain to the west (Tarahumara Alta). These revolts also attracted recalcitrant Indians among the neighboring groups that had mostly submitted to the mission regime.⁴³

All these seventeenth-century rebellions were postconquest responses to the first serious demographic invasions by Spaniards and to the labor demands and social and psychological devastation brought by the intruders. In several cases, rebellions were preceded by famine and epidemic that cast doubt on the effectiveness of the fathers' power to control supernatural forces. Indians came to associate the ringing of church bells with death. Insurrections were fomented by leaders who still had access to knowledge of native magic and ritual but who often invoked Christian symbols of temporal power (bishops, popes, kings) to legitimize their actions even as they desecrated supernatural symbols such as crosses, altar ornaments, and church bells. Selective and pragmatic borrowing was not unusual for peoples accustomed to polytheism. Nearly always fueled by utopian or millenarian ideas, leaders promised resurrection to those Indians who died in the fighting and an abundance of foodstuffs for all. Witches prophesied that "even the pines would bear squash and corn." The rebels rarely discriminated in their targets, vowing to kill all Spaniards, civilians and clerics alike. Their goal was to obliterate the intrusive presence and to return to a state of affairs that, though unpredictable, seemed more amenable to their own attempts at regulation and balance through familiar and reassuring ritual activity. In particular, they sought to revitalize those ritual practices that reinforced social networks and familiar kinship structures.⁴⁴ Jesuit insistence on the elimination of polygyny and drinking parties was simply incomprehensible.⁴⁵

In no case did the first-wave rebellions rid whole Indian societies of the Spanish presence, although the Tepehuan revolt seriously threatened the Nueva Vizcayan mining economy for several years.

Paradoxically, rebellions owed part of their organizational success to the coherence imposed by the mission system on previously disaggregated settlement patterns. Spaniards found it useful to weaken cohesion at the state level among the peoples of central Mexico, but they were frustrated in dealing with the more loosely identified northern groups and encouraged them to form stronger intertribal ties, even naming captains-general for the entire Tarahumara and Tepehuan nations.[46]

After the desperate first-generation millenarian rebellions demonstrated the futility of attempting to expel the invaders by force, it was clear that other strategies would have to be substituted. Warfare could no longer be a means of reinforcing group solidarity. Furthermore, daily subsistence demands discouraged collective protest. Mission Indians in Nueva Vizcaya responded in a variety of ways, ranging from partial accommodation or constructive collaboration to passive resistance or resistant adaptation, and less frequently to active resistance—in this case, expressed in flight and raiding rather than widespread rebellion.[47] A closer look illustrates this continuum of responses.

Partial accommodation was linked to the issue of perceived benefits. This response, of course, varied according to the status of the Indian. Indian officials chosen by or with the blessing of the priest served as middlemen who had to try to persuade their fellows to conform to the new economic and religious regime. They gained the most from Spanish distribution of goods and perhaps even kickbacks that accrued to the missions for each Indian supplied in *repartimiento* (forced labor draft).[48] Whether they passed on any of these benefits to others is not clear, since we know practically nothing about cargo systems (ritual redistribution of wealth related to community fiestas) in the colonial north. There is evidence that some Indian officials tried to extract certain commodities from the people they governed.[49]

The scant evidence indicates that the first village officials may have been former wartime leaders (thus helping explain why the leadership of the early revolts often included Indian governors and captains) but that later the missionaries chose from among those most willing to do their bidding and even from non-Indian *castas* (mixed-race groups). In both cases, these were individuals with less or no loyalty to any indigenous standard of moral economy.[50] By the third quarter of the eighteenth century this practice was widespread.

In defending himself against Tarahumara complaints that he had appointed an Apache as governor of Tutuaca, the Jesuit Joaquín Trujillo argued that it was indispensable that such recalcitrant Indians be governed by outsiders and that many missions had governors who were *coyotes* (race term for people of mixed ancestry), *mulatos*, and Indians of other nations.[51] Certainly, there were cases in which Indian governors refused to comply with Spanish requests and others in which governors were attacked by their own people when the exactions were excessive.[52] The case of the Conchos, among whom the Spaniards had their earliest successes in labor appropriation, lends credence to the idea that band leaders were able to exercise more coercive power. Forced labor drafts seem to have coincided with bands whose chiefs were adept at delivering labor.[53] For this reason, Concho missions staffed by Franciscans were never very numerous or stable.

Indian military auxiliaries, who supplemented Spanish militias and presidial soldiers in times of crisis or warfare, also benefited disproportionately. Concho Indians, the Tlaxcalans of the north, were particularly used for this purpose, but others including Tarahumaras and Tepehuanes were also conscripted to put down rebellions and sometimes fought against their own people. They were paid for these services in money and in kind, and the families of Indian soldiers who died in battle sometimes received compensation.[54] Spanish officials explicitly recognized this role, as a report of the viceroy's advisory council on matters of warfare demonstrates. It listed Concho, Tarahumara, and Tepehuan villages from which Indian auxiliaries had been recruited and suggested that these allies be well paid for their services in warfare and as spies in their own communities to warn of impending problems and thus ensure the steady flow of labor to mines and haciendas.[55]

Aside from these categories of officials and auxiliaries who received special benefits from Spanish rule, a broader stratum was willing to collaborate where material advantages were widespread. Aware of this connection, the missionaries deliberately employed their material resources in gift giving. Often they were aided in the beginning by generous gifts of livestock from viceregal authorities.[56] Everyone probably benefited from dietary changes, especially from the introduction of meat protein, wheat, fruit, and vegetables.[57] Although some scholars argue that the traditional Indian diet of corn, beans, and squash was not much affected by the production of wheat, vegetables, fruits, chicken, and eggs, there is evidence that mission Indians did consume these non-native products. Chocolate was popular, and missionaries ordered large quantities of it annually from central Mexico. All the missions raised livestock, wheat, corn, and beans.[58] Fiestas, at least, provided the occasion for the consumption of beef, which according to the missionaries became very popular. Indians were known to trade horses for cattle; in other cases, they simply stole them.[59]

The degree to which Indians had control of these resources is not very clear. In the seventeenth century Indian *cofradías*, confraternities dedicated to the cult of patron saints, developed almost exclusively in those missions that experienced imports of Nahua speakers from central Mexico.[60] In the eighteenth century *cofradías* appeared in mission villages that had substantial non-Indian populations. In some parts of Mexico *cofradías* allowed Indians to husband and consume resources that might have otherwise been extracted from the community.[61] We know very little about the *cofradías*, which existed in perhaps a third of the mission communities, but some possessed (mostly without title) small livestock ranches, which produced meat consumed in saints day celebrations.[62] Most were described as very poor with few assets. We know nothing about their internal political and economic structure except that members (male and female) took annual turns in planning and participating in saints day fiestas. Women, in particular, were responsible for cleaning the church and performing ritual tasks.[63] Complaints from missionaries in the eighteenth century told of Indians going out to solicit for *cofradías* as far away as Culiacán and Chihuahua and then consuming the few pesos they collected in drunken parties. Religious authorities believed that *cofradías* provided a cover for the resurgence of idolatrous practices, manifested in ritual drinking and dancing. Reportedly, *cofradías* failed to live up to their obligations of providing wax for candles and paying for masses, indicating that missionaries were frustrated in their attempts to make them a source of remuneration.[64]

Although mission lands were communal, family units enjoyed the fruits of the individual plots they worked. Other lands (either those that fell within the mission boundaries or additional parcels acquired later by purchase or donation) were worked by Indians to support the missionary and the church.[65] For the most part, aside from the crops raised on their own small plots, Indians were dependent on the missionary to provide other, nontraditional foods.

Technological improvements also benefited those mission Indians who survived epidemic disease. Although flood irrigation techniques were used before the Spanish arrived, missionaries introduced more sophisticated ditch irrigation systems (*acequias*). Iron tools such as knives and agricultural implements made everyday tasks easier. Again, we cannot be sure how extensively these goods were distributed, but judging from the *memorias* (lists of commodities ordered by the missionaries annually from Mexico City), certain items such as knives, axes, and hoes were popular.[66] Cloth and shoes were also widely distributed. This gift giving by priests undoubtedly encouraged partial collaboration by the recipients. Although the pre-Columbian patterns of exchange are not clear, there are indications that petty trade and acquisitiveness were not alien to mission neophytes. The missionaries frequently remarked on Tarahumara trading acumen and desire for Spanish goods. "The Tarahumaras are docile, sociable, and addicted to bartering . . . for a needle, an Indian [will trade] two hens; for a knife, two ewes or a lamb . . . and for a measure of cloth, a horse."[67] The lure of material goods had been manipulated by Spaniards for some time; it was the basis of the peace-by-purchase policy that had already proved successful in the aftermath of the sixteenth-century Chichimec wars.[68] In addition to gift giving, missions also provided some training in smithing and building. Tarahumaras, especially, were willing to contribute labor to the mission enterprise, provided they were compensated in material goods. When these were not forthcoming, the Indians were apt to seek remunerated work elsewhere.[69]

The willingness to collaborate is most understandable in the material arena. The accommodations that took place in the religious realm are more difficult to explain. Participation in religious dramas, processions, dances, and fiestas had obvious material benefits, and these events commanded the greatest attendance.[70] Holy Week, Christmas, and saints days were the most popular occasions for congregating and feasting. Despite the relative absence of *cofradías* in mission pueblos that remained more strictly Indian in ethnicity, religious sodalities (such as those of the Tarahumara that sponsored *matachín* dancers) were formed to dramatize events during major fiestas.[71] The *matachín* dances were introduced by the Jesuits to teach about the Christian triumph over the Aztecs, but over time they took on other significance and were performed during the Christmas season and on other occasions. Also introduced were Easter-cycle dramatizations of the passion of Christ, which included representations of Pharisees, Judases, Moors, and soldiers. Missionaries used music, vocal and instrumental (violins, drums, flutes, and bells), to foster participation in festivals and attendance at catechism.[72] Fiestas were even more popular when they coincided with precontact rituals performed at significant times in the agricultural cycle. Certain precontact practices were conflated with Catholic rituals; for example, missionaries lamented that the use of ashes on Ash Wednesday was associated with face-painting for native ceremonies and commented that the frequent practice of self-flagellation as penitence seemed excessive.[73] Indians also identified God and the Virgin Mary with the dual supernatural forces (male/female) that they associated with the sun and the moon. According to the Jesuits, both the Tepehuanes and Tarahumaras had a concept of soul (although very different from Christian beliefs). To what extent it was modified by new teachings is not clear.[74]

A significant number of Indians listened to the priest on matters of Christian doctrine and sacraments, but responses varied widely. Missionary preaching frequently met with laughter, derision, and mockery from adults. Priests were more aggressive in pushing catechism of children and the sacraments of baptism and marriage. In the missions where Indians actually took up residence, parents did allow their children to attend catechism, even though such attendance could disrupt the division of labor within families. Furthermore, disobedient children were occasionally physically punished by missionaries, provoking outrage from parents, who avoided public confrontation and judging others and who must have felt terribly frustrated that they could not protect their own children.[75] Children were often kept overnight in the church for sustained instruction, and each missionary had several acolytes who performed a variety of religious and serving tasks.

Most Indians overcame their fear of churches as places where Spaniards buried their dead (*casas de los muertos*). Before contact they abandoned dwellings in which people had died and performed rituals to keep the dead from spiriting them away.[76] Although early dissidents who participated in revolts often tried to connect baptism with epidemic disease and death, eventually most Indians conceived of it as ensuring additional protection, both spiritual and material, in the form of godparents, and complained when the priest was unable to perform this service before an infant died. The concept of baptism may have been more readily accepted by natives who had precontact initiation rites for adolescents.[77] The church's insistence on marriage eventually met with at least nominal compliance by mission residents, although Indians often lied about the degree of consanguinity involved in a match, and many continued to take other partners informally.[78] Sometimes women, in marriages that had been forced by missionaries, aborted pregnancies started with other partners by drinking herbal potions.[79] Yet a significant degree of compliance characterized the sacraments connected with key points in the life cycle.

On the other hand, confession and communion were less easily comprehended. Many Jesuits did not aggressively encourage Indians to partake of the Eucharist, arguing that they were not sufficiently indoctrinated. Confession was required annually, but Jesuits often lamented that confessions were marred by denials and falsehoods. In these more abstract areas of Christian dogma the problems of translation posed greater obstacles. This situation was partially overcome by the eighteenth century for most of the Tepehuanes and Conchos, who were also fluent in Spanish, but not as easily in the case of the western Tarahumaras. Even in the eighteenth century missionaries often complained that women were less likely to fulfill the minimum requirement of confessing once a year. Communion was not celebrated widely, but the variations seem to have depended not so much on the capacity of the Indians as on the leniency and language ability of the priest.[80] Missionaries were more likely to ignore the fusion of native and Catholic beliefs when it did not conflict with basic doctrine, a practice that occasioned critical remarks from Spanish officials.[81]

Indians also took advantage of the priests' curing powers. In some cases, Spanish medical practice was more effective than that of shamans and native healers. The most common indigenous curing rites involved the magical extraction of foreign objects from the body through the sucking of wounds and sores. The devastation of epidemic diseases proved the inefficacy of these means and encouraged a greater fear of sickness. During epidemics Indians reportedly abandoned the very ill.[82] By administering food and water, Jesuits kept at least some of them alive. Although missionaries did learn which Indian remedies were effective and used them, they also kept supplies of herbs and powders sent from Mexico City to treat various ailments.[83] Just as priests manipulated one-on-one confrontations with shamans to establish their superior supernatural connections, they occasionally produced timely remedies to discredit individual curing specialists.

Where there were practical reasons for cooperating, Indians were likely to adapt to Spanish innovations, but the degree of accommodation was also strongly correlated with the strength of coercive mechanisms. Here the links between missions and civil society are important, particularly in terms of labor coercion. It is no coincidence that the Tepehuanes, Conchos, and lower Tarahumara Indians, who lived in the areas of densest Spanish settlement and greatest Spanish military force, proved to be the most adaptive. Missionaries did not always assert themselves as buffers against encroachments on Indian labor and land and sometimes collaborated with non-Indian neighbors. Acculturation was also furthered by a rapidly growing racial mixing (mestizaje) that seriously undermined the Indianness of mission villages by the eighteenth century.[84] The shifts in ethnicity do not necessarily imply cultural change, but descriptions by Spanish observers beginning in the second quarter of the eighteenth century suggest that in all the Tepehuan and some of the lower Tarahumara villages, recent mestizo and mulatto arrivals were engendering new behavioral patterns (usually described as pernicious and vice-ridden) as well as accelerating the rate of racial mixture. Ecclesiastical and crown officials argued that many of the missions should be secularized because they no longer possessed the unadulterated indigenous characteristics that conferred mission status.[85] A more detailed study of these villages in the late eighteenth and early nineteenth centuries, drawing on parish and notarial records, would shed more light on their ethnic and cultural makeup and help us understand the transition from indigenous to peasant economies.[86] But even without this information we can make some observations regarding strategies, whether devised by biological Indians or by mestizos, that retained some culturally Indian features in attempting to thwart incorporation.

There was always at least some measure of social space outside the purview of the missionary in which villagers could manipulate and construct strategies of passive resistance. Often in the period of first contact with Indian *rancherías* missionaries would be told day after day to come back later, or the Indians would suspend their hospitality and suddenly stop providing food to the would-be proselytizers. Native elders who correctly associated Spanish intrusion with labor requirements argued that they could not become Christians because they were too old to work. Missionaries also experienced frequent slights and manifestations of disrespect, enduring derisive laughter and name calling. They were extremely frustrated by customary Indian refusal to engage in debate on the source of cosmic power. In this early period missionaries often feared for their lives, especially as Indians became more aggressive during drinking parties. As one missionary expressed it, "We dwell like sheep in the midst of wolves."[87]

As time went on, even in the most acculturated villages, foot dragging, evasion of or minimal compliance with communal labor obligations, and dissimulation continued to confound the missionaries.[88] In the eighteenth century Jesuits complained bitterly of the sloth and perversity of Indians. The following description is not atypical: "The Indians of the sierra are predominantly *ladinos*—lazy, impertinent, and badly influenced by Spaniards. They barely attend to the needs of their missions, planting 3 or 4 *almudes* of corn, and this only in some missions.... In sum, they are without shame, without fear, and without respect. We have learned from experience that the only way to live with them is to expect nothing."[89]

These "weapons of the weak" enabled Indians to thwart mission goals of producing agricultural surpluses, which had little justification in their own rationale. When Indians did have extra produce to market, they often went around the priest and sold it to traders/brokers (*rescatadores*). The Tarahumaras were particularly adept at bartering corn for cloth with Spanish traders.[90] Mission cattle that ran wild were frequently pilfered by their own villagers as well as by outsiders. Theft could be rationalized in several ways. Wild cattle were seen as fair game, and Indians could understand the justice in appropriating livestock that destroyed their *milpas* (plots) or stealing a few head here and there when priests did not meet their obligations in remunerating labor or supplying gifts. What was perceived by the Jesuits as discretionary gift giving often became established in the minds of natives as entitlements.[91]

When the missions failed to provide sustenance because of drought, disease, neglect of lands (often due to prolonged absence in labor drafts), and collaboration of the missionaries with the civil society, their inhabitants not only pilfered but also went out and foraged, surviving because they had never lost their knowledge of wild food sources.⁹² The most frequent complaint of eighteenth-century missionaries was that Indians rarely resided permanently in the missions.

Finally, when Indians perceived that the missionary could not or would not sufficiently protect them against labor demands and land encroachments from outside, they had a variety of possible remedies, many of which were offered by their very oppressors. The villages most exposed to outsiders learned to appeal to civil authorities directly, against their own priests and other Spaniards. Some Indian families left the missions to seek more permanent work on haciendas. Others actively sought mestizo or mulatto marriage partners who had moved into their communities from the earliest days of their founding and had greater access to resources and fewer restrictions on their mobility. In spite of laws restricting Indian travel, migration and flight to other Indian villages were widespread in the eighteenth century.⁹³

Expressions of disrespect, mimicry, grumbling, and gossip became more ingrained in subtle, anonymous ways. Bilingual Indians had even more camouflage for rejecting the values of the oppressors who no longer mastered indigenous languages so efficiently. Epithets of cheater, liar, thief, murderer, and cuckold were ascribed to the padres with impunity.⁹⁴ It is no wonder that missionaries complained constantly of the fickleness of their charges. Moving beyond these social hostilities, Indians also revived or invented witchcraft to bring harm to their exploiters. In the eighteenth century *hechiceros* (Indian and mestizo) continued to surface even in more densely settled areas. In some cases, they performed acts intended to exact revenge against priests who had punished transgressors. Several missionaries claimed they nearly died from strange illnesses passed to them by witches. Shamans also conducted curing ceremonies with combinations of the traditional sucking and blowing rituals and Christian symbols such as crucifixes. Others directed harvest ceremonies.⁹⁵

In some cases, these forms of passive resistance did not succeed in preserving the integrity of the indigenous community, especially when the defense was too piecemeal against rather formidable odds. The Jesuits themselves recognized this when they decided to secularize the Tepehuan and lower Tarahumara missions in the 1740s.⁹⁶ Some Indian and mestizo inhabitants fought hard to keep their mission status because of tax and tithe exemptions, on one occasion sending a delegation to the viceroy to protest the transfer to parish status.[97] Many of these villages did survive as dynamic mestizo communities, and we need more study to determine the extent to which indigenous ways were socially reproduced there in the late eighteenth and early nineteenth centuries.

In the upper Tarahumara missions Indians were more active in their resistance and more able to avoid being swamped by the non-Indian population, because the area had fewer resources coveted by outsiders.[98] By refusing to abandon their *ranchería* dwelling patterns to live permanently in mission centers, they were able to continue certain religious and social practices, much as they had always done. In such cases, missions served primarily as ceremonial centers where Indians congregated on holy days to celebrate and to conduct business. Away from the missions most of the time, they continued to host drinking parties, to change sexual partners, and to hunt and gather wild plants such as *mescal*. Leaders with oratorical ability (always seen by the missionaries as *hechiceros* in the power of the devil) continued to deliver public sermons on proper behavior. The Tarahumaras even celebrated Christian holidays without the priest. These celebrations incorporated Catholic prayers as well as feasts and ritual that retained features of native curing ceremonies. They included mention of God, Jesus, and the Virgin but had little relationship to Christian doctrine. After the expulsion of the Jesuits in 1767 the upper Tarahumara remained largely without priests for more than a hundred years, facilitating the continuation of ritual practices, which were primarily indigenous with some Catholic elements. In the Tarahumara region today public sermons and Holy Week celebrations embodying unique fusions of Indian and Christian elements continue in many communities.[99] The refusal to settle in mission pueblos did not mean that these Tarahumara tried to divorce themselves from all Spanish society; many even sought temporary jobs outside their *rancherías* in agriculture, mining, and wood cutting.[100] They were determined, however, to preserve certain physical locations in which their social networks could operate without interference.

Those Indians, mainly Tarahumaras and other groups in the western escarpment of the Sierra Madre, who did not want to make any accommodation to the ideology of the mission system found another solution short of rebellion.[101] They simply fled beyond the area of effective Spanish penetration, to the most inaccessible mountain canyons. Even here, however, they took their sheep and cattle to provide wool, hides, and manure for cultivation. No area of the Tarahumara, therefore, remained untouched by Spanish "civilization," but at least a part managed to preserve certain cultural practices that distinguished it more clearly from the non-Indian society. Nevertheless, these least acculturated Tarahumaras did not conserve an undisputed ethnic purity; they tended to absorb through intermarriage other Indian groups who fled the Spanish in Sonora and Sinaloa (Pimas and Jovas, for example) to the refuge of the sierra.[102] These Tarahumaras also accepted and mixed with marginal mestizos and mulattoes, perhaps acquiring geopolitical knowledge that helped them preserve autonomy. Tarahumaras, in particular, have been able to preserve cultural integrity in direct proportion to their ability to flee, and certain Tarahumara communities seem to have had the cohesion to resist as whole entities. By the time of the Tarahumara rebellions of the 1690s, tribal differences concerning acceptance of or resistance to outsiders were not centered within communities. Instead, dividing lines separated entire *rancherías* from one another, with those of the most isolated northwestern corner of Tarahumara country leading the resistance.

The upper Tarahumara Indians found another outlet for their hostility to the Spanish in the late eighteenth century. Because of demographic pressures in the plains area of the United States, Apache Indians were being pushed southwest and were successful in conducting raids on Spanish farms and livestock as far south as Durango. The rugged mountainous terrain of western Chihuahua provided sanctuary as well as Tarahumara recruits for Apache raiding activities.[103]

Nonetheless, active resistance through flight and direct aggression by raiding were not representative of most Nueva Vizcayan Indian responses by the end of the eighteenth century. Where indigenous communities had maintained ethnic purity and preserved a distinct cultural identity, primarily in the old Jesuit mission area of Alta Tarahumara, they had achieved it through the combination of a dynamic strategy of adaptive resistance and a fortuitous lack of interest in their region by outsiders. Many other former Indian villages had been transformed biologically into mestizo communities with social and economic structures that combined indigenous and imposed features.

The Indian history of this area of Nueva Vizcaya reflects a complex interplay of Indian and Spanish strategies. As in other areas where invading cultures tried to dominate or incorporate technologically weaker and less centrally organized societies, what emerged was a dynamic mixture. Above all, Spaniards directed their energies to the appropriation of Indian labor, but the invaders also had cultural priorities that they insisted on imposing, including ritual obeisance to Catholicism and Spanish domination of public places. Jesuits considered other Spanish cultural ideals, such as "orderly" urban living in monogamous unions, to be of great importance but equivocated about imposing them rapidly in the face of native resistance. Furthermore, they despaired of instilling an appreciation for abstract Christian concepts of virtue and sin, and the social and linguistic distance that separated them from their charges allowed them even to ignore the continuation of precontact ritual and social practices.

Indigenous peoples evinced a similar or perhaps even more extensive range of responses to Spanish impositions. Some they were prepared to resist by means up to and including rebellion. Others were perceived as less threatening and provoked little reaction. The Indians accepted many Spanish material introductions eagerly and turned them to their own purposes. By obfuscating and feigning deference publicly, and sometimes even by manipulating the Spanish system itself, they were able to evade some of the obligations imposed on them. More important, they also carved out spaces in which they could act out their critique of the dominant society and reinforce social and economic networks, enabling them to defend their material interests and reproduce themselves biologically and culturally.[104]

Indigenous peoples did not create autonomous social spaces uniformly, nor did agents of Spanish civilization impose their idiosyncratic desires everywhere in the same measure. Class and personality differences created divisions within each group. This chapter has only been able to hint at the range of indigenous responses without reference to particular individuals. Although individual actions are more difficult to document for Indians, further study could identify how individual Jesuits diverged in compressing their moral rules to a bottom line. Finally, as if analyzing the interaction of the wide-ranging strategies of subordinate and dominant human actors were not complicated enough, natural phenomena such as regional topography, climate, soils, and natural resources should also be considered. A broad stratum of factors make up the extremely complex mix of adaptation, rejection, and resistance evolved by Indian societies in response to the imposition of the mission regime. The evidence suggests, however, that even when subordinate groups were biologically swamped, they persistently refused to adopt some fundamental elements of the dominant ideology.

Notes

1. Gerard Decorme, *La obra de los jesuitas mexicanos durante la época colonial, 1572-1767* (Mexico City, 1941), pp. 86-87.
2. Report on missions, 27 Dec. 1793, Archivo General de la Nación, Mexico City (hereinafter AGN), Historia, vol. 42, fols. 20-26, 79-84.
3. Andrés Pérez de Ribas, *My Life among the Savage Nations of New Spain*, edited by Thomas A. Robertson (Los Angeles, 1968), p. 10. See, for example, Laura Fishman, "Claude d'Abbeville and the Tupinambá: Problems and Goals of French Missionary Work in Early Seventeenth-Century Brazil," *Church History* 58:1 (1989), 20-35. It is interesting to note how this analysis anticipated the eighteenth-century critiques of such Enlightenment thinkers as Voltaire and Montaigne.
4. Certainly, these themes are important, especially in this region, where Spanish settlement in the north was most concentrated. See Susan M. Deeds, "Rural Work in Nueva Vizcaya: Forms of Labor Coercion on the Periphery," *Hispanic American Historical Review* 69:3, 425-49; and "Mission Villages and Agrarian Patterns in a Nueva Vizcayan Heartland, 1600-1750," *Journal of the Southwest* 33:3 (1991), 345-65.
5. See, for example, James C. Scott, *Weapons of the Weak: Everyday Forms of Peasant Resistance* (New Haven, 1985); and Steve J. Stern, editor, *Resistance, Rebellion, and Consciousness in the Andean Peasant World, Eighteenth to Twentieth Centuries* (Madison WI, 1987).
6. On the Tepehuanes, see Campbell W. Pennington, *The Tepehuan of Chihuahua: Their Material Culture* (Salt Lake City, 1969), and "The Northern Tepehuan," in *Handbook of North American Indians*, vol. 10: *Southwest*, edited by Alfonso Ortiz (Washington DC, 1983), pp. 306-14. In the sixteenth century Tepehuanes also inhabited parts of Nayarit and Jalisco. Today surviving Tepehuanes dwell in the mountain canyons of southern Chihuahua.
7. On the Tarahumaras, see Campbell W. Pennington, *The Tarahumar of Mexico: Their Environment and Material Culture* (Salt Lake City, 1963); Campbell W. Pennington, "Tarahumara," in *Handbook of North American Indians*, 10:276-90; William L. Merrill, "Tarahumara Social Organization,

Political Organization, and Religion," in *Handbook of North American Indians*, 10:290–305; William L. Merrill, *Rarámuri Souls: Knowledge and Social Process in Northern Mexico* (Washington DC, 1988).

8. On the Conchos, see William B. Griffen, *Indian Assimilation in the Franciscan Area of Nueva Vizcaya* (Tucson, 1979); and Arturo Guevara Sánchez, *Los conchos: Apuntes para su monografía* (Chihuahua, 1985).

9. See Ralph Beals, *The Comparative Ethnology of Northern Mexico before 1750* (Berkeley, 1932); and Carl Sauer, *The Distribution of Aboriginal Tribes and Languages in Northwestern Mexico* (Berkeley, 1934). The Acaxee and Xixime are discussed in Susan M. Deeds, "First-Generation Rebellions in Nueva Vizcaya" (unpublished manuscript).

10. Basil C. Hedrick, J. Charles Kelley, and Carroll Riley, editors, *The Mesoamerican Southwest: Readings in Archaeology, Ethnohistory, and Ethnology* (Carbondale IL, 1974); and J. Charles Kelley, "Settlement Patterns in North Central Mexico," in Gordon R. Willie, editor, *Prehistoric Settlement Patterns in the New World* (New York, 1956), pp. 128–47. The following discussion of cultural characteristics draws on the anthropological sources mentioned in the previous notes and on Edward H. Spicer, *Cycles of Conquest: The Impact of Spain, Mexico, and the United States on the Indians of the Southwest, 1533–1960* (Tucson, 1962), pp. 25–45; 371–565.

11. For an analysis of similar practices among modern-day Tarahumaras, see Merrill, *Rarámuri Souls*, pp. 53–84.

12. Daniel T. Reff, *Disease, Depopulation, and Culture Change in Northwestern New Spain, 1518–1764* (Salt Lake City, 1991).

13. Carta ánua, 1608, P. Juan Font, Zape, in Luis González Rodríguez, *Crónicas de la sierra tarahumara* (Mexico City, 1984), pp. 160–65; relación de lo sucedido en la jornada que Don Gaspar de Alvear . . . hizo a los tarahumares . . . hecha por el P. Alonso de Valencia, Apr. 1620, University of Texas Nettie Lee Benson Collection (hereinafter UTNLB), Joaquín García Icazbalceta Collection, Varias Relaciones, I.

14. Carta ánua, 1607, P. Juan Font; and P. Juan Font to P. Prov. Ildefonso de Castro, Durango, 22 Apr. 1608; both reprinted in González Rodríguez, *Crónicas*, pp. 156–60 and 178–86, respectively.

15. The contemporary ethnographic descriptions from which this synthesis is taken include the following: report of Joseph Tardá and Tomás de Guadalajara, 1676 (I have used a copy transcribed by William L. Merrill and Luis González Rodríguez from a copy in Rome: Joseph Tardá and Tomás de Guadalajara, Letter to Francisco Ximénez, 15 Aug. 1676, Archivum Romanum Societatis Jesu, Mexicana 17, 355–72) (hereinafter Tardá and Guadalajara report, 1676); report of Juan María Ratkay, Carichic, 20 Mar. 1683, translated copy from the Latin in the Bolton Collection, Bancroft Library, Mexicana 17 (University of Arizona Special Collections ms. 2261 (hereinafter Ratkay report, 1683); and many individual letters of missionaries found in

Documentos para la historia de México, 4th series (Mexico City, 1857) (hereinafter DHM), vol. 3, and in Felix Zubillaga and Ernest J. Burrus, S.J., Monumenta mexicana, 7 volumes (Rome, 1956–81).

16. Ratkay report, 1683.

17. Ritual cannibalism was reportedly practiced by Tepehuanes but not Tarahumaras: Tardá and Guadalajara report, 1676; Juan de Estrada, Breve noticia de las misiones de la Compañía de Jesús de la América septentrional (Mexico City, 1948).

18. Carta ánua, 1611, P. Juan Font, in González Rodríguez, Crónicas, pp. 186–93. The importance of kinship networks in reproducing indigenous and peasant communities in northern New Spain is best analyzed in Cynthia Radding, "Ethnicity and the Emerging Peasant Class of Northwestern New Spain, 1760–1840" (Ph.D. dissertation, University of California, San Diego, 1990).

19. Visita of Capt. Juan Fernández de Retana to Huejotitlán, Feb. 1693, Archivo General de Indias, Sevilla (hereinafter AGI), Patronato, leg. 236, fol. 447.

20. Carta ánua, 1607, P. Juan Font, Ocotlán, in González Rodríguez, Crónicas, pp. 156–60.

21. Francisco Ramírez to Governor of Nueva Vizcaya, Bachíniva, 15 May 1690, AGI, Patronato, leg. 236, fols. 89–90.

22. See note 8.

23. Deeds, "Rural Work"; Chantal Cramaussel, La provincia de Santa Bárbara en Nueva Vizcaya, 1563–1631 (Ciudad Juárez, 1990); Chantal Cramaussel, "Encomiendas, repartimientos y conquista en Nueva Vizcaya," in Actas del Primer Congreso de Historia Regional Comparada (Ciudad Juárez, 1989), pp. 139–60. See also Robert C. West, The Mining Community in New Spain: The Parral Mining District (Berkeley, 1949).

24. Report of P. Hauga to Bishop of Durango, San Miguel de las Bocas, 30 June 1749, Archivo de la Catedral de Durango (hereinafter ACD), Varios 1749; cartas ánuas, 1611, 1612, P. Juan Font, in González Rodríguez, Crónicas, pp. 171–74; 186–93.

25. George Collier, "Mesoamerican Anthropology: Between Production and Hegemony," Latin American Research Review 26:2 (1991), 203–10.

26. Tardá and Guadalajara report, 1676.

27. Testimony of Gerónimo, governor of Papigochic, 16 May 1690, AGI, Patronato, leg. 236, fols. 84–86.

28. P. Joseph Pallares to P. Prov. Bernabé de Soto, Batopilas, 24 Apr. 1689, in González Rodríguez, Crónicas, pp. 139–42; testimony of Capt. Luis de Valdés, 9 June 1690, AGI, Patronato 236, fol. 165.

29. Tardá and Guadalajara report, 1676; Ratkay report, 1683. The issue of generational relations has been analyzed in detail for the Pueblo Indians of New Mexico by Ramón Gutiérrez in When Jesus Came, the Corn Mothers

Went Away: Marriage, Sexuality, and Power in New Mexico, 1500–1846 (Stanford, 1991), pp. 75–81.

30. For a modern description of *tesguinadas*, see John G. Kennedy, *Tarahumara of the Sierra Madre: Beer, Ecology, and Social Organization* (Arlington Heights IL, 1978), pp. 97–126.

31. Peter M. Dunne, S.J., *Early Jesuit Missions in Tarahumara* (Berkeley and Los Angeles, 1948), pp. 166–67.

32. Reff, *Disease, Depopulation, and Culture Change*. The high rates of decline were replicated in the Tepehuan and Tarahumara missions. Susan M. Deeds, "Population Movements in Eighteenth-Century Villages of Nueva Vizcaya" (Paper presented at the Rocky Mountain Council on Latin American Studies, Estes Park CO, 1986).

33. Carta ánua, 1612, P. Juan Font, in González Rodríguez, *Crónicas*, pp. 171–74; on hired labor, see the accounts in Cuentas de la Real Caja de Durango, 22 May 1599, AGI, Contaduría, leg. 925.

34. Testimonios jurídicos de las poblaciones y conversiones de los serranos por el año de 1600, AGN, Historia, vol. 20, exp. 19. As time went on, missionaries themselves were more prone to take disciplinary action, enhancing the likelihood that they would become targets of rebellion. Thus, after rebellions this function was increasingly entrusted to Indian intermediaries.

35. Griffen, *Indian Assimilation*, pp. 45–46; report of José Rafael Rodríguez Gallardo, 18 Aug. 1750, AGN, Provincias Internas, vol. 176, fols. 216–17.

36. Carta ánua, 1616, México, AGN, Jesuitas, III-29, exp. 21.

37. Many of the Jesuit annual reports (*cartas ánuas*) are devoted to this theme. Andrés Pérez de Ribas used such anecdotal accounts in compiling his *Historia de los triunfos de nuestra Santa Fe entre las gentes más bárbaras y fieras del nuevo orbe* [1645] (Mexico City, 1944).

38. See, for example, the cartas ánuas of 1595 and 1607, AGN, Historia, vol. 19.

39. Carta ánua, 1636, México, AGN, Jesuitas III-15; relación de la guerra de los tepehuanes por P. Francisco de Arista, Dec. 1617, AGN, Historia, vol. 311, exp. 1.

40. The severity of such punishments was limited by Jesuit rules; see Párrafos . . . acerca de . . . el castigo de los naturales, copy transmitted by P. Juan de Almonaziz, Matapé, 31 Dec. 1684, AGN, Archivo Histórico de Hacienda (hereinafter AHH), Temporalidades, leg. 1126, exp. 3.

41. Thomas H. Naylor and Charles W. Polzer, S.J., editors, *The Presidio and Militia on the Northern Frontier of New Spain: A Documentary History*, vol. 1: 1500–1700 (Tucson, 1986), pp. 149–244; Deeds, "First-Generation Revolts."

42. On the Tepehuan rebellion, see Naylor and Polzer, *Presidio and Militia*, pp. 245–93; Charles W. Hackett, *Historical Documents Relating to*

New Mexico, Nueva Vizcaya, and Approaches Thereto to 1773 (Washington DC, 1926), 2:100–15; Pérez de Ribas, Historia de los triunfos, 3:164–218.

43. These rebellions are analyzed in Susan M. Deeds, "Las rebeliones de los tepehuanes y tarahumaras durante el siglo XVII en la Nueva Vizcaya," Colección conmemorativa quinto centenario del encuentro de dos mundos, vol 4: El contacto entre los españoles e indígenas en el norte de la Nueva España, coordinated by Ysla Campbell (Ciudad Juárez, 1992), pp. 9–40.

44. Documentation for the Tarahumara rebellions can be found in AGI, Patronato, leg. 236, and Audiencia de Guadalajara, leg. 156.

45. The Jesuit father provincial singled out these two basic areas of conflict in calling for military backup for the Tepehuan missions in 1614, citing instances in which missionaries had been physically threatened in attempts to bring an end to "amancebimientos, borracheras y vicios." P. Provincial Rodrigo de Cabredo to Viceroy Marqués de Guadalcázar, México, 5 Aug. 1614, AGN, AHH, Temporalidades, leg. 278, exp. 7.

46. Carta ánua, 1674, P. Joseph Tardá, San Joaquín y Santa Ana, 24 Feb. 1674, AGN, Jesuitas, III-29, exp. 27; viceregal order, 1 Oct. 1746, Archivo General de Durango, cajón 9, exp. 2.

47. Some of the theoretical bases for this analysis come from Spicer, Cycles of Conquest (constructive collaboration is implied in Spicer's incorporative model); Stern, Resistance, Rebellion, and Consciousness; and Scott, Weapons of the Weak.

48. The naming of Indian officials is treated in Testimonios jurídicos de las poblaciones y conversiones de los serranos ... por el año de 1600, AGN, Historia, vol. 20, exp. 19. A Franciscan report alleges that the Jesuits got one peso for each Indian supplied in repartimiento: Relación simple de las misiones que tienen los padres de la compañía en Parral, n.d. (18th century), Thomas Gilcrease Institute, Hispanic Documents, 176–6.

49. Report of Rodríguez Gallardo, 18 Aug. 1750, AGN, Provincias Internas, vol. 176, exp. 6, fols. 216–17; P. Constancio Gallarat to P. Vis. Juan Manuel de Hierro, Sn. Felipe el Real, 12 May 1735, UTNLB, W. B. Stephens Collection (hereinafter WBS), 66:213–16.

50. Decree of Gov. Joseph Sebastián López de Carbajal, Parral, 7 Aug. 1724, Archivo de Hidalgo de Parral (microfilm copy in the University of Arizona Library), reel 1723b, frames 608–9 (hereinafter AHP with reel and frame numbers); P. Agustín Carta to P. Prov. Juan Antonio Balthasar, Chihuahua, 7 June 1751, AGN, AHH, Temporalidades, leg. 2009, exp. 41; response to Tepehuan complaints in Viceroy to Governor of Nueva Vizcaya, 18 Nov. 1754, AGN, General de Parte, vol. 38, exp. 161, fol. 185.

51. P. Trujillo to P. Vis. Bartolomé Braun, Tutuaca, 6 Apr. 1764, UTNLB, WBS, 66:17–19; report of P. Juan Antonio Balthasar to Viceroy, 1754, UTNLB, WBS, 1719.

52. Quejas dadas contra Nicolás de Valenzuela y Nicolás el Vagre, Atotonilco, 18 July 1720, AHP, reel 1720b, frames 1360–67, 1532–49.
53. Testimony of Concho Indians, Casas Grandes, 20 Mar. 1690, AGI, Patronato, leg. 236, fol. 772; Deeds, "Rural Work," pp. 433–34; Griffen, *Indian Assimilation*, pp. 45–46.
54. Autos del Gobernador Juan Isidro Pardiñas, Parral, 3 Apr. 1690, AGI, Patronato, leg. 236, fols. 20–25; report of Junta de Guerra, México, 4 Aug. 1704, AGN, Historia, vol. 20, exp. 1; muster lists of Jan.–May 1716, AHP, reel 1716a, frames 311–65. Radding has analyzed this phenomenon for the Opata Indians of Sonora in "Ethnicity and the Emerging Peasant Class."
55. Report of Junta de Guerra to Viceroy, México, 4 Aug. 1704, AGN, Historia, vol. 20, exp. 1.
56. Carta ánua, 1597, AGN, Historia, vol. 19, exp. 6; Tardá and Guadalajara report, 1676; P. Juan Font to P. Prov. Ildefonso de Castro, Guadiana, 22 Apr. 1608, in González Rodríguez, *Crónicas*, pp. 178–81.
57. A helpful discussion of these dietary changes is found in Miguel León Portilla, Susan Schroeder, and Michael C. Meyer, "Early Spanish-Indian Contact in the Borderlands" (unpublished manuscript).
58. Deeds, "Mission Villages."
59. Report of P. Diego Larios, 1614, AGN, AHH, Temporalidades, leg. 278, exp. 7; Pedro Gomez Castellano to Salvador de Acosta, Santa Cruz, 24 Aug. 1749, in ACD, Varios 1749.
60. Carta ánua, 1612, P. Juan Font, in González Rodríguez, *Crónicas*, p. 171.
61. Murdo J. MacLeod, "The Social and Economic Roles of Indian Cofradías in Colonial Chiapas," in Jeffrey A. Cole, editor, *The Church and Society in Latin America* (New Orleans, 1984), pp. 73–98; John K. Chance and William B. Taylor, "Cofradías and Cargos: An Historical Perspective on the Mesoamerican Civil-Religious Hierarchy," *American Ethnologist* (1985), 1–26.
62. Reports to the Bishop of Durango from P. Pedro Retes, Santa Catalina, 15 Aug. 1749; P. Lázaro Franco, Zape, 8 Aug. 1749; P. Hauga, Las Bocas, 30 June 1749; all in ACD, Varios 1749. See also the inventories of 1753 in AGN, Misiones, vol. 13, fols. 24–57.
63. P. Joaquín Basurto to Bishop, Badiraguato, 13 June 1749, ACD, Varios 1749.
64. Quoted in Gerard Decorme, Atanacio Saravia, and Pastor Rouaix, *Manual de historia de Durango* (Mexico City, 1952), pp. 86–87; see also the report of P. Joseph Chavez to Bishop, Cariatapa, 18 July 1749, ACD, Varios 1749.
65. P. Benito Rinaldini to P. Prov. Andrés García, Huejotitlán, 13 Oct. 1749, Archivo Histórico de la Provincia de los Jesuitas, Mexico City (hereinafter AHPM), no. 1389; Deeds, "Mission Villages."

66. These lists are found scattered throughout the many legajos of the Temporalidades branch of the AGN, AHH.

67. Letter of P. Juan Ratkay to P. Nicolás Avancini, 25 Feb. 1681, in Mauro Matthei, editor, *Cartas e informes de misioneros jesuitas extranjeros en Hispanoamérica* (Santiago, Chile, 1969), pp. 155–59.

68. Philip Wayne Powell, *Soldiers, Indians, and Silver: The Northward Advance of New Spain, 1550–1600* (Berkeley, 1952).

69. Carta ánua, 1662, San Miguel de las Bocas, AGN, Misiones, vol. 26; Ratkay report, 1683; autos regarding the founding of new presidios; 1730, AGN, Provincias Internas, vol. 69, exp. 4, fol. 181.

70. Carta ánua, 1608, P. Juan Font, in González Rodríguez, *Crónicas*, pp. 160–65; report of P. Felipe Calderón to Bishop of Durango, Santa María de las Cuevas, 21 July 1749, ACD, Varios 1749; report of P. Visitador Agustín Carta to P. Provincial, Santiago Papasquiaro, 14 Aug. 1753, AHPM, no. 1391.

71. Kennedy, *Tarahumara of the Sierra Madre*, pp. 153–56; Merrill, *Rarámuri Souls*, pp. 46–50. Edward Spicer, *The Yaquis: A Cultural History* (Tucson, 1980), pp. 59–118, analyzes in detail the evolution of these ritual practices among the Yaquis. The differences between modern Yaqui and Tarahumara practices suggests that the Christian rituals were incorporated into previous belief systems.

72. Carta ánua, 1596, México, AGN, Historia, vol. 19, exp. 5.

73. Tardá and Guadalajara report, 1676.

74. Carta ánua, 1611, P. Juan Font, in González Rodríguez, *Crónicas*, p. 159. See Merrill, *Rarámuri Souls*, pp. 46–47, 85–120.

75. Testimony given during the visita of Retana to San Pablo and Huejotitlán, 1693 Feb. AGI, Patronato, leg. 236, fols. 847–48; Tardá and Guadalajara report, 1676.

76. Carta ánua, 1597, DHM, 3:36–41; Ratkay report, 1683.

77. Pérez de Ribas discusses this practice among Cahita-speaking peoples; he interpreted it as an adoption ceremony for orphans: *Triunfos*, pp. 166–67.

78. Ratkay report, 1683.

79. Carta ánua, 1623, P. Pier Gian Castini, Chinipas, in González Rodríguez, *Crónicas*, p. 51.

80. Carta ánua, 1608, P. Juan Font, in González Rodríguez, *Crónicas*, pp. 160–65; Ratkay report, 1683; report of P. Gerónimo Figueroa, 8 June 1662, AGN, Historia, vol. 19, exp. 16; visita report of P. Juan de Guendulaín, 18 May 1725, Chihuahua, AGN, AHH, Temporalidades, leg. 2009, exp. 99; report of P. Balthasar to P. Prov. Escobar, México, 15 Aug. 1745, AGN, AHH, Temporalidades 2009, exp. 20; report of P. Benito Rinaldini to Bishop of Durango, Huejotitlán, 29 July 1749, ACD, Varios 1749. See also William L. Merrill, "Conversion and Colonialism in Northern Mexico: The Tarahumara Response to the Jesuit Mission Program, 1601–1767," in Robert W. Hefner, editor, *Conversion*

to Christianity: Historical and Anthropological Perspectives on a Great Transformation (Berkeley, 1993), pp. 129–63.

81. Charles W. Polzer, S.J., Rules and Precepts of the Jesuit Missions in Northwestern New Spain (Tucson, 1976), p. 40. Reporting on the Topia mission of Otaez in 1745, P. Vis. Juan Antonio Balthasar recommended the removal of P. Felix Ortier, who had stirred up discontent by trying to reform certain customs of the Indians that most experienced missionaries would have left alone: Durango, 12 Mar. 1745, AGN, AHH, Temporalidades, leg. 2009, exp. 20. Informe del Gen. Pedro de Rivera, 3 Nov. 1728, AGI, Guadalajara, leg. 135, exp. 3.

82. Carta ánua, 1625, P. Pier Gian Castini, in González Rodríguez, Crónicas, pp. 50–51.

83. In addition to providing basic necessities during epidemics, Jesuits reported using sangrías, purgas y sudores (bleeding, purges, and sweat baths) in treating those who were ill; e.g., P. Luis de Ahumada to P. Provincial Martín Pelaez, Parras, 13 Nov. 1608, AGN, Historia, vol. 19. Medicinal remedies were frequent items in missionary supply orders (memorias); many of these are found in AGN, AHH, Temporalidades, legs. 279, 282, and include such reputed cures as treacle, myrrh, camphor, and vitriolic spirits.

84. See the articles by Deeds mentioned in note 4; see also Michael M. Swann, Migrants in the Mexican North: Mobility, Economy, and Society in a Colonial World (Boulder CO, 1989).

85. Susan M. Deeds, "Rendering unto Caesar: The Secularization of Jesuit Missions in Mid-Eighteenth-Century Durango" (Ph.D. dissertation, University of Arizona, 1981).

86. See Radding, "Ethnicity and the Emerging Peasant Class," for an example of how this work can be done.

87. Ratkay report, 1683.

88. Puntos de annua desta mission de Taraumares, 14 Nov. 1668, AGN, Jesuitas, III-15, exp. 4.

89. Report of P. Vis. Andrés Xavier García, ca. 1740, AGN, AHH, Temporalidades, leg. 1126, exp. 4. Such references abound in missionary reports and are too numerous to cite.

90. Letter of P. José Pascual to Gov. Bravo y Serna, 18 Sept. 1639, reprinted in Francisco Orozco y Jiménez, Colección de documentos inéditos relativos a la Iglesia de Chiapas (San Cristóbal de las Casas, Mexico, 1906, 1911), 1:93–95.

91. Much of the testimony gathered during the Tarahumara rebellion of the early 1690s speaks to this issue: AGI, Patronato, leg. 236. See also Scott, Weapons of the Weak, chap. 7; and James C. Scott, Domination and the Arts of Resistance: Hidden Transcripts (New Haven, 1990), chap. 6.

92. Report of P. Hauga to Bishop of Durango, Las Bocas, 30 June 1749, ACD, Varios 1749.

93. Report of P. Hernando Santaren, n.d., 1590s, AGN, Jesuitas, II-4; bigamy case, 1640–43, in Archivo Parroquial de Parral, caja 17a, exp. 1–1; testimony of Indians before the Juzgado de Indios, 11 Sept. 1692, in Lesley B. Simpson, *The Repartimiento System of Native Labor in New Spain and Guadalajara* (Berkeley, 1958), p. 61; report of P. Juan A. Balthasar to P. Provincial, ca. 1740, AGN, AHH, Temporalidades, leg. 1126, exp. 1; visita que hizo el Gobernador López de Carbajal a Santiago Papasquiaro y disposiciones que dictó, Apr. 1724, AHP, reel 1722b, frames 659–687; P. Pedro Retes to P. Prov. Escobar, Santa Catalina, 17 July 1746, AHPM, no. 1406; Pedro Gómez Castellano to Salvador de Acosta, Santa Cruz, 24 Aug. 1749; ACD, Varios 1749.

94. Tardá and Guadalajara report, 1676.

95. Causa criminal contra Mateo de la Cruz, 1703–5, AHP, reel 1703, frames 973–982; various letters of Padres Manuel Ignacio Cartagena and Fernando Caamaño to Bishop of Durango, June 1745, ACD, Varios 1745.

96. Often families were divided in their loyalties, making community cohesion even more difficult to achieve: carta ánua, 1608, P. Juan Font, in González Rodríguez, *Crónicas*, pp. 160–65. Deeds, "Rendering unto Caesar."

97. P. Agustín Carta to P. Prov., 14 Aug. 1753, Santiago Papasquiaro, AHPM, no. 1391; petition to viceroy, Nov. 1754, ACD, Varios 1755.

98. Tardá and Guadalajara report, 1676; P. Diego Ortiz de Foronda to P. Rector, Yepómera, 22 Feb. 1690, AGI, Patronato, leg. 236, fol. 7; report of P. Juan Antonio Núñez to Bishop of Durango, Satebó, 19 July 1749, ACD, Varios 1749.

99. P. Joseph Miqueo to P. Provincial Cristóbal Escobar y Llamas, Yoquivo, 1745, AGN, Jesuitas I-16, exp. 11; Merrill, *Rarámuri Souls*, pp. 68–84; Kennedy, *Tarahumara of the Sierra Madre*, pp. 153–56.

100. P. Ignacio Xavier de Estrada to P. Provincial Juan Antonio de Oviedo, Themeichic, 23 Nov. 1730, AGN, AHH, Temporalidades, leg. 278, exp. 7. This ability to use the Spanish world without losing ethnic solidarity has a parallel in Yaqui history: Evelyn Hu-Dehart, *Missionaries, Miners, and Indians: Spanish Contact with the Yaqui Nation of Northwestern New Spain, 1533–1820* (Tucson, 1981), and Spicer, *The Yaquis*.

101. Report on Alta Tarahumara, n.p., n.d. (ca. 1780), in DHM, IV-4, 117.

102. See note 100.

103. P. Balthasar Rauch to P. Provincial Juan Antonio de Oviedo, Sisoguichic, 17 Oct. 1730, AGN, AHH, Temporalidades, leg. 273, exp. 7; report on Chihuahua, 1760s, AGN, Provincias Internas, vol. 95, exp. 1; William B. Griffen, *Apaches at War and Peace: The Janos Presidio, 1750–1858* (Albuquerque, 1988), pp. 30, 59–60.

104. Scott, *Domination and the Arts of Resistance*, pp. 108–35, describes how spaces are created by dissident subcultures to enable them to enact their "hidden transcripts."

Paul Farnsworth and Robert H. Jackson

Cultural, Economic, and Demographic Change in the Missions of Alta California: The Case of Nuestra Señora de la Soledad

The Franciscans and the Spanish Crown founded the missions of Alta California with the intent of controlling the indigenous populations on the coast with minimal expenditure of royal funds. Control was to be achieved by gathering the California Indians in the missions, changing their entire culture, and turning them into a docile, Christian, peasant labor force. The missions failed in the goal of culture change but did succeed in using native labor to finance the colonization of the region.

Indian labor was meant to support the missionary enterprise and, if possible, produce surpluses for trade. In California, however, the missionaries came to realize that it was not possible both to transform the Native Americans into peasants and to maintain high levels of economic production. Consequently, the effort to change the Indians' culture was abandoned, except for the addition of a veneer of Christianity deemed acceptable to the church and the introduction of those European skills necessary for economic production.

The change in strategy appears to have taken place midway

We wish to express our appreciation to the students and volunteers who participated in the excavations at Mission Soledad. We also thank the Catholic Diocese of Monterey and the Mission Soledad Restoration Committee for granting permission for the excavations. Funding was provided by the University Research Expedition Program (UREP), the Mission Soledad Restoration Committee, the Native Daughters of the Golden West, and the following UCLA institutions: Summer Sessions, Graduate Division, Friends of Archaeology, Program on Mexico, Institute of Archaeology, Institute of American Cultures, and American Indian Studies Center. Finally, we thank Laurie Farnsworth for her help in the preparation of this chapter.

through the mission period in Alta California, in the early nineteenth century, and the results can be seen in both the historical and archaeological records. In this chapter we trace the effects of this strategy in relation to Mission Nuestra Señora de la Soledad. The analysis relies, in part, on the joining of historical documentary and archaeological evidence, which provides important insights into the process of change experienced by a people without a voice. Historians are able to reconstruct elements of Indian life from documents written by Spanish civil and religious officials, but there is a dearth of information on the day-to-day lives of the mission Indians. Archaeologists use the record of material culture, the artifacts left behind by the converts living at Soledad, to fill the information gap.

We focus here on establishing the relationship of several factors: the political economy of the missions and colonial policy objectives, demographic patterns and the development of the mission labor force, and cultural persistence. Royal officials in Mexico City relied on the missions to subsidize the cost of the military garrisons stationed in California, placing considerable pressure on the Franciscans to maintain production levels and exploit a large labor force. With the onset of civil war in Mexico after 1810, the military garrisons in California depended even more heavily on the missions.

Demographic patterns in the missions undermined the political objectives of Mexico City policy makers, because high mortality rates among both adults and children created a constant need to recruit adults. Continuous recruitment retarded acculturation and evangelization, leading in the first decades of the nineteenth century to a resurgence in traditional culture driven by the large percentage of the mission Indians who were recent converts only marginally assimilated.

The Franciscans established Mission Nuestra Señora de la Soledad in 1791 to fill the gap between San Carlos Borromeo de Carmelo (Carmel mission) (founded in 1770) and San Antonio de Padua (founded in 1771) (map 1) and to control the Chalon Costanoan and Esselen Indians. Control was to be achieved by modifying the native culture and social structure. Since these cultural changes were related to the role of the missions in California, when that role was modified, so too was the degree of cultural change. The social and cultural changes mirrored the evolving economic focus of Mission Soledad, which, in turn, affected the demographics of the mission

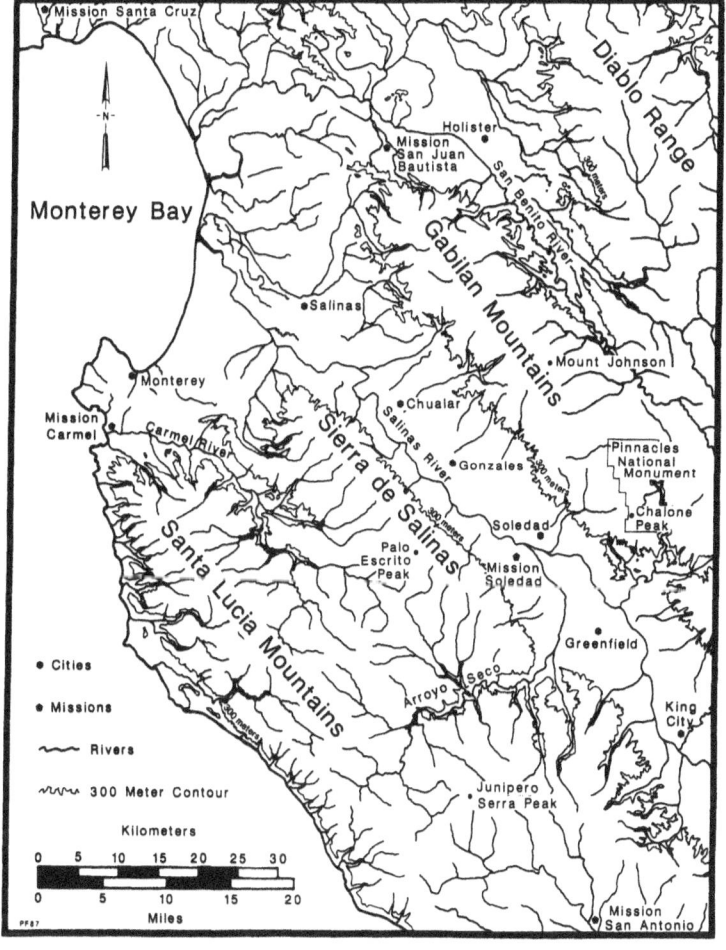

Map 1. Mission Soledad in Alta California.

population. The demise of the missions came at the hands of settlers who wanted to share in the wealth generated by the exploitation of Indian labor. The result was the near destruction of the native populations and the cultural extinction of the Esselen and the Chalon Costanoan by the middle of the nineteenth century.

Salinas Valley Ecology and Geography

Mission Soledad is located about fifty-three kilometers southeast of Monterey Bay and forty kilometers inland (map 1). The mission is one kilometer southwest of the Salinas River and one and a half kilometers from its confluence with the Arroyo Seco. Here the Salinas Valley is seven to eight kilometers wide, flanked by the Gabilan Mountains on the northeast and the Sierra de Salinas on the southwest. Further southwest lie the Santa Lucia Mountains. The Indians recruited into the mission occupied the Gabilan and the Santa Lucia Mountains.

The Indians and Spanish missionaries had different concepts of ecology and the utility of the land. For the Indians, the Salinas Valley was a rich source of food, whereas for the missionaries, it was a sterile environment with limited potential for economic development. This view is clear in the writings of missionary Francisco Uria, who wrote the earliest description of the mission's land: "This soil is very sterile. Only when there is a heavy rainfall is it somewhat covered with vegetation. The two sierras that form the canyon are very barren and unsuitable.... In the way of groves and forests the mission has only some poplar, alder, and willow trees along the river valley, and on the brow of the hills some very crooked live oak and similar crooked trees. Other kinds of timber are unknown."[1]

The mission was close to a wide variety of ecological zones, which the Native Americans fully exploited. In contrast, the missionaries focused their activities almost entirely on the valley floor and used the woodlands only for timber. To the European agriculturalists the land beyond the valley floor was "barren." They pastured their own grazing animals there and planted grains, fruits, and vegetables in comparatively small areas near the mission, using irrigation as far as possible to modify the environment for these mainly unsuitable crops.

Three indigenous groups occupied portions of the region: the Salinan, the Costanoan, and the Esselen. The Franciscans at Soledad baptized only twenty-two Salinan Indians.[2] The Costanoan occupied the territory from San Francisco Bay south to around the present King City in the Salinas Valley. Scholars divide the Costanoans into eight major language groups. One of them, Chalon speakers, occupied the middle portion of the Salinas River Valley. Unlike the other Costanoan language groups, the Chalon speakers were organized into only one politically autonomous unit, or tribelet, called Chal-lon.[3] The Chalon Costanoan lived in the Gabilan Mountains to the east of the mission and the valley floor west as far as the Salinas River. The Esselen occupied the Santa Lucia Mountains to the west of the mission and the valley floor east as far as the Salinas River. The mission stood in Esselen territory.

The Esselen were the first California Indian group to become culturally extinct, during the first half of the nineteenth century.[4] Early extinction resulted from their small initial population and the effects of Franciscan activities in three missions close to Esselen territory. Consequently, the ethnographic data about them are sparse and unreliable. Most of the ethnographic work that relates to the Esselen took place around Monterey and Carmel.

Population estimates for the Esselen vary considerably, from around five hundred to thirteen hundred.[5] The latter figure, derived from mission baptismal records, is based on a total of 951 baptisms from villages considered by Sherburne F. Cook to be Esselen, multiplied by a factor of 1.5 to correct for Indians dying from introduced diseases before baptism. This multiplication factor is based on similar work at other missions, but because of the isolation of the Esselen tribelets it may be too high. Esselen territory may have been more extensive than Cook allowed, so these factors probably balance out his estimate. Thus thirteen hundred appears to be the most realistic figure.

The Costanoan numbered between 7,000 and 9,800, although Cook estimated their numbers as high as 11,000.[6] The Chalon speakers may have numbered around 900, although Cook's calculation of 1,326 Costanoans baptized at Mission Soledad suggests a much larger population, in the region of 1,500 or more.[7] Cook underestimated the size of Esselen territory, however, and this figure could be inflated by both Esselen and other Costanoan Indians. Fifteen hundred seems to be a reasonable estimate.

Religion, an integral part of California Indian life, was targeted for elimination by the missionaries. The Costanoan offered prayers to the sun accompanied by blowing smoke toward the sky. Offerings of seeds, tobacco, and shell beads were made. Small feathered sticks were used as charms to promote good luck in fishing and hunting. Frequently, offerings such as tobacco leaves, feathers, strips of rabbit skin, feather headdresses, and capes of grass were attached to the tops of poles.[8]

Dreams played a major role in Costanoan religion, serving as a guide for an individual's future actions. Omens included the twitching of leg muscles, indicating a journey; a bird entering a house or hovering in one's path, or a dog howling near a house, were all bad omens. The call of the great horned owl foretold death.[9]

Shamans were believed to be able to control the weather, causing the rain to stop or start. They cured diseases by cutting the skin, sucking out disease objects, and exhibiting them to onlookers. Herbal cures were also used, and shamans were hired whenever people were very ill. Diagnosis of diseases was done by singing and dancing. Shamans also performed ceremonies to ensure the abundance of acorns and fish. Grizzly bear shamans were largely responsible for witchcraft. They wore bearskins, had bear teeth, and had claws filled with poison to kill their victims. If discovered, they were killed with bow and arrow.[10]

The Limits of Cultural Change

Spanish indoctrination may have had some success among children living at Soledad mission, but demographic and recruitment patterns prevented meaningful conversion. High infant mortality greatly reduced the number of children in the mission community, the group generally targeted for more complete indoctrination. The missionaries were aware that they were unable to keep the Indians alive long enough to change many of their traditional beliefs and practices. Further, the Franciscans knew that, as long as they had to recruit "pagan" Indians to maintain the population, they would not be able to eliminate traditional practices entirely. A large percentage of the mission population consisted of adults only superficially converted to Christianity and Spanish culture. Cultural persistence can be seen in the record of material culture uncovered during archaeological excavations at the mission.

Archaeological research at Mission Soledad started in 1983 and continued to 1989. Most work was done in and around the mission's west wing, which was completely excavated, but the neophytes' barracks were also tested and a portion of the aqueduct system explored. These excavations' data illuminate the cultural changes occurring in the mission. Two series of subassemblages, representing well-dated and largely undisturbed data sets, are especially significant. Changes in the material record are corroborated by documentary evidence concerning the ebb and flow of recruitment of Indian converts from outside the mission community.

The first series of subassemblages comes from garbage pits located under the south end of the west wing (area A in figure 1). Three of these pits represent Indian food preparation and consumption activities (pits A, C, and E). According to annual reports to the father president of the missions, the west wing was built between 1799 and 1809; archaeological evidence indicates that it was constructed before 1805.[12] Thus, the garbage pits can be firmly dated to the last decade of the eighteenth or the early years of the nineteenth century. Their chronological sequence was established using a modified form of Stanley South's mean ceramic date formula, which yields a California mean ceramic date (CMCD).[13]

The second series of subassemblages comes from a sequence of floors in a room also in the west wing, approximately fifteen meters north of the garbage pits (area D in figure 1). This series represents the mission's kitchen, at least for part of its period of use. The base of a stove (hornillo) was found in one corner of the room, and the artifact subassemblages reflect other kitchen activities.

The three subassemblages from this room represent a sequence of garbage that became embedded in a succession of adobe floors, divided into early and middle subassemblages, and a buildup of garbage directly on the last floor level. Thus, the sequence is defined stratigraphically, although the dates assigned are again CMCDs. The building disappeared between 1834, when it was still in use, and 1850, when a sketch of the mission does not show it at all.

A quantification of the artifacts in each subassemblage, based on a classification described in detail elsewhere,[14] measures the continuity of the traditional Indian activities represented. This analysis is derived from material culture and cannot measure most continuities in the Native American belief and social system. The true degree of continuity is probably underestimated.

The degree of continuity of indigenous traditional activities changed significantly during the mission period. During the first de-

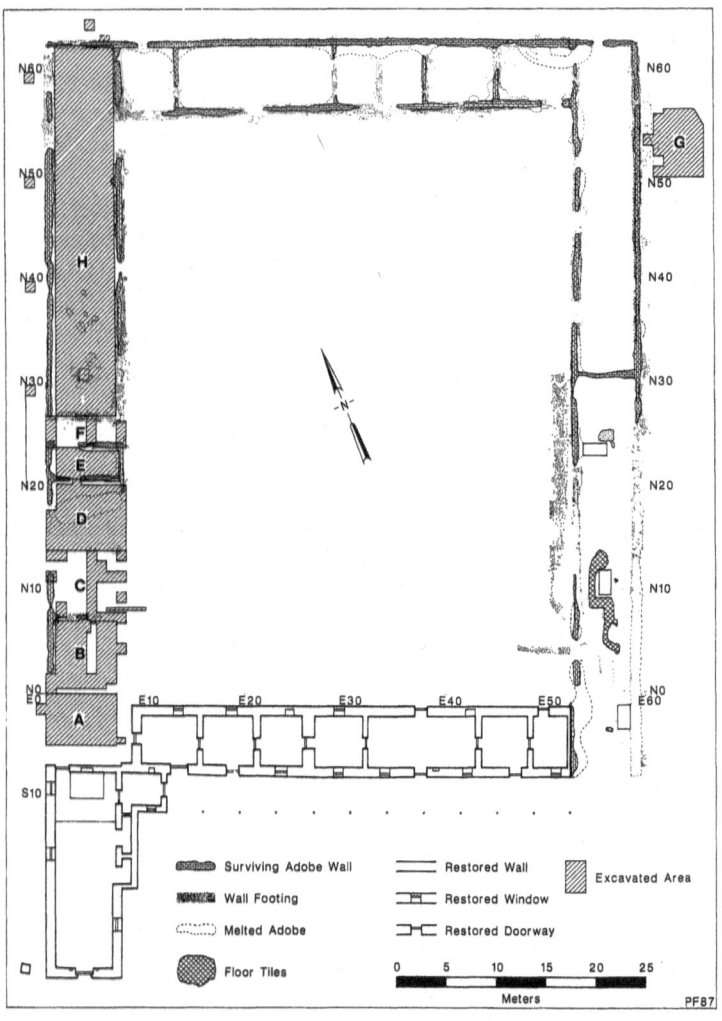

Figure 1. Excavations in the Central Quadrangle at Mission Soledad.

cade the artifacts that represented continuity of traditional activities increased from under 30 percent around 1795 to approximately 45 percent of the subassemblage by the early part of the nineteenth century. In this period the number of Indians at the mission grew rapidly, tripling from 240 in 1795 to 725 in 1805. In contrast, during the first four years (1791–94), the population grew slowly. With a lower ratio of Indians to Spanish and fewer "pagans" being baptized, the missionaries were able to influence their charges more during the mission's early years.

The decade 1800–1810 saw a new trend. The continuity of traditional activities declined from 40 percent of the subassemblage from the early floor in the kitchen, dating from approximately 1800, to 30 percent of the subassemblage from the middle period floor, dating from around 1810. During the period 1805–10 the mission's population was gradually declining, and the number of new baptisms was lower than during any previous five-year period. The decline in recruiting gave the missionaries the opportunity to change the culture of the Native Americans who had been brought to the mission in the previous decade.

An increase in overall continuity of traditional activities was found in the assemblage from the early 1820s, when the proportion of these artifacts grew to 40 percent of the subassemblage. During this time the mission's population continued to experience a gradual decline, in spite of the importation of non-Christianized Indians from the Central Valley. Only in 1822 was the number of new baptisms comparable to baptismal figures in the years of heavy local recruiting, between 1799 and 1805. Therefore, the increase in continuity of traditional activities cannot be explained by an influx of large numbers of "pagan" Indians.

The analysis revealed some significant trends at Mission Soledad. An initial period of relatively slow population growth to 1795 resulted in the Indians' rapid acceptance of Spanish material culture. Next a period of rapid population growth through recruitment brought about an increase in traditional cultural elements. After a decline in recruiting in 1805, elements of traditional culture decreased again. Finally, during the ensuing period of continued population decline and relatively limited recruiting, the proportion of elements indicating continuity of traditional culture rose again. The evidence suggests, then, that a change occurred in the relationship between the degree of cultural change and patterns of recruitment of Indian converts from outside the mission community around 1810. The cause of this change is found in the economic function of the mission. The decade 1800–1810 was characterized by a dramatic increase in economic production in California. The missionaries diverted labor from surplus food production to diversified agricultural production, craft specialization, and the specialized production of livestock. Livestock was the major source of Spanish trade wealth both within California and internationally.

The archaeological record shows that between 1800 and 1810 the missions changed their emphasis from attracting, controlling, and changing the culture of the California Indians to exploiting their labor for economic production. Of course, the missionaries still demanded a certain level of European culture, especially from the males, who were the prime labor force, for they had to be able to carry out the introduced European agricultural tasks, industrial processes, and crafts needed to produce the missions' wealth. In other aspects of their lives, though, greater continuity of native traditions could be tolerated, except in religious practices. As long as the Indians carried out Christian religious activities and the tasks assigned to them, the missionaries did not enforce other aspects of Spanish culture as rigorously as before. The result was increased continuity of traditional native activities.

The concrete elements of culture (material items and explicit behaviors) move between cultures much more rapidly and easily than symbolic, ideological, and valuational elements. In view of the fact that the California Indians were able to maintain 30 percent or more of their material culture, albeit in modified form, their retention of the nonmaterial elements must have been far higher, even in the area of religion. This figure becomes even higher if allowance is made for perishable items. Therefore, after the change in the missions' main emphasis between 1800–1810, there was not much change in these nonmaterial and religious realms of culture.

An end point in the cultural change of the California Indians occurred by 1810, not at the secularization of the missions in 1834, as is often assumed. Thereafter, a measurable return to traditional activities occurred. The ultimate result of Spanish-Indian contact was a form of stabilized pluralism in which the Native Americans adopted a culture that was neither native nor Spanish but exhibited elements of both. In material culture this blend was around 40 percent Indian.

In ideology, symbolism, and values, however, the Indian percentage was far higher, with only a thin veneer of Spanish culture.

The foregoing directly contradicts the usual model of Indian cultural change in the missions, which assumes that the longer the Indians were in the missions, the more acculturated they became, which was almost certainly the case for each individual Indian. With the constant influx of un-Christianized Indians throughout the mission period, however, this steady increase in the level of European culture was not the pattern for the mission population as a whole. Furthermore, the amount of Spanish culture acquired by individuals diminished after the 1800–1810 change in emphasis of the missions to economic production.

The Economy of Soledad Mission

From its inception one of the central activities developed at Soledad was European-style agriculture, which served the double purpose of supporting the resident population and producing surpluses that could be distributed to the military or sold to the settlers.[15] The Spanish Crown, which theoretically held title to all lands in the Americas, assigned to each mission a roughly defined territory within which to develop agriculture and ranching. The territory of Soledad mission stretched from nine to twenty leagues east to west and three leagues north to south, primarily in the Salinas Valley.[16] Grants of land to private individuals in the 1830s and 1840s from the former Soledad mission territory totaled 187,605 acres, approximately the amount of land available for economic development.[17]

The Salinas Valley is in the rain shadow of the Santa Lucias. Rainfall decreases south up the valley to Soledad, where the average rainfall is 8.94 inches, and then increases.[18] The Spanish were probably not aware that they had chosen the driest point in the valley for the settlement. Agricultural returns suggest that a lack of water was a major problem. Mission Soledad did not develop the extensive irrigation facilities of many other missions. As a result, it was hard hit when droughts struck, and they came frequently: in 1795, 1796, 1800, 1805, 1807, 1808, 1809, 1815, 1817, 1820, 1822, 1826–27, and 1829.

The hydrology of the Salinas Valley had a major impact on the development of Mission Soledad. The river flows in a broad sandy channel into which the waters sink in summer, becoming an underground river. At Soledad these waters reappear, and the river is perennial from this point to the ocean. This was undoubtedly a major factor in the choice of the mission's location. The Arroyo Seco, the most northerly of the Salinas River's main tributaries, discharges primarily from January to March. Mission Soledad is located just one and a half kilometers west of the confluence of the Arroyo Seco and the Salinas River, a point that was extremely vulnerable to flooding. The mission was on the edge of an alluvial terrace, on a low promontory that projects northwest into the valley about six meters above the land to the west, north, and northeast.

The point where the Arroyo Seco emerges from its steep-sided canyon into the broad Salinas Valley was also prone to flooding. This area was vitally important to the mission, as it was where the water for the irrigation system was drawn. The early years of the mission's development were hampered by the lack of an irrigation system, and one was not built until 1796 or later. In March 1799 Fr. Mariano Payeras wrote that the heavy volume of the river had damaged the dam and irrigation ditch (zanja) that were crucial for agriculture at the mission.[19]

Fr. Payeras also warned about the danger of heavy rains and flooding. The mission and its fields and irrigation systems were more vulnerable to waters flooding from the Arroyo Seco than from the Salinas. In addition, flash floods from the Sierra de Salinas, emerging from the canyons south-southwest of Soledad, had only about a kilometer of the valley floor to cross before reaching the mission. Not surprisingly, floods did occur at the mission, especially in 1824, although there was flood damage in 1799, possibly in 1820, and probably in 1831–32. The danger from flooding was extreme, and it may be that the mission escaped lightly. After the flood of 1824 it took two years to rebuild the structures destroyed, and the missionaries were continually making repairs from that time until the mission's secularization.[20]

As discussed earlier, land in the Salinas Valley is fertile, but the limitations of labor and the inability to develop irrigation reduced the importance of agriculture at Soledad. Not much land in the Salinas River floodplain could be irrigated, and thus a great deal of the grain production depended on variable rainfall. Because of ecological factors, agricultural production at Soledad varied from year to year, and production levels were low when compared with those of neighboring missions with better prospects for agriculture.

Cultural, Economic, and Demographic Change in Alta California 121

Table 1
Ratio of Seed Planted to Harvest at Soledad Mission, Selected Years

Year	Wheat	Barley	Corn
1792	1:21	1:29	—
1793	1:15	1:17	—
1794[a]	1:6	1:14	—
1795[a]	No harvest		
1796[a]	1:10	—	—
1797	1:9	1:11	1:78
1798[a]	1:6	1:24	1:55
1810	1:17	1:60	1:100
1811	1:15	1:60	1:75
1812	1:14	1:14	1:67
1813[a]	1:14	1:28	1:20
1814	1:15	1:25	1:100
1815[a]	1:8	1:14	1:83
1816	1:10	1:24	1:133
1817	1:16	1:25	1:167
1818[a]	1:8	1:9	1:33
1819	1:13	1:14	1:100
1820[a]	1:12	1:17	1:20
1821	1:14	1:5	1:105
1822[a]	1:6	1:3	1:40
1823[a]	1:10	1:13	—
1824[a]	1:9	1:3	—
1825	1:16	1:26	1:300
1826	1:10	1:14	1:133
1827[a]	1:4	1:11	1:7
1828	1:15	—	1:100
1829[a]	1:11	—	—
1830[a]	1:6	1:11	—
1831[a]	1:6	1:10	1:50
1832[a]	1:11	1:2	1:32

Source: Soledad Mission Annual Reports, Santa Barbara Mission Archive-Library.

[a] Poor return for at least one crop.

A more detailed examination of crop returns at Soledad, in this case the ratio of seed to harvest (table 1), highlights the unreliability of agriculture and documents the frequency of poor harvests.[21] Three grains formed the staple of mission agriculture: wheat, corn, and barley. Wheat was the most important crop by volume of production. In normal years of rainfall all three crops gave good returns. There was a poor harvest at Soledad about every other year, however, as demonstrated by a low return of seed to harvest. Moreover, poor harvests came with more frequency in the 1820s and 1830s, when the military increasingly pressed the mission economies to produce large surpluses. The ecological limitations on agriculture prompted the Franciscans stationed at Soledad to specialize in ranching.

The lands of the mission domain in the Salinas Valley were ideally suited for ranching, and the missionaries oversaw the development of herds of cattle and sheep. Livestock were run on three ranches located within the mission territory. The relative importance of ranching can be judged by the value of the ranches and livestock at secularization: 31,136 pesos of a total value of 47,297 pesos.[22] Cattle supplied some meat but were primarily used for hides and tallow; sheep supplied wool used for textile production. Annual reports in the 1820s and 1830s mentioned that Indians worked at looms, the only specific reference to an activity other than building construction.[23] Conditions unique to Soledad apparently prompted the Franciscans to specialize in textiles, and the provision of blankets and clothing may have been viewed by the missionaries as their major contribution to the military.

Although the mission population was small, a significant proportion of the Indians, as much as 70 percent of the population, were considered able-bodied workers. Moreover, the missionaries did not occupy the available labor force in major building construction projects, as at other missions. The mission building complex had been completed before 1810, and the annual reports after that date merely record the maintenance, renovation, and repair of existing buildings. The only large project during this period was the construction of a chapel to replace the church damaged in a flood.[24] A conscious decision appears to have been made not to enlarge or replace the buildings constructed in the 1790s, and to direct labor to other activities, such as textile production.

The records of other missions document the volume of food, clothing, and footwear provided to the military during the difficult period of transition from colony to nation. These subsidies helped finance continued colonization in Alta California.[25] No such documents for Soledad have been found, but an extant mission account book records transactions with soldiers and settlers for food, clothing, boots, and shoes.[26] Using the labor of the resident Indian population, the Franciscans at Soledad materially contributed to the perpetuation of the colonial order in Alta California.

Demographic Patterns at Soledad Mission

Population levels at Mission Soledad were directly related to the ability of the missionaries to recruit new converts. The mission population could not reproduce itself, and it expanded only during periods of active recruitment and contracted when the number of new recruits and children born at the mission did not match mortality levels. Several factors limited the ability of the missionaries to attract recruits: the availability of soldiers to participate in the recruiting expeditions, competition among neighboring missions for recruits, and the supply of food. Poor harvests were frequently followed by a reduction in recruiting efforts. In 1822, for example, missionaries baptized 124 recruits. The harvest in that year was poor, and the number of recruits brought into the mission dropped in the following year to nine. Indian resistance also limited the Franciscans' ability to recruit.[27]

Death rates were high in the mission community, and patterns of mortality by age and gender had a considerable impact on the Indian population's reproduction and survival. In 1797 California governor Diego de Borica attributed the high rates of mortality to the changes in life style enforced in the missions.[28] This view is consistent with the observation that only a few epidemics of contagious disease such as smallpox or measles attacked the mission population.

Borica identified four factors related to high native mortality. The first was the Indians' loss of liberty. The second was the heavy workload, which could have affected the fertility of women incorporated into the labor regime, reduced the amount of milk produced by nursing women, and interrupted a normal pregnancy if the woman was made to work at difficult tasks. The third factor was the poor hygiene practiced by the mission population, attributable to changes in clothing and housing and the lack of attention given to hygiene by the missionaries. The congregation of the Indians into compact settlements facilitated the spread of respiratory ailments and diarrhea caused by contact with polluted water. The high rates of infant and child mortality may have been caused, in part, by dehydration associated with diarrhea. Finally, Borica cited the common practice of locking up single women and the wives of absent Indians in damp and fetid dormitories at night as damaging to their health.

The 1813 responses to a government questionnaire on conditions in Alta California, sent to obtain information on the missions for the liberal Spanish Cortes, which was considering mission secularization, indicate another cause of Indian depopulation at Soledad mission. According to missionary Antonio Jayme, O.F.M., "the dominant malady among them is venereal disease [mal qalico-syphilis] killing them off nor can we find a remedy to stave it off."[29] The factors outlined above contributed to exceptionally high mortality rates at Mission Soledad and the destruction of the Indian population within several generations. An analysis of patterns of fertility, migration, and mortality shed further light on this demographic collapse. Because of the disappearance of the burial register for Soledad, figures on mortality had to be extracted from the extant annual reports.

Several patterns emerge.[30] Death rates were consistently high, and higher than birth rates. In the 1790s birth rates were high, as evidenced by a gross reproduction ratio (GRR) of 4.92 during the 1793–97 quinquennium. Then birth rates dropped; more significantly, infant mortality rates were extremely high. The net reproduction ratio stood at 0.08 during the same quinquennium, indicating that the high birth rates had a negligible impact on the population, which would have experienced a net decline of 92 percent over a generation had death rates remained at similar levels. Conditions at the mission deteriorated after the 1790s as birth rates declined, the net reproduction ratio approached zero, and, during the decade 1800–1810, death rates soared because of high epidemic mortality. The death rate during the 1798–1802 quinquennium reached 326 per thousand population, and 183 per thousand between 1803 and 1807. More than 90 percent of the population disappeared over a generation. Life expectancy was extremely low, and congregation into the mission led to the virtual destruction of the local indigenous population. Continued recruitment accelerated this trend but prolonged the life of the mission.

The resettlement of Native Americans into what in effect were death camps was an integral aspect of Spanish Indian policy in Alta California. Living conditions at Soledad were such as to raise mortality rates to levels that were significantly higher than among contemporary European populations. The consistently high mortality that caused the demographic collapse of the California Indian populations was unique in the late eighteenth century to the missions, and at a more general level to the European–Native American interface.

Mortality rates were even higher for young children, girls, and women in Mission Soledad. These patterns can be documented by comparing the population of young children and females to the total population. With the exception of the first period of heavy recruitment in the 1790s, young children formed only a small percentage of the total population, less than 20 percent and as low as 9 percent. Missionaries recruited from a cross-section of the Indian population, and native women living in the mission bore children. More than 90 percent of the children died before reaching age ten, however, which shows up as the low percentage of the 0–9 cohort in relation to the total population.[31]

There was also a considerable sexual imbalance in the mission population.[32] Except in the first phase of recruitment, girls and women formed a relatively small proportion of the total population, between 30 and 40 percent in the period after 1810. This imbalance stemmed from both the high pattern of infant and child mortality and high rates of mortality among women. The difference between the mission group and other documented populations clearly can be attributed to the unique conditions of the missions, such as the practice of incarceration in dormitories. Young girls in the age cohort 0–9 formed an equally small percentage of the total female population.

The age and sex imbalance of the population of Soledad mission was most pronounced in the period after 1810 and highlights an important factor in the expansion of the mission economies after that date: the low dependency ratio, or the relation between the productive and unproductive members of the population. Therefore, a large percentage of the total population could be put to work in agriculture, livestock tending, building construction, and artisan industry such as textile production. In the long run, however, and especially in the absence of recruitment of new converts from the hinterland, the mission population was doomed to extinction, as the pool of potential mothers declined and the children born at the mission rarely survived past age ten. In the short term, the peculiar demographic characteristics of the Soledad mission population facilitated the emergence of a specialized textile artisan industry that contributed to the financing of the continued colonization of Alta California.

The goals of the missionaries and government changed during the course of the colonization of Alta California in response to the needs of the state. Visitador General José de Gálvez organized the occupation of Alta California in 1769 for geopolitical reasons. The perceptible shifts in economic structure and the approach to Indian cultural change occurred not as a result of a modification in the ideology of the missionaries but rather because of the needs of the colonial state. Pressure to supply the military with food and clothing, more than any other factor, brought about the changes documented at Soledad mission.

Between 1800 and 1810 the missions directed their efforts to exploiting the labor of the California Indians for economic production. Archaeological analysis shows that the result was an increase in the continuity of traditional native culture, except in activities for which a degree of European culture was needed for economic purposes. The California Indians maintained over 30 percent of their material culture throughout, and their retention of the nonmaterial elements was far higher. After 1810 there was a measurable return to traditional cultural activities, with only a thin veneer of Spanish culture. This conclusion fortifies the interpretation that, as far as the Alta California missions were concerned, the political and economic goals of the colonial state were more important than the spiritual imperative of the Franciscans.

Living conditions at Soledad mission and other factors undermined the viability of the native population of the mission. The Franciscans responded to the rapid decline in population by bringing in more converts to replace those who died. The missionaries rationalized the high mortality rates ideologically by baptizing the Indians before their death and populating heaven with the souls of thousands of new Christians. There was also a pragmatic side to the generally Spanish-born Franciscans. They reorganized the Soledad mission economy to meet the needs of the secular state, recognizing that these needs superseded the transformation of the culture, social organization, and world view of the Chalon and Esselen Indians. The converts living at Soledad mission paid the price for the implementation of the mission program in the Salinas Valley and saw the material benefits of their labor largely expropriated by prominent settlers after secularization in the mid-1830s.

Notes

1. Francisco Uria to Governor Echeandia, 1828, Santa Barbara Mission Archive-Library (hereinafter SBMA), document no. 3121.

2. Robert Gibson, "Ethnogeography of the Northern Salinan," in Robert Hoover and Julia Costello, editors, *Excavations at Mission San Antonio: The First Three Seasons, 1976–1978* (Los Angeles, 1985), p. 165.

3. Gary Breschini, Trudy Haversat, and R. Paul Hampson, *A Cultural Resources Overview of the Coast and Coast-Valley Study Areas* (Salinas CA, 1983), p. 289.

4. Thomas Hester, "Esselen," in *Handbook of North American Indians*, Vol. 8: *California*, edited by Robert Heizer (Washington DC, 1978), p. 497.

5. The first estimate is from A. L. Kroeber, *Handbook of the Indians of California* (Washington DC, 1925), p. 545; the second is from Sherburne F. Cook, "The Esselen: Territory, Villages, and Population," *Monterey County Archaeological Society Quarterly* 2:1 (1974), 11.

6. Kroeber, *Handbook*, p. 4664; Richard Levy, "Costanoan," in *Handbook of North American Indians*, 8:485; Sherburne F. Cook, *The Conflict between the California Indian and White Civilization* (reprint; Berkeley and Los Angeles, 1976), p. 186.

7. Levy, "Costanoan," p. 485; Cook, *Conflict*, pp. 184–85.

8. A. L. Kroeber, "A Mission Record of the California Indians," *University of California Publications in American Archaeology and Ethnology* 8:1 (1908), 22; Kroeber, *Handbook*, p. 471; Levy, "Costanoan," p. 489.

9. Levy, "Costanoan," p. 489.

10. Kroeber, "Mission Record," p. 23; Kroeber, *Handbook*, p. 472; C. Hart Merriam, "Village Names in Twelve California Mission Records," *Reports of the University of California Archaeological Survey* 74 (1968), 373–74; Levy, "Costanoan," p. 489.

11. Paul Farnsworth, "The Economics of Acculturation in the California Missions: A Historical and Archaeological Study of Mission Nuestra Señora de la Soledad" (Ph.D. dissertation, University of California, Los Angeles, 1987), pp. 340–93; Paul Farnsworth, "The Economics of Acculturation in the Spanish Missions of Alta California," *Research in Economic Anthropology* 11 (1989), 217–48.

12. Zephyrin Engelhardt, O.F.M., *Mission Nuestra Señora de la Soledad* (Santa Barbara CA, 1929), p. 21; Farnsworth, "Soledad," p. 349; H. H. Bancroft, *History of California* (San Francisco, 1886), 2:153.

13. A mean ceramic date is based on the mean date for the production of all the shards in the level or feature. This method is derived from the work of

Stanley South, *Method and Theory in Historical Archaeology* (New York, 1977), pp. 207–14. California mean ceramic dates are modified versions of the mean ceramic date concept, with additional Mexican, Spanish, Chinese, and nineteenth-century British ceramic types included. In addition, historical factors are used to narrow the date ranges. Although the CMCDs provide a convenient method of expressing the approximate date for each level or feature, they should not be considered absolute dates, for they represent the mean of a range of possibilities. In essence, a CMCD is the most likely date at which a level or feature was formed, based on the ceramic artifacts.

14. Farnsworth, "Soledad"; Farnsworth, "Economics"; Paul Farnsworth, "Mission Indians and Cultural Continuity," *Historical Archaeology* 26:1 (1992), 22–36.

15. For a more complete discussion of the economic relations of the missions, the military, and the settlers in Alta California, see Robert H. Jackson, "Population and the Economic Dimension of Colonization in Alta California: Four Mission Communities," *Journal of the Southwest* 33:3 (1991), 387–439.

16. Engelhardt, *Soledad*, p. 34.

17. Farnsworth, "Soledad," p. 249.

18. Homer Hamlin, *Water Resources of the Salinas Valley, California* (Washington DC, 1904), p. 45; Robert Durrenberger and Robert Johnson, *California: Patterns on the Land* (Palo Alto CA, 1976), p. 130.

19. Document no. 429, SBMA.

20. Soledad Mission annual reports, SBMA.

21. The ratio of seed to harvest at Mission Soledad can be compared with agriculture in another part of Latin America that functioned at similar levels of technology and depended on significant labor inputs: Cochabamba in Bolivia. The following seed-to-harvest returns were reported for Cochabamba agriculture in the 1920s: irrigated corn, 1:100; unirrigated corn, 1:50; wheat, 1:10; and barley 1:10. It should be noted, however, that corn was the principal grain grown in Cochabamba and that wheat and barley were produced on lands of lesser quality. See Robert H. Jackson, "Liberal Land and Economic Policy and the Transformation of the Rural Sector of the Bolivian Economy: The Case of Cochabamba, 1860–1929," (Ph.D. dissertation, University of California, Berkeley, 1988), p. 23.

22. Engelhardt, *Soledad*, pp. 41–42.

23. Soledad Mission annual reports, SBMA, 1827, 1830, and 1831.

24. Soledad Mission annual reports, SBMA, 1810–32.

25. See, for example, Jackson, "Population."

26. Mission Soledad account book, Bancroft Library, University of California, Berkeley.

27. Soledad Mission baptismal register, Monterey Diocese Chancery Archive, Monterey CA; Soledad Mission annual reports, SBMA.

28. Robert H. Jackson, "Causes of High Rates of Indian Mortality in the Alta California Missions: A Contemporary Analysis," *Noticias* 3 (1988), 6–9.

29. Maynard Geiger, O.F.M., and Clement W. Meighan, translators and editors, *As the Padres Saw Them: California Indian Life and Customs as Reported by the Franciscan Missionaries, 1813–1815* (Santa Barbara CA, 1976), pp. 71–80 (quotation, p. 76).

30. The inverse projection method developed by historical demographer Ron Lee is used to calculate estimates of demographic statistics through the microcomputer program Populate. Populate analyzes annual totals of births, deaths, and population and produces quinquennium data on crude birth and death rates per thousand population, gross and net reproduction ratios that measure a population's production of children and its net growth through natural reproduction, and mean life expectancy at birth. A net reproduction ratio of 1.0 indicates a doubling of a population over a generation, and a figure of 0.50 means a halving of the population over a generation. Robert McCaa and Hector Perez Brignoli, *Populate: From Births and Deaths to the Demography of the Past* (Minneapolis, 1989).

31. For a more complete discussion of infant and child mortality in the missions, see Robert H. Jackson, "Patterns of Demographic Change in the Missions of Central Alta California," *Journal of California and Great Basin Anthropology* 9 (1987), 251–72.

32. For a more complete discussion of the sexual imbalance in the mission populations, see Jackson, "Patterns of Demographic Change."

Lance R. Grahn

Guajiro Culture and Capuchin Evangelization: Missionary Failure on the Riohacha Frontier

This chapter examines the dynamics of eighteenth-century indigenous responses to mendicant evangelization in the Guajira peninsula of northern New Granada. In this case, which ended in self-admitted missionary failure, the contours of mission ethnohistory especially reflected the Guajiro Indians' cultural adaptability, survival, and independence. Colonial Christianity, even when backed by military force, failed to take hold among the Guajiros—the predominant Indian group in the region—because, in the main, it did not displace native spirituality and mores. The priests, and especially the Capuchin friars who dominated this mission field, did not meet a primary responsibility of evangelization. The ability of the Guajiros to maintain their foundational cultural supports allowed them to deflect Spanish ideological and physical attacks.

The work of Michel Perrin demonstrates that colonial-era Guajiro leaders adapted traditional mythologies to the new realities of imperialism,[1] but the stories' essence and pre-Columbian significance persisted. For example, Christian patriarchy failed to replace Guajiro matrilineality, a basic principle of Guajiro culture and society. Catholic doctrine and ecclesiastical structure, rooted in male dominance, did not overturn the indigenous centrality of the mythic twin motif of the sexual duality of Guajiro religion. Instead, Guajiro clans generally maintained a significant degree of cultural autonomy and stability in the face of Catholic pressures to assume positions of socioreligious dependence. Moreover, violent Guajiro attacks on Catholic churches, their accoutrements, and their clergy throughout the eighteenth century signaled the Indians' outright rejection of Christianity.

Indian reactions to European intrusions also illustrated the capacity of Native Americans to use imperialism against itself, accomodating some of its elements to combat what they deemed its more destructive components. Guajiro headmen quickly learned the techniques of European trade and realized its benefits. They not only mythicized European-introduced livestock but also used it in profitable commercial intercourse with British and Dutch traders, establishing a useful and powerful counterweight, including access to superior weaponry, to Spanish influence in the area. This same trade supported regional contraband trafficking, of which even Spanish colonists and administrators took advantage. Guajiro participation in Caribbean trade networks, then, enabled clans to resist Spanish subjugation. On one hand, the Guajiros proved too astute commercially for the Spaniards to defeat them politically, militarily, or ideologically. On the other hand, the Guajiros were too important to the vitality of the local economy for Spanish authorities to risk their annihilation.

The confrontation between Guajiros and Capuchins on this strategically located imperial frontier demonstrated the historical dialectics of theory versus praxis and of metropolitan policy versus colonial reality that characterized New World imperialism. It also exhibited the intermingling of religious, political, and materialist expressions of cultural values, goals, and behaviors—both among and between Guajiros and Spaniards. Missionay evangelization, which pitted a Western worldview against a non-Western one, took place in a context equally defined by Indians and Europeans. In the end, the late-eighteenth-century finality of the Guajiro victory over Spanish pretensions made it clear that Native Americans were central players in the imperial enterprise, shaping and determining its character and impact.

The Cultural Confrontation of Evangelization

Spanish efforts to convert and so to civilize the Guajiros and other smaller neighboring tribes, such as the Chimilas and Motilones, displayed the early modern European adherence to religious conversion as part of imperialism. Christian evangelization was a foundational principle that justified Spain's presence in the Americas. Lost souls had to be saved; it was the Christian mandate. Even the increasing secularization of Spanish imperial rule in the eighteenth century did not nullify the western European axiomatic equation of Christian salvation and true civilization. Conversion and acculturation, in turn, were to produce and maintain political stability, especially on American frontiers, and so buttress Spanish imperial dominion there. Viceroy Pedro Solís Folch de Cardona (1753–61), for example, saw the conquest of the Guajiros as a necessary and critical expression of Spanish power and authority and so called it "a very useful project" to which "all possible energy" should be given.[2] Antonio Julián, a Jesuit missionary dispatched to the Guajira by Solís, declared,

> No doubt one of the reasons for this precious pearl [of the province of Santa Marta] having been hidden is that in it have been left the fatal vestiges of three barbarous nations [the Guajiros, Motilones, and Chimilas] that surround it. Indomitable, [they remain] rebellious until now against religion, the Crown of Spain, and peaceful civility. Impudent, terrible, and dominating the best lands, these [Indians] impede to great extent free commerce [throughout the province] and even throughout the New Kingdom [of Granada]. The pacification of these nations and their removal from the darkness of infidelity in which they still deplorably lie would be of great service to God our Lord, the Crown of Spain, and merchants and nonmerchants who wish to come to the New Kingdom of Granada; and then the wealth of rich goods and treasures which have been hidden in the province would be brought to light.[3]

This political baggage of evangelization notwithstanding, missionization remains fundamentally a spiritual and religious enterprise, a contest between Western and indigenous religious views. We now recognize that the failure of Catholic Christianity to quash Native American spirituality was not simply a result of "the large number of idolators . . . in contrast to the small number of missionaries," the difficulty of communication (specifically, communicating a Western faith system to non-Western peoples with their own fully developed cosmologies), and the overt irony of Christian teachings of love versus Christian brutish behavior.[4] These factors, of course, played a part in Indian-missionary relations, but they ascribe to the "hearers of the gospel" only a passive role in the exchange. As the Guajiro Indians' responses to missionary efforts attest, Native Americans were active and equal participants in this spiritual duel.

Upholding traditional cosmology and spirituality, the Guajiros sustained their own colonial-era historical agency, ultimately determining their response to Christianity. They could accept or reject conversion, and if the former, select the elements of Catholicism to incorporate into their own culture. In so doing, they filtered Christianity through several layers of analysis, such as their own cultural values and systems, internal and external political rivalries, and economic motivations and traditions. For the Guajiros, becoming Christian was a logical response to changing external conditions that, at the same time, maintained their cultural stability: "The native view of reality stood behind accepted ways of dealing with practical situations, and the life style confirmed their perception of the cosmos. Religion united world view and ethos into a mutually supportive system, rationalizing the nature of existence and directing human participation in it."[5]

The traditional Western assumption regarding conversion to Christianity is, Why not? Strictly interpreted, Christianity assigns to itself universal validity and superiority over all other forms of religious expression. Its adherents, especially in the early modern period and those from Catholic Spain (or Puritan England), naturally acted on that premise. The Guajiros, however, resented that presumption. They recognized, as has the modern scholar Tzvetan Todorov, that "the Christians' position is not, in itself, 'better than that of the [Indians (Todorov, of course, refers specifically to the Mexica)],' or closer to the 'truth.' Religion, whatever its content, is certainly a discourse transmitted by tradition and important as a guarantee of a cultural identity. The Christian religion is not in itself more rational than the Indian 'paganism.' "[6] Like other Native American groups described in this volume, the Guajiros posed to those who sought to evangelize them, and to us as well, the weightier question, Why? What did Christianity have that was superior? Could it, and did it, uphold that claim? Would conversion lead to something better, however that "better" was defined? To the Guajiros, did conversion make sense, not only in the context of native culture and traditions but also in the context of change occasioned by European imperialism and rivalries in the area? By thus probing the soundness of Christian theology and missiology and their political, economic, and social ramifications, the indigenous inhabitants of the Guajira peninsula largely defined the character and direction of both religious and secular colonialism in their homeland.

Significantly, the general rejection of Christian theology and worship by the Guajiros did not mean that they were immune or opposed to all change. Rather, they could, and did, change when they decided it was in their best interest, and that very adaptability was a major factor in their successful rebuff of Spanish subjugation. It also reflected the Guajiros' commitment to maintaining an overall cultural stability and their capacity to use change in the service of continuity and survival when a tradition-bound adherence to pre-Columbian patterns might have led to their destruction at the hands of the European newcomers.

The Guajiros' acceptance of the Christians' commercial economy, for example, was an impressive case of indigenous and utilitarian cultural adaptation in response to European encroachment. It represented the careful process of Indian choice in the matter of external cultural pressures, including evangelization. In the sixteenth century, using runaway and stolen Spanish cattle and the agricultural lessons of Spanish clerics, the Guajiros established for themselves an economy based on the raising and sale of livestock.[7] They learned quickly that in their newly established world, commerce was profitable and full of power. Trading with Spaniards, Britons, and Dutch alike, they maintained their own cultural and societal core and became potent players in the social mix and political rivalries of European imperialism along the Spanish Main. The Indians were producers, middlemen, and consumers in the lively, and technically illegal, trade through the area that linked Kingston and Willemstad to markets in the Andean highlands of New Granada. English and Dutch provocateurs also found in their Guajiro partners an audience sympathetic to their anti-Spanish message and to stirring up trouble for local Spanish authorities. After all, it was Spanish officialdom that sought to subjugate the Guajiros and to end their profitable trade with the English and Dutch merchants and Spanish outlaws, whereas it was these very partners who supported the trade and supplied the Guajiros with weapons superior to those carried by Spanish troops.[8]

A confrontation between Guajiro and Spanish soldiers in the mid-1730s illustrates this indigenous decision-making process, the Guajiros' control of their own situation (including, by extension, their ability to deal largely on their own terms with Spanish missionaries), and the natives' clear understanding of power relationships in the colonial world. As part of the Spanish policy to curb the rampant smuggling in the jurisdiction of Riohacha and to pacify the "rebellious" Guajiros, the Santa Marta governor, Juan de Vera y Fajardo (1733–43), posted Captain José Barón de Chaves and a detachment of fourteen soldiers to El Pájaro, a landing on the western coast of the Guajira peninsula known to be a smugglers' haven. When the

Spaniards arrived at the cove, a group of Guajiro warriors surrounded them, disarmed Chaves and his men, and left. Soon afterward, however, the Guajiro band returned and gave back to Chaves the guns they had taken. They told him that they could buy better firearms from their English trading partners. The irony of this incident was not lost on the devastated captain, who took no further action against the Guajiros or illegal coastal trade.[9]

The Guajiros had turned European colonialism on its head. Adapting to an evolving system of international trade and using Spanish mercantilist weaknesses to their own advantage, they adopted colonial features that they found compatible with their own world view and polity. Mary Helms explains the dynamics of Indian contact with the Western world:

Interpretations of the outside world as a place of power, of Europeans as expression of such power [which, for the Guajiros, occurred within the context of international commerce], do derive from the group itself in the sense that traditional cosmographies and cosmologies define the cosmos and its power, assign particular symbolic significance to its parts and manifestations, and differentiate between the qualities associated with the cultural center or heartland of socialized community life and the extraordinary, power-filled supernatural attributes of realms that exist beyond and far off.[10]

Guajiro headmen likely found in international commerce a better, more logical, and more effective access to and explanation of cosmological (not to mention material) power than they did in Christianity, even though that was a fundamental intent of missionization. The friars purposed to explain to Indian listeners the universe, its operation, and the respective stations of the divine and the terrestrial in a way that the clerics naturally assumed was superior to all others. But, as Irving Hallowell states, "learning new religious beliefs and practices ... had to be motivated" by a sufficient want for something, a sufficient drive to do something and to get something, for "man is essentially a pragmatist, and a belief in the existence of supernatural beings and powers cannot be dissociated from his drives. The reality of the supernatural realm must meet the test of experience."[11]

To the Guajiros, European religion failed that test but European economic lessons did not. Consequently, the introduction of Western civilization among the Guajiros had most profoundly an overall economic effect that reformed but did not fundamentally alter their traditional spirituality. Instead, the Guajiro world view demonstrated flexibility and improvisation by pulling into its mythology cattle and the economic ramifications of herding. According to one Guajiro origin story, which illustrates this development, "Maleiwa [the creator deity] began to model clay on the summit of Iitujulu. He was going to make people. After preparing a lot of earth, he fashioned figures looking like cattle for those who were going to own cattle. For those who were to remain poor he did not make any; their world would be worthless, and they would not be able to obtain women. For those who would be poor, he made wretched-looking figures."[12]

Guajiro acceptance of elements of European culture, including the wavering presence of missionaries, then, represented not so much conversion as the vehicle of adoption of economic skills introduced by missionaries, skills that became part of, and so remained consistent with, the core principles of Guajiro cosmology and political economy. For the most part, the Guajiros incorporated lessons of economic "modernization" that actually braked their acceptance of the Christian gospel rather than produced the Christian conversion the missionaries anticipated.

Bolstered by their economic strength, the Guajiros accepted or rejected spiritual conversion as they saw fit. Save for a few notable exceptions that proved the rule, Guajiro clan leaders and their followers chose to reject Christianity and accept economic change that for them made cultural sense. Again, to cite Hallowell, "man is only a creature of culture in so far as he learns and uses the traditional instrumentalities of his society. But even so he is far from a passive instrument since he uses cultural means for attaining satisfying individual ends."[13] Guajiro leaders proved astute enough to know that Christian missionaries, like the political and military authorities who sought the Indians' pacification, were agents of subjugation, even if it was, at best, only subjugation to God. Initial missionary impact in the sixteenth century engendered ultimate failure in the eighteenth.

The Spanish defeat in the confrontation between Christian and indigenous spirituality and world views meant that the missionary efforts, secular initiatives, and promotional propaganda of the colonizers did not produce the desired religious, political, and fiscal realities of a permanent, prosperous Spanish colony in the Guajira. Viceroy Pedro Mendinueta (1797–1803) confessed that the century-long effort to subdue the Guajiros "had not fared well." In fact, their

Christian Hispanicization, that is, reducing "them with gentleness" and "introducing them to [Spanish] laws and religion," was "all but impossible." Hence, Mendinueta concluded, in a fine example of political doublespeak, that though he upheld "the undeniable law of the sovereign" and the ideal of Spanish sovereignty in the peninsula, his only realistic choice was to do as his predecessors had done: accept the Indians' rebellious (rebellious, that is, in the context of Spanish imperial goals) independence.[14]

The Capuchin Mission to the Guajiros and Indigenous Response

As was (and remains) the usual case with Western missionization among native inhabitants of the Americas, Asia, and Africa, Christians initiated the contact, and the cultural change and conflict it engendered, with the Guajiros of the Spanish Main. Consequently, Capuchin activities form a useful framework for an examination of Guajiro responses to missionary efforts. It should be remembered that ethnic cosmological conflict within missionization has political, economic, and strategic contexts, all which the Capuchin missions in the Guajira illustrate as well.

Catholic evangelism among the Guajiros began with Martín de Calatayud, a Hieronymite priest and bishop of Santa Marta from 1543 to 1548, when he walked across the peninsula in 1544 (not by choice but as the result of a navigational error that landed him and his party on the eastern side of the peninsula by mistake), lived for a time in Cabo de la Vela, and often resided in the port town of Riohacha, which even then was described as an open seaport "subject not only to the invasions of maritime enemies but also those of the Guajiro Indians who surround it."[15] The Guajiros (and their neighbors as well) had not only survived the initial stages of European military and spiritual conquest; they were also willing and able to vent their hostility toward the newcomers. They had rejected the initial attempts to introduce them to the "light" of the Christian gospel, the Roman Catholic church, and the "civilized" culture of Spain. The Guajiros' reputation at the end of the eighteenth century as an "irreconcilable enemy of Spain" and Roman Catholicism, then, was a long-standing tradition.[16]

The longest sustained period of Spanish attempts to evangelize the Guajiros began in 1691, when Father Juan Cuadrado de Lara stopped at a Guajiro settlement just south of the port of Riohacha while on a canonical visit through the diocese of Santa Marta. There he baptized two adults and several children. His optimistic report coincided with two other developments in the region: the desire of the leadership of the Capuchin Province of the Most Precious Blood of Christ of Valencia to expand the group's missionary efforts beyond the llanos of Caracas and the request by a band of Otomaco Indians, who lived west of Maracaibo in the jurisdiction of Riohacha, for a priest. Aware of this convergence and hopeful of reasserting hegemonic control over Tierra Firme, Charles II and his councilors responded with an August 1694 *cédula* that authorized and ordered the Capuchins to evangelize the Guajiros of Riohacha.[17]

The 1694 royal order set in motion the weaving of a complex web of evangelical enterprise led by the Capuchins and a series of clashes between Western and indigenous cultural systems. Gregorio de Ibi, Buenaventura de Vistabella, and Antonio de Ollería walked into the southern Guajira in 1694, even before word of their royal authorization arrived. They soon reported quick success. Reflecting the traditional Capuchin missiological emphasis on agriculture, they converted and resettled a group of Aratomo Indians in a mission village where the lessons of civility and civilization could be better taught. But in less than a year all three clerics were dead and few faithful converts remained. Coyamo Indians killed Ibi because they feared that he would lead Aratomo expansion into their territory. Fathers Vistabella and Ollería died in Maracaibo of illness contracted in the harsh physical and work environment of the Guajira.[18]

In this case, native resistance to the missionaries' message probably rested on cosmological and territorial grounds. Evangelization was not yet part of a fully articulated, multifaceted imperial program to subjugate and dominate the Indians for religious, political, and economic purposes, as it would be later in the eighteenth century. Consequently, the indigenes' commercial motivation for maintaining cultural independence, fully present in the 1730s, is not yet so viable. Like their more powerful Guajiro neighbors, the Aratomos moved forcefully to protect their cosmological and geographical domain, and so their identity as well, from the intrusive priests.

This response pattern was exhibited by Native Americans throughout the colonial era in northeastern New Granada. Father Pedro Aguado noted in his well-known sixteenth-century history of colonial New Granada that the Indians of Santa Marta province were famous for their obstinate defense of their home territories, "by which they conserved their liberty and heathenism (gentilidad)."[19] More than two hundred years later Spanish authorities—civil, military, and ecclesiastical—held the same opinion. In 1778, for example, Antonio de Narváez y la Torre, the highly capable governor of Santa Marta and Riohacha from 1777 to 1786, reminded the viceroy that the long history of Guajiro depredations had produced a series of royal orders unmatched for their rigor. Yet the Guajiros remained unconquered.[20]

Undeterred by the deaths of the first three clerics, the Capuchin order immediately sought to replace its deceased brothers in the field. Moreover, the Crown approved its request to build up an even larger mission among the Indians of the Guajira peninsula. In 1696 four Capuchins already working in the llanos of Caracas, led by Pablo de Orihuela, were transferred to what was designated the Santa Marta and Maracaibo mission. They were joined by a group of seven Capuchins from Spain headed by Mauro de Cintruénigo. The eleven gathered in the port of Riohacha, on the southwestern coast of the Guajira peninsula, and set up their residence in the nearby village of Laguna de Fuentes.

Like Ibi, Vistabella, and Ollería, the new arrivals at first reported good fortune. They established five mission villages in the Riohacha district: San Juan de la Cruz, San Antonio de Orino, San Nicolás de los Menores, Chimare, and El Toco. They also converted a clan chieftain baptized as Juan Moriscoti and one hundred others whom the missionaries hoped to set about the physically grinding work of gathering pearls. Delighted with the Capuchins' work, Spaniards predicted a quick Catholic pacification of the Guajiros. The work of the second group soon soured, however. By 1697 sickness, poor diet, and the rigor of their work felled seven of the missionaries, whereupon Orihuela and Cintruénigo returned to Spain to report on their missions' affairs. Only two priests remained in the field.[21]

Clerical mortality and pastoral difficulties led ecclesiastical and political administrators to restructure the Capuchin mission to the Guajiros. They transferred its locus to the city of Maracaibo and to the jurisdiction of the missionary province of La Grita and Mérida in Venezuela, regions purported to be "very fertile and salubrious sites and places of innumerable Indians" and therefore more conducive to missionary success.[22] Again, work among the Aratomos was to be the springboard to subsequent Guajiro evangelization.

In 1700 Father Cintruénigo returned to the town of Riohacha to oversee the transfer of the remaining work to Nuestra Señora de los Remedios near Maracaibo. What he found was an understaffed mission in even more serious disarray than before. In his absence the Guajiros had begun to raid Spanish ranches and steal livestock. Their aggression soon swelled into a rebellion against the Catholic presence in their homeland. Joined by mission Indians from La Cruz, Orino, and El Toco, the rebels pushed the civilian and military colonists of Menores southward toward Valledupar. The Capuchin friars fled to the safety of the port of Riohacha.

The results of the rebellion were manifest when the governor of Santa Marta province, Diego Peredo (1701–3), toured the Guajira peninsula. He encountered no priest nor any Christians. By his account, he took on himself the conversion of the Guajiros. He claimed to have reduced one clan, persuading its members to accept catechization.[23] It is not unlikely that this was the already reduced Moriscoti group.

The Guajiro majority remained unimpressed by the Christian gospel and Spanish will. According to Juan de la Rosa de Amaya y Buitrago, an eyewitness to the uprising, "after the rebellion . . . the Guajiros' arrogance grew; [they hurled] their disrespectful threats [at the Spaniards], telling them that as long as they do not drive them to the Sierra Nevada to live with the Arhuaco Indians, the challenges [would] not cease."[24] The municipal authorities of Riohacha took seriously these threats but responded with bravado of their own. They promised to make the upstart Guajiros beg for missionaries to instruct them in the holy faith, call themselves vassals of the king, and pay royal tribute. Unlike the Indians, however, the Riohachans could hardly back up their brave words. Their town was defenseless, its fortifications in shambles as a result of previous foreign attacks and Spanish inattention, so they posed little threat to the numerically stronger Guajiros.

The Indians reinforced their rejection of Christianity with a second uprising. After the accidental shooting of an Indian at Orino, the Guajiros again took up arms, forcing another Spanish retreat south toward Valledupar. They quickly established the upper hand and then agreed to a cease-fire. As Rosa de Amaya explained, the two rebellions in quick succession demonstrated the hopelessness of Guajiro reduction and conversion, for now it was "natural that the missionary fathers returned to their cloisters, . . . seeing how ineffectual they had been" in the Guajira mission field.[25]

The Guajiros had clearly asserted their military superiority in the peninsula. They used their military strength to good effect in the defense of their autonomy and their control over their homeland. But their rebellions also reasserted their belief in the viability and relevance of their own cosmology and world view vis-à-vis Catholicism. As the Coyamos' murder of Father Ibi in 1694 had presaged, the Guajiros by and large found nothing of theological use in Christianity, nor did it fulfill any cultural niche in native society beyond the agricultural ramifications of evangelization already established before 1700.

These rebellions, coming as they did after several years of Capuchin presence in the Guajira, also may have represented an indigenous refusal of the Christian cultural context of male dominance. Hispanic *marianismo* notwithstanding, early modern Christianity was a religious system largely based on the heroic attributes and actions of men, primarily designed for men, serviced exclusively on mission frontiers by men, and governed only by men. The maleness of pope, king, Trinity, and priests, and the Christian demand to accept male dominance of heaven and earth as a fundamental tenet could hardly escape the notice of an "unequivocally" matrilineal society like the Guajiros.[26] Family membership and identity, wealth, and political position passed exclusively through the mother's line. Though headmen were male, each Guajiro sib, or *parcialidad*, over which they exercised authority was nevertheless defined matrilineally.[27]

Moreover, eighteenth-century Guajiro cosmology likely reflected this feminine societal organization and vice versa. John Bierhorst explains: "The Guajiro . . . preserve a fully developed mythology based on a variant of The Twin Myth, in which the hero *Maleiwa*, after driving off the jaguar that had killed his mother, goes on to drill fire, save the world from the great flood, and establish human reproduction. But this mythology, at least today [and so likely in the eighteenth century as well], is largely rejected. Instead the Guajiro pay close attention to the lore of *Pulowi*, who is the underground mother of game animals." Central to the Guajiro cultural core, Pulowi was a "woman of great riches, immense riches, wearing jewels on her ankles, chains of gold around her wrists," according to the stories. Nonetheless, she was loath to part with her animal children, and she sought destructive vengeance on hunters who killed them. So vengeful was she that another story described her as a voracious monster whose companion, the rain spirit, brings her bottles of human blood to drink. The understanding of Pulowi may also reflect the Guajiros' economic reliance on Spanish-introduced domesticated animals, such as cattle, mules, and horses, giving Pulowi double significance in a confrontation with Catholicism.[28]

Nonetheless, unwilling yet to forgo Christian pacification, the Council of the Indies ordered in 1704 at least two Capuchin brothers into the diocese of Santa Marta to revitalize the Riohacha missions. Things moved slowly, but twelve years later, Pedro de Muniesa, prefect of the "missions of Maracaibo, Mérida, La Grita, and the Guajiro Indians," reestablished the mission village at San Juan de la Cruz, not far from the port town of Riohacha. His colleague, Mariano de Olocau, revived the mission of San Nicolás de los Menores on the royal road between Riohacha and Maracaibo.

By the early 1720s the Capuchins' missionary presence had expanded. San Juan de la Cruz housed 270 Indians. San Antonio de Orino, not far away, had 375 Indians and a "fine herd of cattle," which might well indicate that some Guajiros had relaxed their opposition to Catholicism for economic, not cosmological, reasons. Farther up the coast 200 Indians dedicated to pearl fishing, again a typical colonial Guajiro economic enterprise, inhabited the mission of San Agustín de Manaure. San Nicolás de los Menores also had about 200 native residents. Closer to Maracaibo the newest mission village, San José del Rincón, established by Fr. José de la Soria, procurator of the Capuchin mission in Riohacha, had some 160 Indians. The missions of San Pedro Nolasco, founded by the bishop of Santa Marta, Antonio Monroy y Meneses (1716–42) and staffed by seculars, and San Felipe de Palmarito, a settlement of 400 Indians established in the Capuchins' temporary absence from the region, also operated in the province. Altogether, however, these missions housed only 2 to 3 percent of the total Guajiro population.[29]

In light of subsequent events, these figures raise again the issue of motivation behind the Guajiro reply to evangelization. Given the numbers of mission Indians, it seems that some genuinely accepted Christianity. Bona fide conversions probably did occur, although, as James Axtell makes clear, sincerity is not always easy to determine precisely.[30] The missions' direct link with traditional colonial Guajiro economic activities also indicates the possibility that a minority adopted mission life for what they perceived to be its relatively greater economic security and for the status protection it likely afforded headmen.

At the same time, these same Capuchin data illustrate limited missionary success, a point not lost on the friars themselves or on their bishop. The Capuchins, fearing attack and martyrdom at Indian hands, took armed escorts when they ventured into Guajiro territory. The Guajiros made it clear to the priests that they and their ideology remained unwelcome.[31] The priests also correctly surmised that the size of the missions of San Juan de la Cruz, San Antonio de Orino, and San Felipe de Palmarito did not signal a long-lasting evangelical renewal. In 1721 Father Soría again requested military escorts for the friars, this time going to the viceroy of the newly created viceroyalty of New Granada, Jorge de Villalonga (1719–23), instead of appealing to local officials.[32] In 1730 Father Andrés de Oliva reported that the recent vitality of the missions had evaporated. "It is impossible to bring forth any fruit [among] these Indians," he said. "They have not given rise to even the slightest hope in all the time that so much work has been dedicated with indefatigable zeal to their conversion."[33]

The small successes around 1720 more likely revealed another fundamental reason for Guajiro animosity toward Hispanic Christianity. As Guajiros sought to protect their territory and their sense of self from uninvited external intrusions, so they protected their commercial prerogatives. Quite possibly, even though a relatively few looked to the missions for economic reasons, the majority rejected them because they threatened economic opportunity and its benefits. Note, for example, the Chaves incident cited earlier. The Guajiro band involved was trading with foreigners for guns that afforded them military superiority over Spanish soldiers. Unpacified Guajiros knew that subjection to the Spaniards' Christ and church would end that intercourse.

Significantly, this connection between Guajiro trade and resistance received considerable attention from colonial officials. A growing official uneasiness in the 1720s and 1730s with the strategic problems inherent in Guajiro trade with English, Dutch, and Spanish smugglers (evidenced by the creation of the viceroyalty of New Granada, first in 1718 and again in 1739) placed greater importance, and so greater pressure, on the Indians' spiritual conquest at the very time the Capuchins were under fire for their poor record. The Capuchins' failure to pacify all the Guajiros left political administrators with what they considered a grave problem. In 1731 José Andía de Rivero (1726–33), Caicedo's successor as governor of Santa Marta province, commissioned a study of contraband trafficking in the jurisdiction of Riohacha. It concluded that the fundamental cause of illegal trade there was Indian independence, specifically Guajiro freedom to trade openly with foreign merchants and New Granadan contrabandists. Not until Spain subdued all Guajiro clans, not just one or even a few, could imperial designs to curb or eliminate smuggling in Riohacha succeed.[34]

Guajiro commercial intercourse with foreigners and contrabandists almost certainly contributed to Viceroy Sebastián Eslava's (1740–49) irritation with the Capuchins. Despite their accumulation of several hundred wards, their attempts to reduce the Guajiro Indians as a whole had failed to meet metropolitan expectations. Consequently, Eslava, who generally supported missionary activity, complained to metropolitan officials about Capuchin ineffectiveness in Riohacha.[35] Eslava's complaints were not without foundation. Beyond the geopolitical and commercial considerations of Guajiro trade, the Indians were still so independent and in control of affairs that travelers, including the missionaries, between Santa Marta and Maracaibo had to pay Guajiro tolls or take an armed escort.[36]

The discomfiture within both political and ecclesiastical hierarchies over Capuchin results led Monroy and Eslava to propose first the expulsion of the Capuchins from the Riohachan mission field and then the division of the friars' territory into two districts. Santa Marta or Riohacha in the west and Maracaibo in the east would serve as local headquarters of Capuchin activity. That change would place mission administration closer to the field and so better regulate and promote evangelization on both sides of the peninsula. The vice-prefect of Capuchin missions and Philip V concurred, and the jurisdictional change was made.[37] Eslava recommended Jesuits for the Riohachan missions, a suggestion that his successor, José Alonso Pizarro (1749–53), implemented. Among the several Jesuits dispatched to the Guajira was Antonio Julián.

In 1753 these reforms showed promise when they coincided with the personal plans of three Guajiro headmen. One, Cecilio López de Sierra, already known to local and viceregal authorities as a supporter of Spain, offered to help the Spanish reduce other Guajiro clans (including the placement of missionaries among them) in return for support of his lifestyle, his political supremacy over his rivals (specifically, the chiefs Coporinche and Masquare), and his greater control over pearl fishing, brazilwood harvests, and livestock trade. Building on previous contacts between Cecilio and Viceroy Eslava and on the approval of the merchants of Santa Marta of the arrangement, José Xavier de Pestaña y Chumacero, the lieutenant governor of Riohacha, and Cecilio negotiated the deal in the Capuchin mission village of Boronata. At the same time, Coporinche and Masquare sought similar arrangements for Spanish leverage in their own pursuits of prestige and power. Each indicated to Spanish authorities a willingness to treat with them if it would lead to the defeat of his competitor. Like Cecilio's, Coporinche's and Masquare's offers to the provincial government included a provision allowing priests to be placed among their respective clan members.[38]

The decisions and actions of these three headmen highlight the interplay between personal wealth and Christianity in the Guajiro response to Christian missions. Cecilio, Coporinche, and Masquare saw the two as complementary. Their peers, who outnumbered them five to one, maybe even nine to one, however, judged them to be contradictory forces. Robert Lowie describes the economic functions of avuncular inheritance within the Guajiro matrilineal sib, in which a well-established sense of personal acquisitiveness was not overthrown but accentuated by the colonial cattle complex. "This comparatively new type of property, along with personal possessions, theoretically passes from matrilineal uncle to sister's son in accordance with the matrilineal system of the people. However, it is only the man's eldest sister's senior son who ranks as legatee. What is more, a man will deliberately strive to thwart the principle by transferring livestock to his own sons during his lifetime, so that actually few, if any, head of cattle remain for the nephew after his uncle's demise."[39] It is reasonable to posit, therefore, that Guajiro elites factored into their response to Catholic missions their perceived ability to promote thereby their status and wealth. If they saw a negative correlation, as most did, conversion carried with it serious liabilities. But, as was the case three decades earlier, a handful of Guajiro leaders judged direct contact with Christianity a useful tool.

Mission populations indicate that the administrative reforms and Guajiro rivalries somewhat enlivened missionary work in Riohacha during the 1750s. By 1759 the six Capuchin missions in Riohacha had more than one thousand Indian wards. The number of Indians at San Juan de la Cruz alone had doubled to nearly four hundred and fifty. At San Antonio de Orino, the location of hostilities earlier in the century, there were more than three hundred.[40]

Nonetheless, these Capuchin victories and the pacification of

Guajiro clans remained highly localized; neither the priests nor civilian authorities proved able to take full advantage of the opening given them by the three chiefs. Even inside the functional missions the pronounced economic motivation of Cecilio indicated that Guajiros accepted reduction more to uphold personal prestige than for any other purpose. The vast majority of Guajiros continued to reject Christianization and Hispanicization in favor of contact with English and Dutch smugglers and Spanish lawbreakers and what was for them, within the geographical confines of the Spanish empire, cultural independence. The Capuchin Andrés de Oliva reported in 1754 that "the mission is in a deplorable state; as there [are] only five of us, there is almost nothing that we can do among the Guajiros, nor do we serve any purpose except to bear witness to their evil deeds. Fortunately, we will leave their territories to new missionaries, and we will return to Spain."[41]

Perhaps the Capuchins realized that even within their villages Indian Christian forms and practices were outward expressions only, that a Christian ethos merely hid a Guajiro world view, that the Christian "logos" had never really defeated the Indian "mythos."[42] Antonio de Alcoy, prefect of the Capuchin missions in the Guajira in the early 1760s, reported in 1764 that the missionaries currently serving there were growing old and disheartened. Their zeal to plant "in the [Indians'] hearts" the "sweet seed of the Christian doctrine" failed to overcome the Guajiros' "notorious contumacy and natural arrogance." The Capuchins' only reward for their apostolic self-sacrifice was "tears of blood." Under those conditions, Alcoy admitted, the missionaries then present could no longer fulfill the royal mandate that sent them to the region. Therefore, he added, the Capuchins under his charge should be replaced.[43] Alcoy recognized that the evangelized, not the evangelizers, had made possible the brief upsurge of Capuchin missions in the previous decade. Despite their best efforts, the missionaries could not ensure the fruits of their labors; the choice to believe or not, to convert or not, rested with the Guajiros, not the Valencians.

Political authorities were equally dismayed and perplexed at the Guajiros' continued autonomy, so much so that Viceroy Solís contracted with an ex-convict and former slaverunner, Bernardo Ruiz de Noruego, to conquer the Guajiros. Accompanied by several priests, Noruego invaded Guajiro territory and bullied the residents of four villages into accepting Christianity and Spanish authority. That glimmer of hope for colonial officials died when he alienated the men under his command with his bombastic, self-serving, autocratic attitude. Noruego failed to subjugate any more Indians, turning metropolitan officials against him as well and prompting them to dismiss him from duty.[44]

Guajiro intransigence toward Capuchin evangelization exploded into open rebellion in 1769. Indian belligerence that year substantiated previous pessimism about mission work in the Guajira and shattered for the time being whatever illusions of success may have remained in Capuchin thinking. The hostility flared after the governor of Riohacha, Gerónimo de Mendoza, directed fifty Guajiro men chosen from the missions at Boronata, Rincón, Orino, La Cruz, and Camarones to punish nearby Cocina Indians for their continued obstinacy toward Spanish rule in Riohacha and Santa Marta. The armed mission Indians turned instead against the government and led a general Guajiro revolt against Spaniards and their influence.

Reminiscent of the decidedly anti-Catholic Pueblo revolt of 1680 in New Mexico, the Guajiro uprising targeted missions and missionaries. According to one Spanish survivor, Capuchin priest Pedro de Altea, the Indian rebels not only burned down the churches at La Cruz, Orino, and Rincón (where the fire destroyed the Capuchin archives) but also "in the midst of the flames profaned the sacred vessels, drinking from the holy chalices their evil *chichas* and liquor, which is the drink that they use for their intoxications, and [sharpened] their tools on the altar stones."[45] These desecrations were not accidental. No doubt the Indians knew full well the religious significance of the items on which they vented their anger. The Guajiros' abuse of the Christian artifacts forcefully evidenced their detestation of Catholicism and what it stood for, both ideologically and realistically.

Within weeks Guajiro attackers had destroyed six of the eight Capuchin missions, driven colonists and missionaries from the field, and threatened to overrun the port of Riohacha itself.[46] The 1769 revolt disheartened the Valencia Capuchins; unlike the 1700 rebellion, this violent and deliberate rejection of their work represented a defeat from which they never fully recovered.

Not surprisingly, secular authorities used these events to substantiate the futility of missionary pacification and to promote war against the Guajiros. Viceroy Pedro Messía de la Cerda (1761–72) laid the blame for the lack of Spanish progress in the Guajira directly at the Capuchins' feet. He claimed that these friars lacked the necessary "dedication for a ministry that requires apostle-like zeal so that privations may be suffered without repugnance."[47] The viceroy's close associate and confidant, Antonio Moreno y Escandón, even declared that the missionaries not only failed to subdue the Guajiros but provoked them to insolence with their own weakness and ineffectiveness.[48]

What the Spanish administration failed to recognize or to acknowledge was the Guajiros themselves. A wavering Capuchin commitment notwithstanding, the Guajiros were still in charge of their own religious fate. Christianity, which provided them no better explanation of the cosmos than did their own traditional mythology, threatened their cultural core and independence, both of which most of them refused to concede.

Moreover, the 1769 revolt exhibited a deep hatred of Spanish intrusion, an animosity whose roots sank deep into Guajiro self-identity. Eliseo Reclus, the famous chronicler of mid-nineteenth-century Colombia, wrote that the Guajiros still hated Catholicism because they saw in it only the "despised faith of their oppressors, the faith in whose name their ancestors were decapitated [and] reduced to slavery." The goal of Christian acculturation, he concluded, had produced among the Guajiros an aversion for anything Spanish and deepened their own native religion: "the love of liberty."[49] As in the 1700s, indigenous spiritual and cultural independence in the 1800s was linked to the Guajiros' enduring military strength: "The city of Riohacha is at the mercy of the Guajiro Indians. They could, if they wished, easily destroy it."[50]

With the missions in disrepute after 1769, the viceregal government tapped the military to solve its Guajiro problem. According to Moreno y Escandón, the Guajiros' armed rebellion, thievery, open rejection of Catholic Christianity, corruption of pacified Indians, and contact with foreign enemies of Spain justified a forceful Spanish response. The planned invasion of the peninsula stalled, however, when the commanding officer of the expeditionary force refused to move inland from the port of Riohacha, claiming that he needed one million men to ensure a total Spanish victory over Guajiro forces.[51]

Viceroy Manuel Guirior (1772–76) launched an investigation into the causes of the disastrous 1769 rebellion, which, in the end, highlighted local Spanish political corruption and abusiveness. The Guajiros had not only rejected Western religion but also rebelled against the Spanish church-state combine. Thus, it was just as important to restore political order as it was to bring military peace and religious tranquility to the area. To those ends Guirior and his successor, Manuel Antonio Flores (1776–82), ordered the establishment of four new civilian settlements in the jurisdiction of Riohacha—Bahía Honda, Sinamaica, Pedraza, and Sábana del Valle—to provide an element of "civilized" social stability and so make possible continuing Spanish political control. Four previously destroyed missions were also rebuilt, and four new Indian villages were raised. To serve these new settlements, the bishop of Riohacha, Agustín Camacho, requested twenty more Valencian Capuchins, approved by the Crown in 1774. This more broadly based policy, including a revived Capuchin presence and ably overseen by the military engineer Antonio Arévalo, appeared to succeed, because Guajiro hostilities subsided for a time.

In 1775 the lull violently ended. José Galluzo, the newly appointed governor of Riohacha, sought to extend the colonization campaign with the establishment of a fifth settlement at Apiesi on the eastern coast of the peninsula. A contingent of three hundred Spanish troops supported by Indian allies drove eastward across the peninsula from Bahía Honda toward Apiesi. Near the end of the trek an estimated one thousand Guajiros confronted Galluzo's forces. When asked why they blocked the army's path, Guajiro leaders said that their English and Dutch partners had told them that Galluzo intended to cut off their foreign trade, disarm them, and subjugate them. The chiefs added that their informants living in pacified villages corroborated that assessment. Of course, the Indians were right. Galluzo responded bravely, warning the Indians to let his men pass or prepare to do battle. For the time being, the Guajiros chose to withdraw. The Spaniards moved on to the site for the new settlement, where, with the assistance of Guajiro volunteers, they erected outer walls and built a church. Several days later most of the troops departed, leaving behind about ninety soldiers to protect the new colony and a Capuchin priest to minister to its residents. Almost immediately thereafter, Guajiro warriors, probably aided by those who had helped in the construction, attacked the village. The Indians burned its buildings and killed most of its inhabitants, including the priest and nearly two-thirds of the soldiers.[52]

From Apiesi the Guajiro rebellion spread in the winter of 1776 to

Sábana del Valle, Bahía Honda, and Sinamaica. Rightfully feeling defenseless since Guajiro clans could muster nearly seven thousand warriors,[53] the remaining colonists and priests fled the interior. Some civilians left the region altogether; others sought refuge in the port of Riohacha. Most of the Capuchins escaped to the relative safety of Chimila Indian territory to the south.[54] Not only frightened for their own safety, the priests abandoned the mission field because the rebellion demonstrated that the Guajiro attitude toward Catholicism had not moderated at all since 1769. A Capuchin superior reported in the wake of the Apiesi revolt that his brothers could no longer persuade even Indian children, that is, the innocents, to convert, let alone their parents.[55] The government's attempt to exert its control in the Guajira had failed again. In the end, Guajiro endurance, adaptability, and power defeated Spanish reactions, reforms, and political creativity. As described by Francisco Silvestre, neither "endearment and gifts" nor "fear and rigor" softened Guajiro steadfastness.[56]

Successive viceregal governments recognized their critical weaknesses on the Guajira frontier. In the 1780s they disbanded Bahía Honda and Sábana del Valle, later destroyed Pedraza, and lastly transferred Sinamaica to the jurisdiction of the new captaincy general of Venezuela. Even Charles III seemed to tire of the effort to pacify the Guajiros, publicly assailing missionary ineffectiveness in the province of Riohacha.[57]

During the 1780s and 1790s evangelistic pacification and acculturation continued to wane. By the count of secular authorities, only one band of Guajiros, totaling about six hundred people, remained in a state of reduction in 1789.[58] Over the course of the next decade insanity, senility, and death reduced the Capuchin presence in the Guajira from six to a single priest in 1800.[59] Spanish military pressures on the Guajiros likewise had little effect.[60] "Fearsome and bellicose" Guajiro clans were once again uncontested in the peninsula,[61] a political and imperial fact that Viceroy Pedro Mendinueta acknowledged in his final report. Although he claimed that information on the Guajira missions was difficult to obtain because they were so far from Bogotá, he nonetheless conceded their sad state and ultimate failure.[62]

Antonio de Alcácer, a leading authority on Capuchin missions in Colombia, pronounced this judgment on the eighteenth-century effort in the Guajira peninsula: "In the name of history, we can only use terms of the most intense praise and admiration for these sons of St. Francis, so self-sacrificing, who suffered [the] worst of all hardships, apparent failure."[63] In a fundamental sense, the missions had indeed failed, but so had political and military conquest. In general, the Guajiros were neither Christianized nor pacified. Supported by cultural adaptability and resilience, the advantages gained from international commerce, and the weaknesses of the Spanish state on the northern Colombian frontier, Guajiro autonomy remained both viable and vital.

Colonial-era Guajiros rejected most of what Christian theology and culture offered them. Instead, they incorporated into their cultural ethos and self-identity other aspects of European imperialism, such as pastoralism and commerce, that strengthened their resistance to conversion and subjugation. Long-term Guajiro religious liberty, then, reflected indigenous cultural strength and illustrated the dynamics of interaction among Indians, church, and state on an imperial frontier.

Catholic missionaries in Riohacha province, acting on their ingrained sense of cultural and religious superiority, ran head-on into the stubbornness of a people who steadfastly rejected this Western-defined hierarchy of values. Although some Guajiro headmen and groups adopted a Christian lifestyle, they always represented a small minority of the population. The majority held on to their basic cosmological beliefs. Even Indian "converts" may have sought in the missions their own economic betterment and status protection rather than a new theology. Religiously, Christianity and its agents failed to conquer the Guajiros because they together failed to satisfy Guajiro needs and expectations. To the contrary, Guajiros judged Christianity to threaten their existence as they viewed and defined it. To become Christian was to surrender power and independence—whether defined as control over geographical territory, commercial relationships, cosmology, or self-identity. Apart from an overwhelming Spanish capability to coerce conversion, there was for the Guajiros simply no need to accept Catholicism, its theology, and its politics.

A twentieth-century Catholic assessment, reached after nearly two hundred fifty years of evangelism among the Guajiros, confirms the Indians' cultural perseverance. An official Capuchin report of mission activity among the Guajiros in 1930 declared that "the irreducible condition of the Goajira Indian . . . made the civilization of the Goajiros impossible and, at the same time, the work and sacrifice of the missionaries futile. . . . Of the eight thousand or more Indians who have been baptized it would hardly be possible to find even one who lived in a Christian manner or knew what the word meant."[64]

The Guajiros, bolstered by population numbers, military prowess, and economic skills and contacts, renounced Christianity in favor of self-defined traditions and innovations. In an era of Spanish conquest that did not end for the Guajiros until about 1800, the Indians remained "agents of their own history even though they could not shape society according to their own dreams," to borrow a phrase from Steve Stern.[65] The Guajiros' pastoral commercialism was an adaptation to external intrusions; their economic innovation was not at first nor wholly of domestic design. The political economy of herding and trade, therefore, did not reflect a "society of their own dreams." Significantly, however, the Guajiros embraced that change and incorporated it into their dreams and their daily existence. Recall the cattle myth mentioned above. The cattle-raising complex became part of their self-identity, and its ramifications undergirded their cultural, political, and religious independence in the peninsula. The Indians' cultural and economic adaptability, on one hand, translated into a reason to reject Christianity and, on the other, afforded an explanation for the Guajiros to keep that rejection effective. From the early colonial period to well into the twentieth century, then, a consistent defense of their perspectives and spirituality (or perhaps their intransigence) distinguished the Guajiros in the larger Caucasian-dominated world of which they had become a part.

Notes

1. See, for example, Perrin's *Le chemin des Indians morts: Mythes et symboles goajiro* (Paris, 1976) and a collection of Guajiro myths and tales on which Perrin collaborated: *Folk Literature of the Guajiro Indians*, edited by Johannes Wilbert and Karin Simoneau (Los Angeles, 1986).

2. Relación del estado del Virreinato de Santafé, Santafé, 25 Nov. 1760, in E. Posada and P. M. Ibáñez, editors, *Relaciones de mando: Memorias presentadas por los gobernantes del Nuevo Reino de Granada* (Bogotá, Colombia, 1910), p. 90.

3. *La perla de América: Provincia de Santa Marta* (Bogotá, Colombia, 1951), p. 27.

Guajiro Culture and Capuchin Evangelization 153

4. L. Nicolau D'Olwer, "Comments on the Evangelization of the New World," *The Americas* 14 (1958), 403.

5. Henry Wurner Bowden, *American Indians and Christian Missions: Studies in Cultural Conflict* (Chicago, 1981), p. 36.

6. Tzvetan Todorov, *The Conquest of America: The Question of the Other*, translated by Richard Howard (New York, 1985), p. 83.

7. See, for example, Johannes Wilbert, *Survivors of Eldorado: Four Indian Cultures of South America* (New York, 1972), and Omar González Ñ., *Los Guajiros: Una cultura indo-hispana* (Caracas, Venezuela, 1973).

8. Blas de Lezo to the Marqués de Torrenueva, Cartagena, 4 May 1738, Archivo General de Indias (Sevilla), Audiencia de Santa Fe (hereinafter AGI, Santa Fe), legajo 1093; Governor Juan de Vera y Fajardo [to the Crown], Santa Marta, 22 May 1737, AGI, Santa Fe, 1233.

9. Vera [to the Crown], Santa Marta, 22 July 1737, AGI, Santa Fe, 1233; Lázaro José de Espinal y Herrera to Vera, Riohacha, 24 Apr. 1737, AGI, Santa Fe, 478.

10. *Ulysses's Sail: An Ethnographic Odyssey of Power, Knowledge, and Geographical Distance* (Princeton, 1988), p. 173.

11. A Irving Hallowell, "Sociopsychological Aspects of Acculturation," in Ralph Linton, editor, *The Science of Man* (New York, 1945), pp. 183, 191.

12. *Folk Literature of the Guajiro Indians*, 1:76.

13. Hallowell, "Sociopsychological Aspects," pp. 174–75.

14. Relación del estado del Nuevo Reino de Granada, Guaduas, Dec. 1803, in Posada and Ibáñez, *Relaciones de mando*, p. 559.

15. Antonio de Alcácer, *Las misiones capuchinas en el Nuevo Reino de Granada, hoy Colombia (1648–1820)* (Puente Común, Cundinamarca, Colombia, 1959), pp. 49–50; José Manuel Groot, *Historia eclesiástica y civil de Nueva Granada* (Bogotá, Colombia, 1957), 1:7–8; José Restrepo Posada, *Arquidiócesis de Bogotá: Datos biográficos de sus prelados*, vol. 1: 1564–1819 (Bogotá, Columbia, 1961), pp. 7–8.

16. Quoted in Ernesto Restrepo Tirado, *Historia de la provincia de Santa Marta* (Bogotá, Columbia, 1953), 2:223.

17. Baltasar de Lodares, *Los franciscanos capuchinos en Venezuela: Documentos referentes a las misiones franciscanas en esta República*, 2d ed., rev. (Caracas, Venezuela, 1929–31), 2:342–44; Alcácer, *Las misiones capuchinas*, pp. 41–53.

18. Lodares, *Los franciscanos capuchinos*, 2:364–67, 353; Alcácer, *Las misiones capuchinas*, pp. 54–56.

19. Pedro de Aguado, *Historia de Santa Marta y Nuevo Reino de Granada*, edited by Jerónimo Becker (Madrid, 1916), 1:32.

20. Antonio de Narváez y la Torre to Manuel Antonio Florez, Riohacha, 12 July 1778, Archivo Nacional de Colombia (hereinafter ANC), Miscelánea de la Colonia, t. 142, fols. 567–75, in P. Josefina Moreno Alberto Tarazona, editor,

Materiales para el estudio de las relaciones inter-étnicas en la Guajira, siglo XVIII: Documentos y mapas (Caracas, Venezuela, 1984), pp. 246–54.

21. Alcácer, Las misiones capuchinas, pp. 57, 58.
22. Lodares, Los franciscanos capuchinos, 2:356–57.
23. Alcácer, Las misiones capuchinas, pp. 58–59; Restrepo Tirado, Santa Marta, 2:11–12.
24. Alcácer, Las misiones capuchinas, p. 61.
25. Alcácer, Las misiones capuchinas, p. 62.
26. Robert H. Lowie, "Social and Political Organization of the Tropical Forest and Marginal Tribes," in Handbook of South American Indians, vol. 5: The Comparative Ethnology of South American Indians, edited by Julian H. Steward (Washington DC, 1949), p. 331.
27. John M. Armstrong and Alfred Métraux, "The Goajiro," in Handbook of South American Indians, vol. 4: The Circum-Caribbean Tribes, edited by Julian H. Steward (Washington DC, 1948), pp. 371–75.
28. The Mythology of South America (New York, 1988), pp. 184–86.
29. Soría, Cartagena, 31 Mar. 1721, Biblioteca Nacional, Madrid (hereinafter BNM), Manuscritos, mss. no. 3570, fols. 70–75; María del Carmen Mena Carcía, Santa Marta durante la Guerra de Sucesión española (Sevilla, 1982), pp. 102–4.
30. "Were Indian Conversions Bona Fide?" in After Columbus: Essays in the Ethnohistory of Colonial North America (New York, 1988), pp. 100–24.
31. Muniesa to the Regidor of Riohacha, Riohacha, 15 Feb. 1716, in Lodares, Los franciscanos capuchinos, 2:364; Alcácer, Las misiones capuchinas, pp. 60, 250.
32. Soría to Villalonga, n.p., 31 Mar. 1721, in Lodares, Los franciscanos capuchinos, 2:365–66.
33. Oliva to the Procurador General de la Religión de Capuchinos, Maracaibo, 10 June 1730, BNM, Manuscritos, mss. no. 9728, fol. 2.
34. Auto de José de Ysequilla, Cartagena, 21 Aug. 1722, AGI, Santa Fe, 3764; Carlos de Briones, Informe sobre la forma de contener el trato ilícito de la costa del Río del Hacha, Santa Marta, 25 July 1731, AGI, Santa Fe, 1233.
35. Royal cédula, Buen Retiro, 20 Apr. 1749, in José Félix Blanco, editor, Documentos para la historia de la vida pública del Libertador de Colombia, Perú, y Bolivia (Caracas, Venezuela, 1875–78), 1:62.
36. Viceroy Sebastián Eslava to the Crown, Cartagena, 31 Jan. 1747, AGI, Santa Fe, 289; royal cédula to Eslava, Buen Retiro, 20 Apr. 1749, in Blanco, Documentos, 1:62.
37. Eslava to the Crown, Cartagena, 31 Jan. 1747, AGI, Santa Fe, 289; royal cédula to Eslava, Buen Retiro, 20 Apr. 1749, in Blanco, Documentos, 1:62.
38. Eslava, [Relación del estado del Virreinato], comp. Antonio de Berastegui, [Santa Fe, Sept. 1751], in Posada and Ibáñez, Relaciones de mando, p. 40; Groot, Historia, pp. 78–79; Lieutenant Governor Joseph Xavier de

Guajiro Culture and Capuchin Evangelization   155

Pestaña y Chumacero to the Marqués de Villar, Riohacha, 17 Feb. 1753, ANC, Milicias y Marina, t. 124, fol. 218, in Tarazona, *Materiales*, pp. 41–43; Manuel Marqués de Escobar to Solís, Riohacha, 5 Sept. 1754, ANC, Milicias y Marina, t. 128, fols. 906–7, in Tarazona, *Materiales*, pp. 54–55; Pestaña y Chumacero to Pizarro, Riohacha, 20 Apr. 1753, ANC, Milicias y Marina, t. 124, fols. 203–4, in Tarazona, *Materiales*, pp. 44–45.

39. "Property among the Tropical Forest and Marginal Tribes," in *Handbook of South American Indians*, 5:366–67.

40. Alcácer, *Las misiones capuchinas*, pp. 140–41.

41. Quoted in Alcácer, *Las misiones capuchinas*, pp. 138–39.

42. Todorov, *Conquest of America*, p. 253.

43. Antonio de Alcoy to Governor Andrés Pérez Ruiz Calderón, Riohacha, 10 Apr. 1764, ANC, Milicias y Marina, t. 97, fols. 925–30, in Tarazona, *Materiales*, pp. 118–20.

44. Solís, in Posada and Ibáñez, *Relaciones de mando*, p. 90; Restrepo Tirado, *Santa Marta*, 2:190–93.

45. Quoted in Alcácer, *Las misiones capuchinas*, p. 167.

46. For information on the 1769 Guajiro revolt and its aftermath, I have relied on Allan J. Kuethe's "The Pacification Campaign on the Riohacha Frontier, 1772–1779," *Hispanic American Historical Review* 50 (1970), 467–81, and his monograph, *Military Reform and Society in New Granada, 1773–1808* (Gainesville FL, 1978), especially chap. 6.

47. Relación del estado del Virreinato de Santafé, Santafé, 14 Sept. 1772, in Posada and Ibáñez, *Relaciones de mando*, pp. 97–98.

48. Antonio Moreno y Escandón, "Estado del Virreinato de Santa Fe, Nuevo Reino de Granada . . . 1772," *Boletín de historia y antigüedades* 23 (Sept.–Oct. 1939), 573–75.

49. *Viaje a la Sierra Nevada de Santa Marta* (Bogotá, Colombia, 1947), p. 97.

50. Reclus, *Viaje*, p. 89.

51. Viceroy Manuel Guirior, in Posada and Ibáñez, *Relaciones de mando*, p. 177.

52. Kuethe, "Pacification Campaign," pp. 476–78; Alcácer, *Las misiones capuchinas*, p. 218; Restrepo Tirado, *Santa Marta*, 2:223.

53. Guirior, in Posada and Ibáñez, *Relaciones de mando*, p. 178; Julián, *La perla de América*, pp. 277–78; Francisco Silvestre, *Descripción del Reyno de Santa Fe de Bogotá, escrita en 1789* (Bogotá, Colombia, 1950), p. 61; Kuethe, "Pacification Campaign," pp. 473–75; Alcácer, *Las misiones capuchinas*, p. 202; Restrepo Tirado, *Santa Marta*, 2:223.

54. Kuethe, "Pacification Campaign," pp. 478–79; Alcácer, *Las misiones capuchinas*, pp. 218–19; Restrepo Tirado, *Santa Marta*, 2:227, 237.

55. Alcácer, *Las misiones capuchinas*, p. 218.

56. Silvestre, *Descripción*, pp. 97–98.

57. Gregorio Arcila Robledo, *Las misiones franciscanas en Colombia* (Bogotá, Colombia, 1950), pp. 168–69.
58. Alcácer, *Las misiones capuchinas*, pp. 228–30; Silvestre, *Descripción*, p. 60.
59. Victor Daniel Bonilla, *Servants of God or Masters of Men? The Story of a Capuchin Mission in Amazonia*, translated by Rosemary Sheed (Baltimore, 1972), p. 48.
60. Restrepo Tirado, *Santa Marta*, 2:260.
61. José de Ezpeleta, Relación del estado del Nuevo Reino de Granada, Santafé, 3 Dec. 1796, in Posada and Ibáñez, *Relaciones de mando*, p. 363.
62. Viceroy Pedro Mendinueta, in Posada and Ibáñez, *Relaciones de mando*, pp. 559, 441.
63. Quoted in Bonilla, *Servants of God*, p. 49.
64. Quoted in Julian A. Weston, *The Cactus Eaters* (London, 1937), p. 44.
65. *Peru's Indian Peoples and the Challenge of Spanish Conquest: Huamanaga to 1640* (Madison WI, 1980), p. xix.

Thomas Whigham

Paraguay's *Pueblos de Indios:* Echoes of a Missionary Past

Six [Indians] do not work as well as one European;
they live with little, and their desires are very limited,
and they never get moving without continuous
and uninterrupted persuasion.
Lázaro de Ribera (1800)

The Jesuit missions of Paraguay have for years evoked an image of a New World utopia, of a vanished Arcadia of hardworking Guaraní Indians ruled by benevolent priests in a setting of almost total isolation. During the eighteenth century even such skeptics as Voltaire stressed the uniqueness of these mission communities. The piety of the Jesuits in Paraguay and the tragedy of their Indian wards even inspired a popular dramatic film, *The Mission*, in 1985. Still, from the vantage point of the Guaraní themselves, the Jesuit interlude was only one chapter in a complex history of Indian-white relations marked less by exclusiveness than by frequent interaction between the two groups. In the long run a successful strategy for Indian survival in the region was not elaborated on the basis of rejecting European civilization. Only by adapting to the demands of the Spaniards did the Guaraní manage to retain a measure of autonomy. In the process, they established communities that served over time to transform all of Paraguayan society.

This ability to adapt is best seen in the various Indian pueblos of Paraguay during the late eighteenth and early nineteenth centuries. These communities, though widely dispersed throughout the province and dissimilar in some ways, were all founded with a mission-

---

The author wishes to acknowledge, with gratitude, the advice and help of Jerry W. Cooney, James Saeger, and Bennett Wall.

ary purpose in mind. Curiously, the traditional historiography has seen fit to deemphasize this common design and has instead imposed an artificial division by calling those Indian villages under Jesuit control *missions* or *reducciones*, and those under Franciscan or secular control *pueblos*. To avoid confusion, I use the latter term exclusively, for indeed, for the Guaraní, such distinctions made little difference. The Indians expected a measure of exploitation from the whites, whether Jesuits, Franciscans, seculars, or civil administrators. Whenever possible, however, the Guaraní used the laws and biases of the Spaniards to their own advantage, and, under different guises, their pueblos managed an institutional survival until 1848, long after the Indians themselves had become thoroughly Hispanicized in everything but language.

Indian communities of many types abounded throughout the Plata region. In the wake of the Jesuit expulsion of 1763–68, Crown officials took pains to preserve and even standardize the outward structure of these towns, an effort that caused no end of administrative problems.[1] The complexity of the situation was monumental. At the time of the foundation of the Platine viceroyalty in 1776, twenty-one *pueblos de indios* existed within the borders of what eventually became the Republic of Paraguay. Of these, only eight, all in the far south, were part of the former Jesuit "empire" of the Alto Paraná. Another three—Belén, San Estanislao, and San Joaquín—had recently been established by the Jesuits in the north of the province as part of a final flurry of missionary zeal. The rest of the pueblos were under Franciscan or secular rule. Mostly located within a short distance from Asunción, they provided labor services for the provincial capital and for individual colonists under an archaic tribute system called the *encomienda mitaria*.

Essentially a method to systematize Indian labor to benefit the colonists, this version of the traditional *encomienda* promoted regular contact between the Guaraní and the Spaniards while keeping intact the community structure. From our perspective, the importance of the *mitayo* communities lies less in the exploitation they clearly experienced than in their continued institutional presence despite such exploitation; unlike most of the former Jesuit villages to the south of the Paraná, these *pueblos de indios* survived well into the nineteenth century.

The durability of community structure was directly linked to administrative practices. Throughout the 1700s the resident missionaries of the pueblos of Itá, Caazapá, and Yuty were Franciscans. Those in charge of Yaguarón, Cuarambaré, Tobatí, Ypané, Altos, and Atyra were secular priests. Franciscans and seculars carried the burden of proselytism in Paraguay by occupying those pueblos vacated by the Jesuits after the expulsion. Apologists for the Society of Jesus have frequently accused the two groups of betraying the Guaraní by allowing outside speculators to operate within the pueblos; however, the openness of the Franciscan and secular systems was beneficial in that it gave the Indians the chance to develop skills useful in resisting total assimilation.

Background

At the time of the conquest the Spaniards viewed Paraguay as a way station, nothing more than a gateway to the silver of Peru. The placid riverine environment, with verdant forests stretching to the horizon, was certainly beautiful, but as it produced no gold or silver of its own, it had little to entice the white men. The Spaniards soon realized, moreover, that Paraguay offered an inadequate route to the silver mines of the Andes. The territory might well have been abandoned (as occurred initially with Buenos Aires) had the local Indians, the Guaraní, not so readily made common cause with the Spaniards.

The Guaraní had every reason to become allies of the newcomers. A semisedentary people who cultivated manioc root and maize, the Guaraní suffered from constant raiding by the Mbayá, Guaná, and Payaguá Indians of the nearby Gran Chaco. The arrival of the Spaniards came as a godsend, and the Carío (as the Guaraní of the Asunción area were called) lost no time in seeking an alliance with the whites. That one accommodation ensured the Europeans a safe base from which they could complete their conquest of the interior of South America—or so they hoped.

In the event, the foundation of Asunción (1537) signaled Spanish control of only the immediate vicinity. The Carío and other Guaraní groups supplied the Europeans with foodstuffs, porters, and native women, who acted as consorts and servants for the Spaniards, who, though they had wrung no mineral wealth from the soil of Paraguay, happily accepted the many services of the Indians in exchange for military protection. By the 1540s this relation took on the formal character of *encomienda*. The Spaniards had no intention of being left without some profit, and though the hard-driving exploitation of their wives' relatives could yield only a tiny harvest of cotton, they rarely hesitated to oppress the Indians. This callous treatment led to several abortive uprisings during the sixteenth century.

Even so, it was the acceptance of Spanish rule that appears noteworthy. Most Guaraní readily adapted to the strictures of life under the Spaniards, seeing in the European-style community their best chance of survival. Few wished to return to the forest. Close contact with the Spaniards apparently brought a rapid acculturation and a sexual intermingling, from which sprang a large grouping of mestizos, or *mancebos de la tierra*. Since no major influx of Europeans into Paraguay was experienced from the time of the conquest until the last generation before independence, these mestizos inherited their fathers' property and legal standing within the colony, though they retained their mothers' language.

The growth of the mestizo population, and the concomitant expansion of settlements into central Paraguay, was coupled with the momentary decline of that portion of the population officially recognized as Indian. One source affirms that by the end of the sixteenth century, there remained within a radius of seven leagues around Asunción only three thousand Indians.[2] This figure probably underestimated the true number of Indians, as some Guaraní succeeded in "passing" as mestizo. In a fluid frontier environment like that of Paraguay, legal distinctions almost always gave way to expedience. In any case, the absolute numbers of Indians remained large.

For all its benefits, Hispanic rule presented the Guaraní with a mixed blessing. Immediate security was now largely ensured, and certain useful adaptations, such as iron implements and the horse, clearly made agricultural work easier. The proximity of European populations, however, exposed the Indians to such epidemic diseases as smallpox and typhus.

Unlike the Andean region, where *mita* obligations took Indians far from their home districts, in Paraguay Spanish demands on native labor failed to disrupt community life greatly. The *yerba mate* (green tea) forests (*yerbales*) were relatively close at hand. Other market-oriented activities, such as the weaving of textiles and the production of black twist tobacco and sugar, could be effected directly within the bounds of the community. Hence, the degree of deviation from early patterns of social organization was quite small. Indian women still performed the bulk of agricultural work, while the men tended animals and hunted. Village elders, transformed into brokers for the Spaniards, nonetheless looked and acted much the same as far as the Indians of the pueblos were concerned. The continuities with the pre-Columbian past were clear to all.

The Early Pueblos

For those Indians who resisted complete assimilation, there was an alternative: the pueblo system. By the mid-1600s the Hispanic presence could no longer be effectively resisted by the Guaraní except through accommodation, and this is precisely what the pueblos represented, an intermediary step between the indigenous and Spanish worlds. Officially, the various communities, both Franciscan and Jesuit, were founded to Christianize the natives and to prevent Portuguese expansion in the north and in the area between the Paraná and Uruguay rivers. The Guaraní saw it differently. From their perspective, the pueblos served another purpose: to preserve as much of Indian culture as possible given the vicissitudes of their "pact" with the Spaniards, and, not coincidentally, to act as a shield from the avarice of those same Spaniards.

Whether under Jesuit, Franciscan, or secular guidance, the different communities had much in common. One defining feature of community structure was the collective nature of land tenure (*tupambae*) practiced within the pueblos. Individual gain was subject to social review, with Indian authorities (invariably heads of kin groups) overseeing the distribution of resources and the resolution of disputes in a manner that consciously mimicked pre-Columbian patterns. In theory, each village had two priests (though in fact most had only one) whose functions were legally confined to the spiritual. The degree of temporal power the priests exercised depended as much on personality and circumstance as any other factor. The Indian *cabildo* could rubber-stamp the policies of the resident priest, or it might occur the other way around. The isolation of the region provided more materially minded clergy wide scope for self-enrichment. As it was, most priests were demonstrably sincere in their dealings with the Indians, acting as honest deputies for native authorities when the need arose.

Such was not the case for the *corregidores* (or *administradores de temporalidades*), the royal officials in charge of the economic affairs of the *mitayo* villages and, after the expulsion of the Jesuits, of all the Indian pueblos. Entrusted with safeguarding native properties and community funds, the officials commonly treated these resources as a personal preserve. Also, by subjecting Indians to all sorts of extralegal exactions, especially those regarding personal service, the *corregidores* managed greatly to supplement their small salaries at the expense of the Guaraní. Scholars have made much of this exploitation.[3] Apparently, the Indians initially accepted this treatment without protest; after all, the cooking of food and the tending of fields presented few problems—Spaniards had always demanded these concessions, and the Guaraní customarily provided them for their own native officials and their families. By the eighteenth century, however, when the assets of the pueblos developed commercial potential, the demands of the *corregidores* grew rapidly, prompting loud Indian grievances.

The history of the Jesuit missions of the Paraná has been covered by Guillermo Furlong Cardiff, Magnus Mörner, and Juan Carlos Garavaglia, not to mention all the earlier panegyrics and defenses.[4] Here we are less interested in the Jesuits—who, after all, were aliens in the Paraguayan environment—than in the Guaraní, the natives, the adherents not of a European religious idealism but of an all-to-American realism and acceptance of harsh realities.

The Indians rarely understood the meaning of Christianity, but they were outwardly willing to accept its institutional and hierarchical forms. This flexibility reflected the growing prestige of a native elite among the Guaraní, an elite that in most pueblos was constituted in a *cabildo*. This body generally included two *alcaldes*, four *regidores*, an *alcalde provincial*, two *alcaldes de la Santa Hermandad*, and a *secretario*, all holding distinctive batons of office, as well as concrete influence in their community. The *cabildo* members organized religious festivals and purchased the fireworks and candles associated with the elaborate processions; they likewise guarded the paraphernalia of the local patron saint. Holy day ceremonies encouraged solidarity among the Indians, who used such occasions to reaffirm community ties through joint prayer and public demonstration of loyalty. To further this communal feeling, all individual resources were consumed in ostentatious fashion by the community as a whole. Little room existed within the pueblos for individual accumulation of wealth, except for *cabildantes* and their families, who lived marginally better lives than other Indians. It is worth noting in this regard that the "primitive communism" of the pueblos was a myth, that both the Jesuits and Franciscans sanctioned property advantages and privileges for a native elite.

In any case, complete isolation for the pueblos within the province of Paraguay was never a real option. The Indians generally did not want to be isolated. Outside earnings fed the community treasury (which in turn profited *corregidores*), and individual Indians could earn wages. The Guaraní accepted this arrangement as a necessary evil, but one with a hidden benefit: by permitting a controlled appropriation of community labor, Indian leaders could direct, and to an extent blunt, the pernicious effects associated with such appropriation. This left most economic activities largely in native hands, and the interactions with Spanish colonists posed no threat to community survival.

Despite the resulting veneer of Hispanicization, the inhabitants of the pueblos had only a shallow comprehension of European customs, at least in terms of detail. They remained Indians in every meaningful way. Writing at the end of the eighteenth century, the Spanish border commissioner Félix de Azara condemned the behavior he encountered in the pueblos:

[The Indians'] religion is Catholic if we consider that to mean baptism alone; but when we look at practices, it appears quite another thing, as they have no understanding of ecclesiastical precepts. Intoning the blessing or some other obligatory ritual constitutes their entire faith, which is mixed with superstition and ignorance. Drunkenness, inconstancy, guile, ingratitude, and petty theft never cause them to blush; they are creatures of the moment, receiving with equal expression a reward or a reprimand—they are easily seduced by evil. Their excesses against the Sixth Commandment are limited only by physical capacity, and it is odd that the French pox is so rarely seen among them (how different it is with the Spaniards, who are left disfigured by their liaisons with Indian women). . . . they need much time to finish any task as they are slow by nature. . . . Honor and shame mean nothing to them, yet they avidly pursue nomination as [town officials]. They treat their horses terribly and never care for them, and they allow bitches to breed uncontrollably, but puppies are never fawned over. . . . For all the rest, they are docile, and look with awe on every Spaniard, especially superiors. They suffer with indifference the lash, hard work, and hunger. When they do eat, however, they thoroughly gorge themselves. They never show anger and proceed with all their affairs in the same cold manner.[5]

Azara's dislike of Indians seems evidence enough in this judgment, and if the truth be told, many of these same criticisms could be directed equally at the mestizo and European inhabitants of Paraguay. What is interesting in the description, however, is the interpretation the Guaraní would have put on it; an attempt to portray themselves as lazy, oversexed, and slovenly was as much in their interest as it would have been with black slaves. If the Indians could appear to be stupid and ineffectual workers, then perhaps the Spaniards would expect less of them. Wage earners and *mitayo* laborers alike gained from such an expectation. In this respect, the Guaraní understood the Spaniards very well.

The Outside Link: The Jesuits

White and indigenous worlds in Paraguay overlapped in myriad ways, some dramatic and some barely perceptible. Every male *mitayo* Indian from eighteen to fifty served a Spanish overlord for two months of the year, a period set by custom and law to ensure that only one-sixth of the able-bodied laborers would be absent from the community at a time. *Cabildo* members and their first-born were not liable for such service. Technically, neither were women, children, or the elderly, though in fact they too often worked in Spanish fields.

The recompense for *mitayo* labor consisted only of daily sustenance and an annual payment of two *reales* per worker to the village cleric. A less tangible reward made this system palatable to community Indians, however. Spanish *encomenderos* assumed the burden of paying the tributes owed by their *mitayo* Indians. More important, the system fostered a level of paternalism that shielded the pueblos from too much contact with outside entrepreneurs. Individual *encomenderos* jealously guarded access to the native communities and acted as intermediaries with other Spaniards. The parameters of exploitation were effectively set in advance.

Mitayo labor gave the Indians responsibility for planting and harvesting the *encomendero's* crops (usually cotton, tobacco, maize, beans, and manioc), tending his livestock, cutting his timber, acting as rowers and yerba gatherers, and occasionally working as domestics in the *encomendero's* household. Few of these tasks involved any real adjustment, since the Indians routinely performed the same work in the pueblos. Indian women also contributed their efforts to the *encomendero*, cooking his food, washing his laundry, and tending his children (some of whom may have been their own). Life under such circumstances, if not always easy, certainly was predictable.

The most common image of these times is of a Mohammedan paradise, with idle Spaniards resting in hammocks, being served cooled drinks by comely Guaraní maidens, while docile Indian menfolk handled all the heavy work. Such sloth was possible in languorous Paraguay, but only for a tiny number of the Spaniards. Indian docility went only so deep, and work never seemed to end. Yet the one aspect of the old apocryphal tale that rings true is the sense of timelessness it suggests. The native communities approved of this arrangement, as did the local government and the *encomenderos*. So long as a cash economy had yet to reach the province, little incentive existed for change. A Spaniard might barter a portion of his tobacco for chickens, but he could eat only a limited number of them. The same held true for land in a province where land was abundant and cheap. Everything worked in favor of continuity, even, in a sense, of stagnation.

This state of affairs ended in the eighteenth century. By that time the Jesuits had successfully integrated their economic activities into a commercial web that reached to Buenos Aires and beyond. The chief factor in this trade was *yerba mate*. Popular throughout the southern half of the continent, the green tea (*Ilex paraguaiensis*) grew only in Paraguay, and in that area of the Plata the Jesuits alone had access to a large labor force. The resulting yerba commerce broke the pattern of isolation that had for so long characterized the region and brought a degree of modernization. It also presented the Indian communities with new challenges in their dealings with the white world.

Scholars have developed the theme of Jesuit yerba ventures at some length.[6] Few, however, have dealt with the effect on Indians per se. Yerba plantations were established near the majority of mission towns, the Jesuits having discovered a way to cultivate the *ilex* shrub. Production of yerba became more efficient, but working conditions were perhaps more monotonous.[7]

In the beginning the Jesuits cultivated yerba solely for internal consumption; only later did it become a profitable crop for individual missions. The colonial government had earlier restricted Jesuit yerba exports to twelve thousand *arrobas* a year.[8] This restriction amounted to a political compromise between the Jesuit Order and the colonists, a compromise that endured but briefly.

Indeed, an abiding enmity characterized the relations between the Jesuits and the Spanish settlers north of the Río Tebicuary and to the south in Corrientes. These colonists had some access to *mitayo* labor through their contacts with Franciscan and secular authorities in the pueblos. But the colonists had neither the technical expertise of the Jesuits nor their political links in Buenos Aires. The Comunero rebellions of the 1710s and 1720s, which began in Paraguay and spread to Corrientes, represented the pent-up frustrations of the colonists against Jesuit influence.[9]

In the long run the Jesuits faced too much opposition, and not solely at the local level. The later Bourbons, especially Charles III, refused the Jesuits the patronage enjoyed under earlier monarchs. Starting in the 1750s, the Crown, acting on the advice of regalist courtiers, began to revoke Jesuit privileges in the empire. In the Plata some of the Jesuit lands east of the Uruguay River were transferred temporarily to the Portuguese.

The Guaraní who lived under Jesuit rule viewed these events with dismay. As much as possible, the father had regulated the Indians' lives, forbidding them even to learn Spanish. The only contact they had had with the outside had been with the occasional royal official, passing through the region on Jesuit sufferance. More important, the Jesuits periodically loaned their Indians to Spanish authorities to serve as soldiers to help repulse foreign encroachments in the estuary. This one irregular contact had a military character bereft of any real sense of mutual understanding.

It is hardly surprising, then, that some pueblo Indians should revolt. The most dramatic example came in 1753–56, when Indians from the seven pueblos east of the Uruguay River rebelled because a treaty assigned their lands and properties to the Portuguese. Lacking the guidance of the Jesuit fathers, who had moved back across the Uruguay in obedience to Crown orders, the Indians turned to their old enemies, the savage Charrúa. The all-Indian alliance lasted only a short time, and despite capable leadership, the Guaraní were soon defeated. A scorched-earth policy left the seven pueblos gutted, their herds dispersed, and their fields abandoned. Ironically, events to the south forced an abrogation of the treaty, and the seven communities returned to Jesuit rule in 1761.[10]

This event, however, was little more than a swan song. About six years later the machinations of court favorites in Madrid paid off in a general decree in 1767 expelling the Jesuit Order from the Spanish empire. In the Río de la Plata the expulsion was effected initially in secret and with great speed. Guards transported the priests down from the Paraná and Uruguay to ships waiting to carry them to an uncertain exile. Thus, the Jesuit interregnum in South America ended, leaving the mission Guaraní without protection from the Spanish settlers and with no sense of place in a world the fathers did not control.

The Outside Link: Seculars and Franciscans

The Jesuits should be given credit for maintaining their ideals. The selflessness and devotion they showed the Indians plus their technical achievements in medicine, architecture, botany, and music have received considerable praise. But ultimately, the Jesuit system failed the Guaraní. Even while seeking the role of cultural brokers between white and native worlds, they paternalistically restricted Indians' contacts with Spaniards. They never sought Indian assimilation into Hispanic society and hence never gave the Guaraní any measure of freedom without Jesuit guidance.

The expulsion of the Jesuits caused the way of life that they had so meticulously cultivated among the Indians to decay rapidly. In theory, the new order brought only a change of personnel—secular administrators for Jesuit priests. In practice, however, the Guaraní chafed under a secular regime more interested in lining the pockets of corrupt officials and outside speculators than in perpetuating a sense of religiosity among the Indians. Secular authorities missed an opportunity in this regard; the Jesuits had successfully masked the harshness of their economic order by giving it the appearance of divine sanction. By comparison, the simple lure of profits for native *cabildantes* had little appeal.[11]

The isolation of the former Jesuit pueblos began to give way to much greater economic exploitation. The communities opened to shady traffickers who joined with the secular administrators in looting town holdings, in setting up long-term contracts (including investments in yerba and a virtual monopoly on the acquisition of cotton cloth), and generally, in forcing the Guaraní into unfavorable debt arrangements.[12] Mission Indians south of the Paraná soon chose to reorder their work habits and, where possible, to abandon

Table 1
Population Decline in the Guaraní Missions, 1768–1802

Departmental divisions[a]	1768	1772	1784	1792–97	1791–2
Candelaria	27,768	28,205	14,472	11,440	10,548
Concepción	14,119	14,137	10,385	9,784	6,068
San Miguel	17,723	15,859	14,769	13,267	12,710
Santiago	13,282	11,508	5,293	5,625	5,369
Yapeyú	15,972	11,182	13,028	11,300	9,982
Totals	88,864	80,891	57,949	51,416	44,677

Source: Ernesto J. A. Maeder, "El caso Misiones, su proceso histórico, y su posterior distribución territorial," in P. H. Randle, editor, La geografía y la historia en la identidad nacional (Buenos Aires, 1981), 2:155.

[a] The Department of Candelaria included the pueblos of Candelaria, Corpus, Itapúa, Jesús, Loreto, San Ignacio Miní, Santa Ana, and Trinidad; that of Concepción included Apóstoles, Mártires, San Carlos, San Javier, San José, and Santa María; that of San Miguel included San Juan Bautista, San Lorenzo, San Luis, San Miguel, San Nicolás, and Santo Angel; that of Santiago included Nuestra Señora de Santa Fe, San Cosme, San Ignacio Guazú, and Santa Rosa; that of Yapeyú included La Cruz, San Borja, Santo Tomé, and Yapeyú.

the region entirely, bringing new populations to the cattle-raising zones of Uruguay, and Entre Ríos, and even Buenos Aires, living the mission area a shell of its former self (table 1).

North of the Paraná circumstances were quite different. The *mitayo* villages, under Franciscan and secular control, continued much as before and even had added to their number the eight formerly Jesuit pueblos between the Tebicuary and Paraná Rivers, as well as the three others, also formerly Jesuit, in the far north. These mission communities underwent no disintegration, yet they too faced outside exploitation. The distinguishing variable was not so much the economic penetration from the outside—in this respect, the *mitayo* and Jesuit pueblos had similar experiences—but the degree of previous direct contact with Spanish settlers. Indians from the *mitayo* communities had had substantial outside connections and understood the motives and behavior patterns of the Spaniards. This knowledge provided a cushion for the pueblos, making their institutional continuity the easiest option. For their part, the Indians of the former Jesuit missions had little notion of how to react to events after 1768; this explains their rush to adopt European ways, to leave their Indian past behind, or simply to escape.

Although the inhabitants of the pueblos north of the Tebicuary never had to set aside the Guaraní identity, they still had to cope with a changing world. Within a decade of the Jesuit expulsion, Paraguay's economy was booming, thanks to the creation of a new Platine viceroyalty that boasted relatively flexible trade regulations. Exports from Paraguay increased accordingly, with shipments of *yerba mate* now arriving regularly at Buenos Aires, Potosí, and even Santiago de Chile. Other local commodities—tobacco, timber, cotton cloth, and hides—followed.

The Indian pueblos participated actively in the export economy. Many communities owned rich *yerbales*. Though technically community property, these *yerbales* produced only moderate profits for the Indians, the rest being taken by merchants in Asunción who were themselves dependent on *porteño* moneymakers.[13] Despite the limited earnings, the wealthier pueblos made enough to pay tributes and tithes, with some left over to purchase adornments for their churches and costly vestments for festivals.[14] Individuals came away with only so much, but the community remained in place. Poorer communities depended in part on alms from their wealthier neighbors.

More and more, however, the lure of the outside affected the young men (and less often, the young women) of the Indian villages, presenting the pueblos with a major threat to their viability. Young Indians recognized the advantages to leaving. In Spanish towns they could work for wages as servants or day laborers and send clothing and food to their families back in the pueblos.[15] Often, however, their ambitions took them much farther afield, not just to the *yerbales* of the north but as far away as Buenos Aires. Commonly, native "fugitives" took work as oarsmen on rafts bound for the viceregal capital.[16] Those who did rarely returned. They abandoned their families to become a permanent underclass in the towns of the estuary and lost their Indian identity in the process. The number of adult males absent at any one time from the pueblos (and carried on the rolls as fugitives) was as high as 20 percent.[17]

The loss of these young men keenly affected the pueblos of Paraguay. Previously, the ties of community helped them weather all sorts of calamities, natural and manmade. The new situation proved different, however, for it carried within it the potential danger of dissolution of the pueblos because of a decrease in community earnings and influence. It also meant fewer tributes for both Crown and *encomendero*, a fact that in itself upset the understanding the pueblos maintained with the white authorities of the province. If the productivity of the pueblos fell, then in Spanish eyes, they would lose their raison d'être. This the various administrators and *cabildantes* sought to prevent in any way possible. No wonder, then, that pueblo officials themselves took the lead in petitioning the colonial governor to punish those aiding the escape of village Indians.[18]

Despite the good intentions of both provincial and local governments, flight from the pueblos remained a problem through the first decade of the new century. Opportunities for Indians in the wider world were simply too great to ignore. At the same time, many Spanish officials found it convenient to wink at the work of labor contractors who came to the pueblos to entice men away—after all, bribes were attractive and effective, especially in isolated areas.

Often the Crown assigned the colonial government contradictory tasks. Tribute had to be maintained at normal levels, while the Indians received orders to supply increased manpower for the royal tobacco monopoly, the textile workshops, the timber and rope industries, and the province's shipyards.[19] Thus, both private and semiofficial industries maintained a voracious appetite for native labor.

But what of the Indians themselves? By 1785 the number of pueblo inhabitants was 27,970, distributed widely throughout the province of Paraguay (table 2).

Table 2 demonstrates some of the pitfalls of dealing with colonial statistics. On the surface, the near parity of numbers between the sexes suggests that tales of male flight from the pueblos were exaggerated. Perhaps some embellishment did occur in government reports, and there can be little doubt that flight constituted a more serious problem in certain pueblos than in others. As we have seen, the former Jesuit communities south of the Paraná were particularly susceptible. Table 2 fails to illustrate one phenomenon, however, that effectively masked the exit of Indians from the community: the concomitant entry of non-Indian peoples onto pueblo lands. The last decades of the eighteenth century witnessed considerable migration of Spaniards, blacks, and mestizos into areas hitherto reserved for the Guaraní. The development of the provincial economy made this movement as inevitable as that of the Indians out of their own vil-

Table 2
Population of the Pueblos de Indios, 1785

Village	Males	Females	Total
Altos	408	334	742
Atyra	431	459	890
Belén	121	202	323
Caazapá	367	338	705
Candelaria	830	918	1,748
Corpus	1,216	1,358	2,574
Guarambaré	151	167	318
Itá	462	467	929
Itapúa	1,334	1,555	2,889
Jesús	624	678	1,302
Loreto	687	772	1,459
San Cosme	506	605	1,111
San Estanislao	339	384	723
San Ignacio Guazú	387	480	867
San Ignacio Miní	357	441	798
San Joaquín	426	428	854
Santa Ana	799	948	1,747
Santa María de Fe	515	547	1,062
Santa Rosa	585	679	1,264
Santiago	551	664	1,215
Tobatí	382	436	818
Trinidad	535	562	1,097
Yaguarón	781	816	1,597
Ypané	106	117	223
Ytapé	29	38	67
Yuty	332	343	675
Totals	13,234	14,736	27,970

Source: Félix de Azara, Geografía física y esférica del Paraguay (Montevideo, Uruguay, 1904), p. 442.

Note: The pueblos of Candelaria, Santa Ana, Loreto, San Ignacio Miní, and Corpus, all located to the south of the Río Paraná, were soon lost by Paraguay to Buenos Aires in a jurisdictional dispute, though in economic matters they were always subject to Asunción.

lages. In any case, though we have no figures indicating ethnic breakdown for the pueblos in 1785, the government did record such information in a census held fourteen years later (table 3). By the end of the century the *pueblos de indios* were no longer inhabited solely by Guaraní.

The social ramifications of this immigration were enormous; in Tobatí, for instance, full-blooded Indians represented only 6.5 percent of the total population, and even though the majority of the newcomers were leaseholders (*arrendatarios*) who lived at some distance from the community proper, their presence had an impact. Many Indians now preferred to list their ethnicity as mestizo or *español-americano* and thus enter secular society by an indirect route. Under the increasingly fluid circumstances, the trick for pueblo officials (both Indian and white) was to meet these new challenges without giving up their institutional segregation. Above all, this required a flexible or accommodating attitude—or at least the semblance of one—and a clear grasp of legal forms and procedures. Paradoxically, in order to defend themselves as Indians, the Guaraní necessarily had to behave like Europeans. Indeed, the viceregal period gave rise to a plethora of finely detailed lawsuits emanating from the pueblos.

Some of this litigation was prepared in collusion with town administrators. Other suits pointedly attacked the same administrators as the source of the problem. In 1783, for instance, the *cabildo* of Santa Ana accused the pueblo's administrator of gross malfeasance. The *cabildantes* claimed that he sold their cattle to a nearby *estancia* (ranch) and traded a quantity of their cotton on the open market in Corrientes. He had formed liaisons with no fewer than sixteen Indian girls (all of whom he set to spinning yarn) and, in general, had established a reign of terror bracketed by flogging and the use of a common torture method called the *cepo*. The *cabildo's* letter to the interim governor, though certainly florid, conformed in every way to standard legal practice.[20] Sadly, we know nothing of the outcome of this case.

Another key Indian complaint involved encroachments on community lands by outsiders. In 1788 Indian officials from the pueblo of Santa María begged the governor to expel some men whose neighboring ranches had expanded wildly at the expense of pueblo lands (and whom they suspected of seizing Indian-owned cattle). In this case, because one of the men had well-placed relatives, the governor passed the deliberation on to the *protector de naturales* (a royal offi-

Table 3
Ethnic Composition of Paraguayan Pueblo Inhabitants, 1799

Village	Spaniards	Mestizos	Indians	Blacks	Slaves	Total
Altos			911			911
Atyra	634		1,059	32	13	1,738
Belén	4		249	1	2	256
Caazapá	420	18	656	68	16	1,178
Guarambaré	6	3	422	8	2	441
Itá			1,148			1,148
San Estanislao	81		695	10	5	791
San Joaquín			931			931
Tobatí	625	41	65	168	83	982
Yaguarón	474	7	1,735	5	15	2,236
Ypané			215	88		303
Ytapé	307	16	138	24	5	490
Yuty	375	34	677	63	15	1,164

Source: Ernesto J. A. Maeder, "La población del Paraguay en 1799: El censo del gobernador Lázaro de Ribera," Estudios Paraguayos 3:1 (1975), 76.

cial charged with overseeing Indian affairs), who mandated a compromise.[21] Formal *arrendatarios* had to take responsibility for some land takeovers, but more commonly, simple squatters did the work. Previously, the pattern of Indian residence was more nucleated, within the pueblos, while mestizo Paraguayans generally lived dispersed among the valleys. Now even this pattern started to break down, with some mestizos moving into the villages and marrying Guaraní women in order to legitimize their land claims.

The most important legal complaints registered by the different pueblos, however, dealt with overall economic conditions. The situation had become desperate in the former Jesuit pueblos of the far south. In 1788 Governor Joaquín de Alós reported that conditions had deteriorated tremendously: "The [community] account books had fallen into disorder and confusion. The warehouses lacked all primary goods. Agriculture was almost abandoned. The tobacco factories [are] inactive. Industry and crafts [have been left] without maestros or directors. Trade [is] ruinous to the communities. The rents of community lands are ridiculously low. The cattle herds have been decimated. There has been no general distribution of clothing since 1768. Food is scarce. The tributes less than half since

1772. The populations of the towns were minimal. And the education of the youth unattended."[22] Despite the alarmist tone of this summary, the situation was less than critical. Alós was interested primarily in the villages south of the Tebicuary, and not in the pueblos as a whole. Paraguay had become involved in jurisdictional disputes with Corrientes and Buenos Aires, moreover, and it was in the governor's interest to stress the inherent failings in the status quo. This pattern was repeated on many occasions.[23] Periodically, as occurred in a 1798 report by Governor Lázaro de Ribera, the government suggested complex rescue schemes for the Indian communities. These projects, however, were designed more to help bureaucrats catch the eye of the Crown than to save the pueblos.[24]

Official commentaries on the status of Indians also attacked the *encomienda*. Provincial authorities, following Bourbon precedents, sought to abolish the institution but encountered a reservoir of opposition among resident priests and the *encomenderos* themselves. Official criticisms of the *encomienda*—originating both in Indian complaints and in periodic inspection tours (*visitas*)—referred to overwork, corporal punishment, and the failure of the *encomendero* to supply food, clothing, and yerba. Indians who had once favored the *encomienda* as the least pernicious system of labor open to them joined with Spanish officials in opposing the old order. Their decision on this point reflected the availability of greater options in an economy increasingly affected by cash transactions.

Starting in the late 1770s, Madrid pressed provincial governors to curtail the system. New titles of *encomienda* in regular two-life possession were no longer awarded, as part of a slow, water-on-stone approach to elite opposition. Frequent protests from the elites over the next three decades contributed greatly to anti-Crown sentiments that ultimately found expression at the beginning of the new century. By then the *encomienda* system had fallen into a state of complete decay and was soon formally abolished.[25]

The Guaraní passed through this transition with difficulty. Royal patrons had addressed their status before on many occasions, but reforms had never been more than temporary. The local elite, on the other hand, was a known entity. Its abuses could be tolerated because the Indians understood them. After all, the economic penetration of the pueblos presented a greater threat to the viability of the communities than any political dispute among the whites. Even independence, gained by Paraguay in 1811, failed to make an immediate impression on the Guaraní pueblos. Eventually, however, they too were swept up in the whirlwind of political change.

The *Pueblos de Indios* in the Early National Period

In most respects, the socioeconomic patterns affecting the *pueblos de indios* during the late colonial period continued until the 1810s. Having been touched by the demands of outside trade, many in the villages (especially young men) cheerfully adapted. These Guaraní sought personal profit wherever possible—in the *yerbales*, along the river, and at home. Little remained of their reluctance to set aside a "precapitalist" way of life, even in the former Jesuit pueblos. Now there was only the issue of power.

The Indians had long since grown accustomed to an authority triad of priest, administator, and native *cabildo*. Whenever friction arose, two of the actors joined hands to oppose the third. With independence, however, a new interventionist state worked its considerable will on the structure of the pueblos. The most important effect of this new actor was to eliminate the temporal authority of the clerics, especially the Franciscans, who frequently had demonstrated a mind of their own.

The pueblos owed a great deal to the Franciscans. Unlike the Jesuits, who were severe taskmasters in everything from farming to religious instruction, the friars took a casual approach toward the supervision of their native charges. The Franciscans allowed them to interact with the larger Paraguayan society and to become familiar in a direct fashion with Spanish ways. Often Paraguayan-born, with relatives (including offspring) in various parts of the country, the clerics easily facilitated contacts of all sorts between pueblo Indians and outsiders.[26] Though poorly educated compared to the Jesuits, the friars retained great influence with both Indians and whites.

This influence cost them dearly. In 1814 Paraguay reached a critical juncture with the rise of José Gaspar de Francia. This stern and taciturn man had earned a doctorate of theology at the University of Córdoba and, like many learned men of his age, took a deistic approach to religious questions. More to the point, he believed that clerics had no business exercising temporal authority in the country. The new dictator decided that the survival of his nation depended on his absolute control of politics. In practice, this meant limiting any potential rival force in the country, including that of the church.

As early as 1815 Francia began to extend his control over the clergy, forbidding the dissemination of religious correspondence without prior approval and ultimately exiling the Franciscan provisor, a Spaniard.[27] Eventually, all regulars were required to swear a loyalty oath as part of their official "secularization."[28]

In the Indian pueblos the effect of these policies was predictable. They engendered concern among the Guaraní and fear among the clerics and resident administrators. Perhaps the influence of the latter would have diminished anyway given the rapid deterioration of trade to the south and the beginning of civil war in Argentina. Francia made the administrators' lives still more difficult by supervising their activities carefully. He never hesitated to correct any malfeasance. In 1823, for instance, he denounced the administrator of Itá for illegally supplying Indian laborers to outside contractors: "The administrators do not have nor have they ever had the right to allow Indians to work outside their pueblo."[29] This ruling flew in the face of tradition, as Francia well knew, but his was not a government where underlings were permitted any leeway in policy matters. As supreme dictator (a position he held until his death in 1840), Francia arrogated all such decision making to himself.

The Indians submitted to the new regime without opposition. As long as they took care to avoid offending the dictator, they could live relatively undisturbed in their pueblos. No longer did a widespread commercial network demand their labor in the *yerbales*. The timber and tobacco industries were generally depressed. Payments in cash also became less frequent. In short, all the key economic forces that had previously attracted the Indians out of the pueblos no longer functioned. During the Francia years the Guaraní (and, for that matter, all Paraguayans) had to return to a subsistence economy resembling that of the 1750s. Most Indians nevertheless regarded Francia as their friend, since in many ways he left them alone, though he did tie them into the Paraguayan military establishment as manufacturers of clothing and intermittently as soldiers.[30] The incorporation of former *mitayo* Indians into the army had never been contemplated during the colonial era, but Francia proved more open-minded. After all, he had to deal with more threatening circumstances. Though the effects of this new policy in the pueblos can easily be overrated, it seems safe to say that it furthered the assimilation of the native population. Hence, though the community structure remained intact, the village leadership increasingly fell into the hands of men who did not act or think like Indians. All the pueblos north of the Paraná experienced this phenomenon.

The Francia interregnum is noteworthy for the persistence of colonial forms long after the break with Spain. Already a middle-aged man by the time of independence, Francia had a conservative political instinct, and he chose to alter only those things that interfered with his power. Since the pueblos could bolster his position, the dictator interfered little. He provided them with honest administrators but generally left their internal governance alone. In this respect, as indeed with his entire rural policy, Francia acted in a far less "supreme" manner than legend would have it.

In the isolation of the dictator's Paraguay, the pueblos were free to look after mundane matters. Population began to grow again in the villages, thanks partly to continued immigration. Land disputes, cattle rustling, contractual disagreements both with outsiders and with other Indians were the problems that appeared most frequently in the archival record.[31] At every juncture in this record, both as individuals and as a community, the Indians appeared more capable, more at home in the secular world, and altogether less Indian than before. Wherever possible, they guarded their legal perquisites as Indians, but in other respects they were now almost indistinguishable from other rural Paraguayans.

Thus did the twenty-one pueblos under Paraguayan control survive well into the nineteenth century. The same cannot be said for what remained of those to the south of the Paraná. In the mid-1810s the forces of the Oriental (modern Uruguay) chieftain José Gervasio Artigas swept through what would later become the Argentine northeast. Pursued by both the Portuguese and rival gaucho troops, the Artiguistas (many of whom were Indians) moved into the already depopulated mission region, which served for a time as their base of operations. A good many Guaraní, tired of their less-than-enviable position between the two opposing forces, joined one side or the other or fled, to the west or into the jungle. Few returned. For the individual Indian, military service presented a useful opening to the larger world. After all, for at least forty years after independence, employment was usually available for any man who could ride, take orders, and handle a lance. These same skills could conceivably lead to steady work in stockraising. Either way, the greater society would benefit. Perhaps Dr. Francia had this in mind when he allowed individual Indians into the ranks of the army.

Although individuals might have benefited from the militarization of society, the system of segregated communities had a difficult time. South of the Paraguayan frontier the situation approached savagery. The remaining Guaraní inhabitants found their home pueblos under constant military pressure. Troops took over their dwellings temporarily and gutted them when they left. Soon the region took on the aspect of a vast no-man's land, claimed by all three of the new nation-states—Argentina, Paraguay, and Brazil—but effectively occupied by no one, not even the tiny number of Guaraní hiding in the Yberá marshlands.[32] The carefully manicured fields of cotton and yerba, once the pride of the Jesuit Order, returned to nature. They can be found so even today, a sad legacy of misfortune and politics.

Carlos Antonio López and the Seizure of the Paraguayan Pueblos

The isolation Paraguay experienced during the Francia years was only temporary. Once the political situation in the Platine estuary stabilized, every reason existed for Paraguay to open its frontiers as in the past. Such opportunities had come and gone during the 1820s. Characteristically, Francia always chose the cautious path of nonintercourse. In general terms, he left the task of political innovation to his successor, Carlos Antonio López, a country solicitor who took power several months after Francia's death in 1840.

Though much of his life had been spent in rural isolation, López was far more modern in his thinking than Francia. He had few illusions about the utility of colonial institutions, and he consciously regarded himself as a modernizer. Despite this, however, López was still an absolutist. Like Francia, he linked the survival of his nation with the power of the state, and extending that power (and that of his family) became his main goal.

This was bad news for the *pueblos de indios*. Up to that time the Indian villages had depended on the strength of established custom and, more particularly, on the innate conservatism of the Francia regime. This shield protected an institutional segregation that even by mid-nineteenth-century standards seemed archaic. With a self-professed modernizer at the helm, things had to change.

López saw that for his regime to be safe, it would have to be secure economically. That required a far-reaching control over the country's resources, and the various Indian properties presented an obvious target. In 1842 López introduced a measure to divide the land and cattle belonging to the pueblos among the Indians living there who met certain criteria. The Paraguayan Congress followed with a decree that authorized such reallocations at the discretion of local officials. The intent of this decree was clear enough—to undercut the communal structure of the pueblos, to set the Indians against one another, all in the name of a new "liberal" order. From this point on, landownership would be restricted to "capable Indians, those most deserving and well behaved."[33]

The decree divided the Indians into two groups: those who could and those who could not own land. Those in the latter group would be subject to legal discrimination, even by other residents of the pueblos. And this was only the first step. The next move came at Itapúa in the south, where López ordered the removal of all Indians and mestizos to make room for expanded port facilities.[34] The inhabitants of the former pueblo were relocated to a boggy site some leagues to the west called Tuparaí (later renamed Carmen del Paraná). There the government reestablished the Indian *cabildo* much as before, but this gave little comfort to Indians placed into an unfavorable physical environment, and it apparently hastened their flight out of the pueblo entirely.[35] Indeed, archival documentation records petitions of several Indians at this time (and not only from Tuparaí) demanding resettlement or redress.[36] The very existence of these eloquent petitions, written by Indians acting as individuals rather than as part of a corporate body, demonstrates how blurred the line between Indian and white behavior had become.

López thus paved the way for the most radical of his "reforms," the elimination of the pueblos as an institution and the incorporation of their holdings into the state's coffers. A precedent of sorts had been established just to the south, in the Argentine province of Corrientes, where the government had already "extinguished" the two Indian communities of Santa Lucía and Itatí by the late 1820s.[37] With Francia gone, Paraguay was ready to follow suit.

In early October 1848 López acted. His carefully worded decree noted that the Indians of the pueblos had been subjected to abuse from time immemorial, that they had long suffered in silence the many humiliations imposed by the conquest. The burden of tribute and of maintaining a "ruinous" communal system, López argued, had been borne long enough. Now had come the time for freedom.

The Indians of the twenty-one pueblos were declared to be henceforth citizens of the republic.[38]

Behind this liberal rhetoric lurked a draconian objective, elaborated in subsequent articles of the decree. Each pueblo was divested of its *cabildo*, administrator, and segregated status. A "voluntary" military draft was established for pueblo Indians. After a lapse of three years they also became responsible for all pastoral and agricultural taxes (including the *diezmo*, or tithe, generally a 10 percent tax on newborn livestock and agricultural produce to support the church). Most important of all, the state seized all cattle, goods, and properties owned by the community and, significantly, by the nonassimilated mestizos living on pueblo land.[39]

This last measure represented the death knell for Paraguay's *pueblos de indios*. In exchange for the dubious honor of de jure equality with other Paraguayans, the inhabitants of the pueblos lost all their communal holdings. In material terms alone, this amounted to a great deal (table 4).

These figures exclude other valuable community properties such as a brick factory and sugarmill at Guarambaré; a soap factory, carpenter shop, and tannery at Yaguarón; several ranches at San Joaquín and San Ignacio; a smithy at Caazapá; and rudimentary textile mills at several pueblos. The government also took thousands of yards of cotton cloth, various religious books, musical instruments, cowhides, and all community buildings, including churches. Many belongings privately held by Indians were also evidently seized. Yet perhaps the most important acquisition to come out of the 1848 takeover was the forty-five thousand inhabitants of the pueblos, who now became ordinary citizens with ordinary ties to the economy as renters and sharecroppers.[40] Their everyday life in the fields and villages continued much as before, but they no longer held legal status as segregated Indians. Many nonetheless were happy to rid themselves of their *administradores* and of their own *cabildantes* and looked forward to a new life under new masters.

López's motivation in ordering the seizure of the pueblos has been the subject of some debate. The most likely explanation focuses on the all-encompassing and authoritarian character of his regime: López simply wanted to eliminate all vestiges of the colonial order, including all the old institutional forms. If such actions could simultaneously enrich the state, so much the better.

Table 4
Holdings of Paraguay's *Pueblos de Indios*, 1848

Pueblo	Cattle	Horses	Mares	Sheep	Cash (in pesos)
Altos	6,785	179	600	2,187	498
Atyra	10,381	200	361	514	257
Belén	694	92	270	678	130
Caazapá	15,336	1,687	2,868	4,685	526
Carmen	1,510	420	740	520	136
Guarambaré	500	40	107	125	40
Itá	4,715	346	891		1,329
Jesús	946	51	267	238	128
San Cosme	1,935	208	344	1,180	133
San Estanislao	3,528	111	185	2,192	394
San Ignacio	23,575	895	4,973	3,921	694
San Joaquín	653	499		1,434	1,218
Santa María	3,900	457	1,523	9,103	330
Santa Rosa	18,118	638	1,555	398	427
Santiago	1,022	882	3,501	2,614	321
Tobatí	3,808	160	348	641	
Trinidad	259	43	75	40	37
Yaguarón	1,721	3,222		1,000	1,206
Ypané	588	43	80	43	73
Yuty	16,507	1,137	4,782	448	290
Totals	116,831	11,331	23,531	32,231	8,442

Source: Inventorio de las temporalidades de las suprimidas comunidades de ... [1848], ANA—Colección Río Branco, I-29:24, nos. 12-24; 25, nos. 1-11.

As for the Indians, they joined the mass of Paraguayans almost without a whimper. No uprisings occurred, as in the 1750s, or even any protests. Other than noting their compliance, about the only comment from the Indians came from the *cabildo* of Altos, which, in its letter of obeisance to López, included a syrupy paean:

Long live his honor and his eloquence,
this ever-constant man,
he never rests even for a moment,
he works at all hours,
he has defeated the Spaniards
and defended the Fatherland
Holy Mother, help our President
with your grace.[41]

In this ironic and anticlimactic fashion, Paraguay's *pueblos de indios* passed out of existence, not with dignity or anger but with a fatalism that in today's age seems more like understatement.

What, then, are we to make of the pueblo as an institution? At the end the segregated communities were widely regarded as antiquated, as being out of step with the times. Indeed, as far as the Indians were concerned, the pueblos had served their purpose, which had been to provide the Guaraní with an institutional framework through which they could negotiate with the Spaniards. This semblance of legal parity between the Indian and white communities served both groups, though more particularly the former, for far more years than anyone might have guessed.

Initially, the pueblos had the legal function of rewarding the conquistadors through grants of *encomienda* and of converting the Indians to Christianity, the better to make them useful subjects of the Crown. This traditional interpretation necessarily places the Indians in the role of victims. The historical character of the pueblos was never one-dimensional, however, and they offered as much as they took.

The conquest had imposed a new reality on the Guaraní. From the mid-1500s on, an outright rejection of the European world was impossible. Remembering that their earliest contacts with the Spaniards had had some mutually beneficial effects, the Guaraní accepted the pueblos as the least pernicious option. They saw, moreover, that they had little other choice. Time permitted adaptation and ultimately assimilation into the wider world.

On the surface, it would be difficult to say who assimilated whom. Ethnocide never entered into the question. The Hispanic and Indian elements of Paraguayan society simply grew to resemble each other so as to be nearly indistinguishable. Non-Indian peasants grew manioc, cotton, and tobacco and spoke Guaraní exactly the same way as Indians in the pueblos. Differences were minimal and increasingly nebulous as time went by.

The eighteenth century presented the pueblos with a great watershed. The expulsion of the Jesuits stripped the southern mission communities of their religious veneer, exposing them at the same time to the full brunt of Spanish economic penetration. This process had been occurring for some time in the Franciscan and secular villages. The commercial renaissance of the late 1700s eventually brought not only the former Jesuit mission communities but even the most distant Indian pueblos of the north into the booming trade.

Many among the Guaraní welcomed the chance to participate in the economic upswing. Some willingly abandoned the pueblos for greener pastures. Others stayed, hoping to preserve the most useful social features of the pueblo system while extracting as much profit as possible from the new economy; both choices involved increased contact between Indians and whites.

The process of penetration was never homogeneous but varied according to local conditions. Some pueblos, because of their position near *yerbales* or along commercial routes, experienced a sustained incursion of entrepreneurs and squatters. A minority of pueblos underwent a less direct penetration, maintaining a higher degree of agricultural self-sufficiency and a minimum of emigration. Yet even the most remote pueblos soon became accustomed to Spanish ways, and on occasion—such as when Indians petitioned to remove a corrupt official—they used those ways to forward their own interests.

By independence the Indian leaders in the pueblos had become practiced diplomatists who could skillfully present their case whenever a dispute arose. With Dr. Francia in power in Asunción, they could count on dealing with a conservative who would never tamper with the institutional structure of the pueblos. Indeed, since trade to the south had collapsed, little incentive for change existed, and he was content to leave the pueblos in peace. But peace did not mean the isolation of old. The contacts between Indians and whites went on unabated, and the process of assimilation continued.

When Carlos Antonio López looked into the question of the pueblos in the early 1840s, he found communities that were Indian largely in name alone. His move to take over the pueblos, to convert their inhabitants into Paraguayan citizens, seemed to him completely appropriate.

What López never understood was that the observable fact of assimilation was part of a long-term Indian strategy of survival. The Guaraní could have resisted and suffered the same sad fate as the Charrúa or Diaguita. They could have retained rigidly segregated communities, as under the Jesuits, but as we have seen, such isolation failed to prepare the Indians for life without the fathers. The only other choice open to them was gradual assimilation, precisely that offered by the pueblos. Thus, the pueblos must be regarded as an instrument of transition affecting the whole of society. It is no accident that today "Guaraní" is considered a synonym for "Paraguayan."

Notes

1. John Lynch, *Spanish Colonial Administration, 1782–1810: The Intendent System in the Viceroyalty of the Río de la Plata* (London, 1958), pp. 110–15, 185–95.

2. Alfred Métraux, "The Guaraní," in *Handbook of Southern American Indians*, vol. 3: *Tropical Forest Tribes*, edited by Julian Steward (New York, 1963), p. 77.

3. See, for example, Viceroy Marques de Avilés to the King, Buenos Aires, 8 June 1799, Archivo General de Indias (Sevilla), Audiencia de Buenos Aires (Hereinafter AGI-BA), no. 85. Secondary works that touch on this question include V. Martin de Moussy, "Memoire historique sur la décadence et la ruine des missiones des Jesuites dans la bassin de la Plata," in his *Description geographique et statistique de la Confédération Argentine* (Paris, 1864), 3:655–734; José M. Mariluz Urquijo, "Los Guaraníes después de la expulsión de los Jesuitas," *Estudios Americanos* 25 (1953), 323–30; Bartomeu Melia, *El Guaraní conquistado y reducido: Ensayos de etnohistoria* (Asunción, Paraguay, 1986); and Ramón Tissera, *De la civilización a la barbarie: La destrucción de las misiones guaraníes* (Buenos Aires, 1969).

4. The list of works on the Jesuit "empire" could go on for many pages. What follows is a representative sampling: Pedro Lozano, *Historia de la Compañía de Jesús en la provincia del Paraguay*, 2 vols. (Madrid, 1754–55); Fr. Pierre François Xavier Charlevoix, *Histoire du Paraguay*, 3 vols. (Paris, 1756); José Sánchez Labrador, *El Paraguay Católico*, 3 vols. (Buenos Aires, 1910–17); P. P. Pastells, S.J., *Historia de la Compañía de Jesús en la provincia del Paraguay*, 4 vols. (Madrid, 1912–23); Pablo Hernández, *Organización social de las doctrinas guaraníes*, 2 vols. (Barcelona, 1913); Enrique de Gandía, *Las misiones jesuíticas y los Bandeirantes paulistas* (Buenos Aires, 1936); Antonio Sepp, *Viagem as missoes jesuíticas e trabalhos apostólicos* (São Paulo, 1943); Magnus Mörner, *Political and Economic Activities of the Jesuits in the La Plata Region: The Hapsburg Era* (Stockholm, 1955); Guillermo Furlong Cardiff, *Misiones y sus pueblos de Guaraníes* (Buenos Aires, 1962); Branislava Susnik, *El indio colonial del Paraguay*, vol. 1 (Asunción, Paraguay, 1965); *Los trece pueblos guaraníes de la misiones*, vol. 2 (Asunción, Paraguay, 1966); Gonzalo de Doblas, *Memoria sobre la provincia de misiones de indios guaraníes* (Buenos Aires, 1970); Richard Alan White, "The Political Economy of Paraguay and the Impoverishment of the Missions: Classical Colonial Dependence," *The Americas* 31 (1975), 417–33; Bra-

nislava Susnik, *Los aborigenes del Paraguay*, vol. 2: *Etnohistoria de los Guaraníes: Epoca colonial* (Asunción, Paraguay, 1979–80); Nicholas P. Cushner, *Jesuit Ranches and the Agrarian Development of Colonial Argentina, 1650–1767* (Albany NY, 1983); Juan Carlos Garavaglia, *Mercado interno y economía colonial* (Mexico City, 1983); Branislava Susnik, *El rol de los indígenas en la formación y en la vivencia del Paraguay* (Asunción, Paraguay, 1985).

5. Félix de Azara, *Geografía física y esférica del Paraguay* (Montevideo, Uruguay, 1904), pp. 415–16.

6. Garavaglia, *Mercado interno*.

7. See my *La yerba mate del Paraguay: Un ensayo de interpretación* (Asunción, Paraguay, 1991).

8. Some of the restrictive laws concerning yerba shipment are listed in the Archivo General de la Nación—Buenos Aires IX (Compañía de Jesús) 7, 1, 1 no. 576.

9. Adalberto López, *The Revolt of the Comuneros, 1721–1735: A Study in the Colonial History of Paraguay* (Cambridge, 1976); James Schofield Saeger, "Origins of the Rebellion of Paraguay," *Hispanic American Historical Review* 52 (May 1972), 215–29. Regarding Corrientes, see Raúl de Labougle, *Historia de los comuneros* (Buenos Aires, 1953), as well as his *Historia de San Juan de Vera de las Siete Corrientes (1588–1814)* (Buenos Aires, 1978).

10. A good summary of the Guaraní war can be found in Philip Caraman, *The Lost Paradise: The Jesuit Republic in South America* (New York, 1975), pp. 235–55.

11. Tulio Halperin Doughi, *Politics, Economics, and Society in Argentina in the Revolutionary Period* (Cambridge, 1975), pp. 18–19.

12. Among the few exceptions was the father of José de San Martín, future liberator of Argentina and Chile. The elder San Martín has generally been portrayed as an honest and efficient administrator at Yapeyú, one of the southernmost Guaraní pueblos. See José Torre Revello, *Yapeyú (ensayo histórico)* (Buenos Aires, 1958).

13. By the 1780s and 1790s the *pueblos de indios* had entered the commercial web of *yerba mate*. See, for example, Guía of Santos Rubledo, Caazapá, 16 Dec. 1789, Archivo Nacional de Asunción, Sección Nueva Encuadernación, (hereinafter ANA-NE) vol. 525. On late colonial river trade, see Jerry W. Cooney, *Economía y sociedad en la intendencia del Paraguay* (Asunción, Paraguay, 1990).

14. One observer noted that the fashions thus chosen "served to ridicule rather than adorn" the Indian celebrations. Gonzalo de Doblas, *Memoria*, p. 38.

15. Sometimes village administrators gave tacit permission for their Indian charges to absent themselves precisely in order that they should send back provisions. See Cabildo of Asunción to the King, Asunción, 13 Sept. 1779, AGI-BA, no. 240. In a few pueblos, such as Yuty and Caazapá, the lack of

provisions was less a problem than labor shortages, and community officials had to go to the free labor market to hire mestizo wage workers to replace absent Indians who themselves were working for wages in Asunción or on estates near the provincial capital.

16. Employment of Indians in this capacity was prohibited but occurred frequently notwithstanding. See Report of Gaspar Francia to Governor Joaquín Alós, Asunción, 6 Nov. 1789, ANA, Sección Judicial Criminal (SJC), vol. 1540; see also my article, "La vida ribereña: El caso correntino," *Folia Histórica del Nordeste* 9 (1990), 143–53.

17. Gonzalo de Doblas, *Memoria*, p. 68; on fugitive rates, see Susnik, *Etnohistoria de los Guaraníes*, pp. 294–98 and passim.

18. The Cabildo to Governor Agustín Fernando de Pinedo, San Joaquín, 29 July 1776, ANA-NE, 456.

19. Regarding these state industries of the viceregal period, see the following articles by Jerry W. Cooney: "A Colonial Naval Industry: The Fabrica de Cables of Paraguay," *Revista de Historia de América* 87 (Jan.–June 1979), 105–26; "Forest Industries and Trade in Late Colonial Paraguay," *Journal of Forest History* 23 (Oct. 1979), 186–87; "Paraguayan Astilleros and the Platine Merchant Marine, 1796–1806," *The Historian* 43 (Nov. 1980), 55–74.

20. Cabildo to Interim Governor Francisco de Piera, Santa Ana, 18 Aug. 1783, ANA, Sección Historia (SH), vol. 439, no. 5.

21. The Corregidor and Cabildo to Governor Joaquín de Alós, Santa María, 17 Sept. 1788, in ANA-SH 152, no. 5.

22. Alós to King, Asunción, 20 Oct. 1788, AGI-BA, vol. 142.

23. Among the many reports from this period are those of Francisco Bruno de Závala (1784), in *Boletín del Instituto de Investigaciones Históricas* 25 (1941), 159–87; Félix de Azara (various dates), in *Memoria sobre el estado rural del Río de la Plata y otros informes* (Buenos Aires, 1943); and Miguel Lastarria (1805), in *Colonias orientales de Río Paraguay o de la Plata (1774–1805)*, in Facultad de Filosofía y Letras, *Documentos para la historia Argentina*, vol. 3 (Buenos Aires, 1914).

24. Ribera had in mind a more rapid Christianization of the Indians (though clerics had to limit their activities to the spiritual), improvements in the cattle industry so as to make it commercially viable, the construction of hospitals, and the submission of regular reports to serve as guides to future planning. See Report of Lázaro de Ribera, Asunción, 18 Oct. 1798, ANA-SH 172, no. 16.

25. Regarding the Paraguayan *encomienda*, see Elman Service, "The Encomienda in Paraguay," *Hispanic American Historical Review* 31 (1951), 230–52; Blanca Rosa Romero de Viola, *Paraguay: Siglo dieciocho, período de transición* (Asunción, Paraguay, 1987), pp. 78–85, 104–9, 159–95, 263–77; and James S. Saeger, "Survival and Abolition: The Eighteenth-Century Paraguayan Encomienda," *The Americas* 38 (July 1981), 59–85. See also Enco-

miendas agregados a la Corona como vacante por muerte, renuncia, o abandono, Asunción, 3 Nov. 1802, ANA-NE 1145.

26. Priests in Paraguay, other than Jesuits, were never especially chaste. A Swiss visitor in the mid-1810s noted with surprise that the "curates and the monks lived publicly in a state of concubinage, and so far from being ashamed of so doing, they were known to boast of it." See Johann Rudolph Rengger and Marceline Longchamp, *The Reign of Doctor Joseph Gaspard Roderick de Francia in Paraguay* (London, 1827), p. 182. Regarding Franciscan approaches to Indian supervision, see Margarita Durán Estrago, *Presencia franciscana en el Paraguay (1538-1824)* (Asunción, Paraguay, 1987).

27. John Hoyt Williams, *The Rise and Fall of the Paraguayan Republic, 1800-1870* (Austin TX, 1979), pp. 56-57; see also Jerry W. Cooney, "The Destruction of the Religious Orders in Paraguay, 1810-1824," *The Americas* 36:2 (1979), 177-98.

28. Decree of Dr. Francia, Asunción, 20 Sept. 1824, ANA-NE 31-7 (records the presence of fifty-three friars in the country).

29. José Mariano Vargas to Francia, Asunción, 23 May 1823, in ANA-NE 3093; for another case in which Francia dealt with corrupt officials in the pueblos, see Expediente del Protector de Naturales Francisco Xavier Arévalo, Asunción, 30 Sept. 1818, ANA-SJC 2053.

30. Rengger and Longchamp, *The Reign*, pp. 174-78; see also Jacinto Ballibian to Francia, Asunción, 1831?, ANA-NE 1889, for an interesting description of textile and yarn production at Yaguarón.

31. Regarding land disputes, see Pedro Francia to Francia, Itá, 3 Nov. 1815, ANA-SJC 1327; and demanda of Mariano Martínez of Yaguarón, Asunción, 8 Nov. 1824, ANA-SJC 1951. Regarding rustling, see denuncia of the Vecinos of Curuguaty against Indians of San Joaquín, Asunción, 25 Nov. 1816, ANA-SJC 1711; and proceso against Juan Silvestre Silva and three Indians of Belén, Concepción, 30 Nov. 1819, ANA-SJC 1818. Regarding contractual problems, see demanda of Juan José Figueiredo (concerning cotton thread from Itá), Asunción, 15 Jan. 1818, ANA-SJC 1919; José Ignacio de Sosa to Francia (concerning tobacco from Jesús), Asunción, 29 Jan. 1832, ANA-NE 2583; and Pedro Pablo Benítez to Francia (concerning yerba from San Joaquín), San Joaquín, 28 June 1832, ANA-NE 2585.

32. Indian refugees from various missions did reach two isolated communities hidden in the swamps, but they came in small numbers and had no hope of doing more than barely surviving. The presence of these two "lost" pueblos and the periodic reappearance of isolated Guaraní in the jungle were anomalies. See Ernesto J. A. Maeder, "Los últimos pueblos de indios guaraníes: Loreto y San Miguel (1822-1854)," in *Anais do V Simpósio Nacional de Estudos Misioneiros* (Santa Rosa, Rio Grande do Sul, Brazil, 1983), pp. 156-72.

33. Message of López to Congress, 1842, ANA-SH 285, no. 11; see also José

Antonio Gómez-Perasso, "Los pueblos de indios y su desintegración en el siglo XIX," *Suplemento Antropológico* 11 (1975), 125–38; and Ramón Gutiérrez, "Los pueblos jesuíticos del Paraguay: Reflexiones sobre su decadencia," *Suplemento Antropológico* 14 (1979), 179–99.

34. Itapúa was thus reorganized as Encarnación, the country's chief port on the Alto Paraná. See Decreto of López, Asunción, 8 April 1843, in *El Repertorio Nacional* (Asunción, Paraguay, 1843).

35. See Basilio Antonio Ojeda to López, Encarnación, 4 Nov. 1843; and Ojeda to López, Encarnación, 18 Nov. 1843, both in ANA-SH 378, no. 2.

36. Petition of Victorio Siya (1844), ANA-SH 271, no. 5; petition of Micaela Cipriana Yaparí, Asunción, 12 May 1845, ANA-SH 273, no. 4; petition of María Petrona Yaharí, Altos, Apr. 1846, ANA-SH 279, no. 6.

37. David Bushnell, *Reform and Reaction in the Platine Provinces, 1810–1852* (Gainesville FL, 1983), pp. 38, 137–38. Similar legislation had been passed in the Andean countries during these same years, though no clear evidence exists to link these different policies.

38. Decree of López, Asunción, 7 Oct. 1848, ANA-SH 282, no. 24.

39. In the same decree López noted that non-Indians constituted nearly the entire population in certain pueblos.

40. Williams, *Rise and Fall*, p. 133.

41. Cabildo of Altos to López, Altos, 21 Oct.? 1848, ANA-Colección Río Branco, I–29:24, 13.

Erick Langer

Conclusion

The contributions in this book demonstrate several approaches to the field of mission history. In large part the contributors received their inspiration from social history and ethnohistory, new interdisciplinary approaches that developed after the heyday of the earlier mission studies from 1900 to the early 1950s. Although social history (and to a lesser extent ethnohistory) has been a dominant interest of the historical profession since the 1960s and has become the mainstream, the use of these new perspectives has only recently revolutionized the way scholars examine missions.

The new historiography of missions is important in two ways. First, missions represent an area of intense interaction between European ideals and indigenous culture, an ideal field for the study of postcontact ethnohistory. Second, the missions can now be integrated into the larger context of the Latin American frontier. Although this point represents in many ways a continuation of the Bolton school—after all, Bolton and his disciples were interested in the missions within the framework of the "Spanish borderlands"—the advances in mission demography, labor studies, and ethnohistory present a strikingly different and more multifaceted picture.

The chapters in this book take into account the indigenous perspective. This approach is laden with methodological problems, since in all but a few exceptional cases we must squeeze out information about native populations from European sources hostile to the Indian point of view. For the missions, we often have a great many sources, written by men who lived with the Indians and were intimately acquainted with their mores, though they used this acquaintance to transform their charges' belief systems and way of life. Moreover, unlike government officials, who usually had little interest in indigenous culture, missionaries were much more aware of cultural aspects, if only to extirpate them. Even so, their descriptions give the new mission historians considerable material that previously had been either ignored or used without full analysis.

It is, of course, impossible to ignore the prejudices of the missionaries when examining the information they offer. Stripping down their accounts to reveal the essential behavior of the Indians works only to a certain degree, for what the missionaries recorded was highly selective and filtered through their own cultural perspectives. Although we cannot retrieve information that is not in the records, the new mission historians, like many other ethnohistorians, have tried to compensate for these methodological problems. Seeing missions within the framework of both native and a particular version of European culture—that of the Catholic missionaries—is an important step forward.

Another advance is the incorporation of studies and concepts of the "ethnographic present," and cultural anthropology in general, to explicate past behaviors. An awareness of problems, such as the dubious assumption that indigenous cultures experienced little change over centuries (an unlikely possibility in the case of the missions), makes possible a sophisticated analysis even with partial information dimly perceived through European eyes. Thus, Susan Deeds' work on northern Mexico usefully combines ideas from James Scott and Edward Spicer, a pioneer in analyzing northern Mexican Indians from an anthropologically sensitive perspective.

The European-Indian interactions illuminated by this multidisciplinary perspective help revise the traditional mission history. Clearly, the missionaries supervised the Indians closely and attempted quite consciously to change them in ways that were not possible in the European-dominated urban centers. This intense interaction, however, did not always have the consequences the official mission histories might have us believe. The Indians were often the victims of the missionary system rather than the happy recipients of European civilization, as David Sweet points out. But it is important to go beyond the vision of Indians as mere victims. Much more was going on in the missions. If we simply reverse the equation—from missionaries as saviors to Indians as victims—we lose much of the complexity of the missions' impact. For example, the demographic effect of the missions on California, combined with the emphasis later in the eighteenth century on production rather than conversion, show that belief systems might not have changed as thoroughly as official policy indicates. As Paul Farnsworth and Robert Jackson show, the Indians in the later period, when the missions presumably were well-established, maintained more of their material culture than earlier in the century.

The focus on the mission regime's internal workings, along with an acknowledgment of the basic fact that the Indians were active participants in their own history, reveals a great deal about the relative power of the mission Indian population. From this perspective, the missionaries' bold assertions of conversion and the triumphs of "civilization" must be viewed with skepticism. The relative economic autonomy the Chiriguanos maintained in their missions, for example, despite the dramatic change in the individual household economy, alerts us to the complexity of the Indian-missionary interaction. It is possible that the Chiriguano case was exceptional and that the republican-era missions had a different dynamic than those of the colonial era. Nevertheless, Susan Deeds finds similar patterns of native autonomy in the colonial Sonora missions.

These considerations lead us to a reevaluation of the relationship between missionaries and Indians. How well did the small numbers of missionaries truly control the large Indian populations? The separation of the sexes, the establishment of patriarchal authority as understood by Europeans, new housing patterns, different foods, high mortality, and new work requirements all argue for substantial European control. Nevertheless, patterns of resistance and the maintenance of earlier practices and beliefs that were either not understood or ignored by the missionaries continued. The conventional duality between continuity and change, or traditional indigenous forms versus conversion to European forms, is too simplistic, however. Indigenous cultures had a dynamic of their own, and the Indians were willing and able to change (indeed, often more than the Europeans). During the mission period and after secularization, the dynamic Indian cultures blended the new and the old. For this reason, it is important to study not only the missions themselves but what happened afterward. Do the secularized settlements have unique characteristics showing the vigor of this new cultural amalgam? Thomas Whigham's study of the Franciscan-controlled pueblos after their secularization, for example, shows that these villages were not fully European but also not completely Guaraní.

Indeed, Whigham identifies a "mission culture," unlike either the surrounding European or Indian community. Indigenous forms and the peculiar religious culture of the missions created a distinctive population that did not identify itself as either European or nonmissionized Indian. This aspect merits investigation for both the mission period and, perhaps more significant, after secularization.

It has long been recognized (not least by Herbert Bolton) that the missions shaped the Latin American frontier, but few have taken up the challenge of relating the mission to larger patterns, aside from the political struggles that inevitably occurred between the missionaries and the settlers. The approaches of the new mission history have much to contribute to frontier studies in general. For example, even "old" topics, such as the struggle over native labor, take on a new hue in the light of demographic factors and internal power relations in the missions. Clearly, the often severe mortality among the Indians greatly restricted the frontier settlers' access to labor. The colonial Brazilian case, described by Alexander Marchant decades ago, was probably universal.[1] As the Indian population dwindled, the competition for labor often sharpened considerably, though, as Farnsworth and Jackson show, this scarcity might have been mitigated in part by a relatively high proportion of adults and males at the missions. Without demographic data, it is difficult to understand fully the effects of the mission regime on the Indians as well as take into account the larger context of the frontier. Demographic studies are lacking for virtually all mission systems outside North America. Although this state of affairs is perhaps not surprising, given the access to records of resource-rich U.S. historians, the longstanding tradition of mission studies as part of the Boltonian project of the "borderlands," and the documentary wealth available, it is necessary to start examining the demographic history of other regions within Latin America.

Despite the value of "borderlands" examples to mission historians of other areas of Latin America, comparisons must be made cautiously. It is likely that, in many ways, the mission experience in what is now the United States represented the extreme case of population decline. In California contact between indigenous peoples and Europeans was sporadic before the missionaries arrived, making disease perhaps a much more serious problem. Moreover, the peoples the missionaries encountered were relatively small ethnic groups organized primarily as hunters and gatherers. The demographic decline had much greater effect on these relatively small groups, since they lacked the population base with which to rebound after contact. Moreover, the relocation of hunters and gatherers to the missions and their conversion to agricultural labor represented a much greater change in culture than the settlement of agriculturalists already used to permanent villages and farming. We need studies of other regions of Latin America to confirm or modify the California model.

The ethnohistorical concerns of the new mission history and the subsequent redefinition of Indian-missionary relations suggest different interpretations of the struggle over indigenous labor on the frontier. Other than in exceptional cases, it is not possible to maintain the traditional stereotype of the selfless missionary protecting the hapless Indian from the predations of exploitative settlers. Missionaries often aided in the exploitation of Indian labor by renting out their workers. More important, the native people played an active role in the use of their labor. We need to know whether Indians refused to work for the settlers, as suggested by the amount of resistance. Often just the opposite of what one might define as resistance occurred, as Deeds and Langer show in their chapters. Indians worked for settlers and in mines or even migrated out of the region, often to the despair of the missionaries, who wanted to keep them at the missions. The role of the traditional chief as labor broker was crucial among the Chiriguanos: did this intermediary role also occur elsewhere? The relative lack of control over native labor by the missionaries (is California here the exception that demonstrates mission controls?) and the Indians' insistence on working elsewhere suggest the complexity of the issue.

Frequently, documentation on indigenous groups is lacking except from the missions. Most other reports on these groups come from military men, government officials, some exceptional settlers (literacy was seldom valued among frontiersmen), and, when we are lucky, a few ethnographically sensitive travelers. The accounts of travelers offer us tantalizing but superficial glimpses of Indian peoples during certain slices of time, making it difficult to trace changes. As a result, the rather dense information provided by the missionaries (despite all its problems) is usually the most valuable that can be found for European-Indian interaction on the frontier.

For these reasons, the missions serve as the best laboratories for an understanding of both indigenous societies along the Latin American frontier and Indian-European interaction. Beyond shedding light on internal dynamics, missions tell us how the Indians reacted to the European invasion.

The missions had a powerful effect not just on the European side of the frontier but also on indigenous societies beyond European control. Our vision of the missions hermetically sealed from the outside world, whether European or Indian (as in the colonial Paraguayan stereotype), is simply wrong. We are beginning to realize that the native economy was often supremely significant in patterns of trade and frontier development. The Indians of the Argentine pampas, for example, formed large political units and supplied cattle to the Chilean markets.

Much still needs to be done to realize the potential of mission research for ethnohistorical insight. Social and ethnohistorical methods will help revitalize mission history, placing it at the center of the study of the Latin American frontier. The new mission history will also illuminate aspects of Latin American society and history more generally.

Note

1. Alexander Marchant, *From Barter to Slavery: The Economic Relations of Portuguese and Indians in the Settlement of Brazil, 1500–1580* (Baltimore, 1942).

The Contributors

Susan M. Deeds is on the history faculty of Northern Arizona University. She has published extensively on Mexico's northern frontier in the colonial period in such journals as *Arizona and the West, The Americas, Hispanic American Historical Review, Latin American Research Review,* and *Journal of the Southwest.*

Paul Farnsworth serves in the Department of Geography and Anthropology at Louisiana State University. He has written on the archaeology of Mexico, California, and the Caribbean for *Historical Archaeology, Journal of the Bahamas Historical Society, Research in Economic Anthropology, Journal of New World Archaeology,* and *American Antiquity.*

Lance Raymond Grahn is a member of the Department of History at Marquette University. He has written on religious, mission, and economic topics in the colonial history of South America for several contributed books and for *Platte Valley Review.*

Robert H. Jackson teaches in the Department of History and Geography at Texas Southern University. He is the author of *The Spanish Missions of Baja California* (1991), *Indian Demographic Collapse in the Mission Communities of Northwestern New Spain* (1994), *Regional Markets and Agrarian Transformation in Bolivia: Cochabamba, 1539–1960* (1994), and, with Edward Castillo, *Indians, Franciscans, and Spanish Colonization: The Impact of the Mission System on California Indians* (1995).

Erick Detlef Langer is a member of the history faculty at Carnegie Mellon University. He is the author of *Economic Change and Rural Resistance in Southern Bolivia, 1880–1930* (1988) and coeditor, with

Zulema Bass Werner de Ruiz, of *Historia de Tarija: Corpus documental*, volume 5 (1988).

David Graham Sweet is member of Merrill College at the University of California, Santa Cruz, where he teaches history. His studies of mission and popular history in Latin America have appeared as book chapters and in such jorunals as *Revista de Historia de América* and *Radical History Review.* With Gary B. Nash he edited *Struggle and Survival in Colonial America* (1981).

Thomas Whigham serves on the history faculty at the University of Georgia. He has written *The Politics of River Trade: Tradition and Development in the Upper Plata, 1780–1870* (1991) as well as other books and articles on Paraguayan history.

Index

Abortion, 12, 93
Abuses, protection of, 17–18
Acaxee Indians, 78, 80, 85, 86
Accommodation: to commercial economy, 134; to mission, 88–95; to pueblo life, 161
Acculturation: through *mestizaje*, 94; for political stability, 132; on *pueblos de indios*, 182, 183; refusal of, 148; religious, 40; retarded by mortality, 110
Administrador de temporalidades, 161, 180
Advantages, material, 35–36
Agriculture, 55–56, 81–82, 85, 119; abandoned, 173; Capuchin emphasis on, 138; crisis, 64; encouragement of, 58; European-style, 119; production, 58–60; reduced in Soledad, 120–21; staples in California, 121–22; surplus to mines, 82; tax on, 180
Aguado, Fr. Pedro, 138
Aguairenda (mission), 51, 55, 56, 59, 60
Alcácer, Antonio de, 150
Alcalde, 83, 162; *provincial*, 162; *de la Santa Hermandad*, 162
Alcoholic beverages, 16; *aguardiente*, 62–63, destruction of, 84; fermented, 34, 84; introduction of distilled, 34–35; use in desecration, 147
Alcoy, Fr. Antonio de, 146
Alliances, Indian-European, 54
Alós, Joaquín de, 173–74
Alta California, xii, xiv, 11, 52, 109–29; colonization of, 126. *See also* California
Alta Tarahumara (mission), 98
Altea, Pedro de, 147
Alto Paraná, 158
Altos (*pueblo de indios*), 158, 180
Amazon River, 15, 26, 30; missions, 32
Amazon Valley, 1, 10, 11; Portuguese, 38; Peruvian, 26, 33
Andean region, vii, 23, 39, 63, 134, 159, 160
Andía de Rivero, José, 143
Anthropology, cultural, 190
Anticlericalism, 58, 65, 175–76; effects of, in Paraguay, 176–77
Apaches, ix, 33, 88, 98
Apiesi, 149, 150
Aqueduct system, 115
Aratomo Indians, 138, 139
Araucanian Indians, ix
Archaeology, xii, 2, 82, 110–27
Arévalo, Antonio, 149
Argentina: in battles and wars, 54, 176–78, 179; and international commerce, 69, 194; migration

198 Index

Argentina (cont.)
  to, xii, 57, 62, 66–67, 68; as mission territory, 10
Arguedas, José, 14
Arhuaco Indians, 140
Arizona, x
Arrendatario, 170, 172
Arroyo Seco (California), 120
Artigas, José Gervasio, 177
Artisanal activity, 62–63
Ashes, used in ritual, 92
Asunción, 158, 159, 160, 169, 183
Atyra, 159
Augustinians, 9
Authority, moral, 83. See also Power
Autonomy, after secularization, 20
Avuncular inheritance, 145
Ax, 34, 35, 91
Axtell, James, 142
Azara, Félix de, 163
Azero province (Bolivia), 66
Aztec Indians, 92

Bahía Honda, 149, 150
Baja California, 11
Bannon, John, x–xi
Baptism, 113, 117; connected to death, 92; obligations of, 41; as protection from disease, 85, 92–93; reason for, 39; as survival strategy, 44. See also Conversion
Barter, 17
Bathing, discouragement of, 13
Belén (mission), 158
Bilingualism, 38
Birth rates, on Soledad mission, 124
Bogotá, 150
Boicovo (mission), 51, 64, 66, 70
Bolívar (fort), 69
Bolivia, ix, 51–72; army of, 54
Bolton, Herbert E., x–xi, 2–7, 8, 10, 37, 43, 44, 50, 189, 192
Boltonians, x–xi, 189

Borderlands, x, 2, 189, 192
Borica, Diego de, 123
Boronata (mission), 145, 147
Brazil, vii, ix, xi, 10, 23, 178, 192
Brazilwood, 144
Bribe, 170
British trade, 131, 134–35, 143, 145, 149
Buenos Aires, 159, 166, 168, 169, 174

Caazapá (pueblo de indios), 159, 180
Cabildante, 162, 167, 170; of Santa Ana, 172; riddance of, 180
Cabildo, 5, 161, 162; abolition of, 180; of Altos, 181; authority of, 175; members avoid labor, 164; of Santa Ana, 172
Cabo de la Vela (Colombia), 137
Cacao, 31
Caicedo, Juan Beltrán de, 143
California, x, 1, 10, 24, 36, 38; Baja, 11; Central, 32; focus on, 2; impact of disease on, 192–93; land management in, 15; mission Indians, 14, 33, 193; missions, 43, 190–91; model, 193; museums of, 7; punishment in, 22; resistance of Indians in, 42. See also Alta California
California mean ceramic date (CMCD), 115
Calatayud, Fr. Martín de, 137
Camacho, Fr. Agustín, 149
Camarones (mission), 147
Camatindi (Bolivia), 70
Campa Indians (Peru), 26, 33, 39
Campos, Daniel, 54
Canada, 3
Candelaria, 168
Candles, 162
Cannabalism, 81
Capitalism, 3, 11, 39
Capuchins, 9, 130–56; ineffectiveness of, 144

Caracas, 138, 139
Carandaití (Bolivia), 66
Cargo system, 88
Carío Indians, 159
Carmelites, 1, 10
Carmel mission, 110, 113
Carmen del Paraná, 179
Castas, 88
Castile, vii
Catechism, 92
Catholicism, viii, 84; acceptance of, 142; hatred of, 148; and patriarchy, 130; practices, 163; and Pulowi myth, 141–42; reasons for failure, 132; rejection of, 137, 141, 147; selection of aspects, 132–33; understanding of, 163. *See also* Christianity; Conversion
Catholic Reformation, 77
Cattle, 34; and cornfields, 58; decimation of, 173; division of, in *pueblos*, 179; economy, 59, 145, 152; government seizure of, 180; Guajiro origin myth, 136, 152; for hides and tallow, 122; Indian ownership of, 61; on missions, 58, 60–62, 64–65, 70, 142; production on frontier, 68; roundups, 62; rustling, 61, 64–65, 91, 95, 134, 140, 177; sale of, 60–61, 172; trade, 118, 122, 194; zones, 168
Cecilio (López de Sierra), 144–45, 146
Celebrations, missionary opposition to, 84
Central America, 10
Central Valley (California), 117
Chaco. *See* Gran Chaco
Chaco War, 72
Chalon Costonoan Indians, 110, 113, 126. *See also* Costanoan Indians
Chané Indians, 67

Charles II, 138
Charles III, 150, 166
Charrúa Indians, 166, 183
Chaves, Juan Barón de, 134–35, 143
Chevalier, François, 49
Chichimec Wars, 91
Chihuahua, xii, 78, 90, 98
Childrearing, 21, 26; among Tarahumaras, 81
Children: discipline of, 92; indoctrination of, 84, 114; labor of, 19, 62–63, 164; mortality, 110, 123; refusal to convert, 150; religious tasks of, 92. *See also* Schooling
Chile, ix, 10, 194
Chimara (mission), 139
Chimeo (mission), 51
Chimila Indians, 131, 132, 150
Chinipa Indians, 78
Chiriguanía, 1, 36
Chiriguano Indians, xii, 33, 49–72; as consumers of coca, 66; economic autonomy of, 191; as laborers, 53–58; migration of, 57–58; and sharing of goods, 67–68, 71; training of, on mission, 55–56, 62–63
Chocolate, 90
Chorete Indians (Bolivia), 57
Christianity: concepts of, 84, 99, 133; and economic opportunities, 143; patriarchal, 141; rationality of, 133; rejection of, 130, 133–34, 136, 140, 143, 145, 147–52; symbols of, in revolts, 87; understanding of, 39–40, 93, 162. *See also* Catholicism
Christmas, 92
Chuquisaca (Bolivia), 51
Church: attacks on, 130; bells, and death, 87; building of, 53, 85, 122; fear of, 92
Cintruénigo, Fr. Mauro de, 139–40
Civilizing function, 3, 8. *See also* Deculturation

Index

Closed corporate community, 39
Clothing, 13, 38; for children, 66; distribution of, 67, 91, 173; production of, 55–56, 122, 126; purchase and use of Western, 66–67
Coca, consumption of, 66, 67
Cocama Indians (Peru), 26
Cocina Indians (New Granada), 147
Coercion, 50, 57, 69; absence of, 85; as cause of mortality, 123; among Concho Indians, 82, 89; to force conversion, 151; linked to collaboration, 94; by mission officers, 83. *See also* Labor, forced; Discipline
Cofradía, 90, 91
Colombia, xiii, 10
Colonialism, 2, 3, 7, 20, 43, 133; natives' understanding of, 134
Comanche Indians, ix
Commerce. *See* Trade
Communion, comprehension of, 93
Community structure: changes in, 36–39
Comunero rebellions (Paraguay), 166
Concepción, 168
Concho Indians, 78, 79, 82; assimilation of, 78, 94; and Christianity, 93; and *encomiendas*, 82, 85, 89; as laborers, 85, 89; rebellion of, 87; as soldiers, 89. *See also* Nueva Vizcaya, Indians of
Concubinage, 22
Confession, comprehension of, 93
Congregación, viii
Consumption: by Indians, 66–68, 82; by hacienda peons, 69; limited, 17
Contraband: by Guajiros, 131, 134–35, 143–44; Spanish reaction to, 144. *See also* Trade
Conversion, 8, 9, 44–45, 57; association with death, 86; of children, 84, 114; for economic advantage, 145, 151; failure of, 114, 136; of Guajiros, 140, 142; as legal function, 182; as part of imperialism, 131–32; as protection from disease, 86; reasons for, 133, 142. *See also* Baptism
Converts, as consumers of Western goods, 67
Cooperation, 84
Coporinche, 144–45
Córdoba, University of, 175
Corn. *See* Maize
Corregidor, 161–62, 163; extralegal exactions, 162
Corrientes, 166, 174, 179
Cosmology: of Guajiro Indians, 141–42; of Nueva Vizcayan Indians, 81; protection of indigenous, 138; and trade, 135–36. *See also* Christianity; Culture; Religion
Costanoan Indians, 112–13; Chalon Costanoan, 110, 113, 126
Costa Rica, 10
Cotton, 160, 182; cloth, 167, 169; decline of, 178; sale to Corrientes, 170; seizure of, 180
Coyamo Indians, 138, 141
Coyote, 89
Crevaux (Bolivia), 69
Cuarambaré, 159
Cuevo (Bolivia), 66, 69, 70
Culiacán (Mexico), 90
Cultigens, introduction of new, 34, 36, 55
Culture: acceptance of European, 136, 157; change in California missions, 110, 112, 117; destruction of, 43; enforcement of European, 118; European bias, 190; hostile attitude to Indian, 25; interest in indigenous, 190; level of European, 118, 163; persistence

of Indian, 33, 114–19; resurgence of traditional, 110; and mission recruitment, 117–18
Cunas, ix

Dance: Indian, 25; religious, 91; Tepehuan, 81
Death. *See* Disease
Debts, 69, 167
Deculturation, 23–27, 45
Demographics, xii, 52, 189; cause for mission establishment, 84–85; population growth, 117; impact of, on missions, 7, 52, 192; demographic collapse, vii, viii, 43, 85, 124–25, 190–91, 193; in Guajiro missions, 142, 145; population losses, 64, 71–72; patterns at Soledad, 123–27; problems with sources, xiv–xv; and revolts, 87; recruitment of Indians, 117, 118, 123; and sexual ratio, 125, 170. *See also* Disease; Guaraní Indians; Mortality
De Nino, Fr. Bernardino, 55
Dependency ratio, 125
Desecration, 147
Desertion: of Indians, 12, 22, 42; of soldiers, 69
Despotism, 20
Devil, 84, 86
Diaguita Indians, 183
Diet, 89–90; and malnutrition, 15–16
Diezmo, 180
Discipline, 5, 21–22, 39, 42; *cepo*, 172; of children, 92; in *encomienda*, 174; of escapees, 170; flogging, 21, 22, 45, 83, 85, 86, 172; head-shaving, 83; incarceration, 21; jailing, 22; self-flagellation, 21; stocks, 21, 22
Discrimination, legal, 179
Disease, 11–15, 30, 32, 59, 80, 123; and abandonment, 93; as cause of revolts, 87; epidemic of 1650 (Peru), 33; exposure to, among Guaraní, 160; venereal, 12, 124, 163
Dominicans, viii, 9
Draft, military, 89, 180
Dreams, 81; as part of religion, 114
Drinking parties, 84, 87, 95, 97. *See also* Alcoholic beverages
Drought, 32; in Bolivia, 64; in California, 119
Dunne, Peter M., x–xi
Durango (Mexico), 77, 78, 98
Dutch trade, xiii, 131, 134, 143, 146, 149

Easter, 92
Ecological zones, 112, 122
Economy: acceptance of commercial, 134; importance of native, 194
Egalitarianism, as ideology, 83
El Toco (mission), 139
Emigration. *See* Migration
Encomendero, 164–65, 174
Encomienda, 3, 82, 85, 87, 159, 182; abolition of, 174; attack on, 174; *mitaria*, 158
Engelhart, Fr. Zephyrin, x
English settlement, ix, 3. *See also* British trade
Entre Ríos, 168
Environment, destruction of, 29–30, 31
Epidemics. *See* Demographics, Disease
Eslava, Sebastián, 144
Español-americano, 172
Esselen Indians, 110, 113, 126
Ethnicity, 23, 173
Ethnocentrism, 2, 8
Ethnocide, 43, 182
Ethnography, 190
Ethnohistory. *See* History
Europe, 34; economy, 51. *See also* Culture

Face-painting, 92
Fairs, 66
Family: destruction of Indian, 26; nuclear, 84
Famine, as cause of revolts, 87
Farinha de mandioca, 16
Favoritism, 83
Fertility patterns, 123, 124
Festivals, 40, 91–92; as reaffirming community ties, 162
Firearms, for hunting, 35
Fiscal, 83
Flight, from mission, 88, 170. *See also* Migration
Flogging. *See* Discipline
Flooding, 120
Flores, Manuel Antonio, 149
Florida, as mission territory, 10
Food: collection of, 15–16, 36, 96; preservation of, 15, 35; production of, 50, 59–60
Forts, 69, 70. *See also* Soldiers
Francia, José Gaspar de, 175–77, 178, 179, 183
Franciscans, viii, xii, 1, 5, 9, 11, 26; authority of, in Paraguay, 175–76; in Bolivia, 51–72; in California, 38, 109–29; compared to Jesuits, 175, 182–83; among the Conchos, 89; and economics of pueblos, 182–83; exile of, 176; and *mitayo* villages, 168; and native elite, 162–63; in Nueva Vizcaya, 78, 85; in Paraguay, 158–88, 191–92; power of, 175; and *pueblos de indios*, 158–59, 161, 175. *See also Pueblos de indios*
French pox (syphilis), 12, 124, 163
Furlong Cardiff, Guillermo, 162

Galiban Mountains, 112, 113
Galluzo, José, 149
Gálvez, José de, 126

Garavaglia, Juan Carlos, 162
Garbage analysis, 115–17
Gauchos, 177
Geiger, Fr. Maynard, x
Genocide, 43, 182
Gibson, Charles, 2
Gift giving, 82, 86, 89–90, 91; among Chiriguanos, 67; as entitlements, 95
Government: on missions, 5–6, 83; officials, 71
Gran Chaco, 10, 54, 56, 61, 65, 66, 69, 159
Gross reproduction rate (GRR), 124
Guajira Peninsula, 130, 133, 134, 136, 139, 140; planned invasion of, 148
Guajiro Indians, xiii; and adaptation, 133–34, 135–36, 152; collaboration of headmen, 144–45; evangelization among, 137–39; invasion of Riohacha, 137; military superiority of, 140–41, 143; mythology of, 136, 141; population on missions, 142, 145; rebellions of, 136–37, 140–41, 147–50; and retention of culture, 130, 132–34, 138, 146, 151; and trade, 131–32, 134–35, 143–44; views on religion, 133, 135–36
Guanaceví (Mexico), 82
Guaná Indians, 159
Guanajuato, 5
Guarambaré (*pueblo de indios*), 180
Guaraní Indians, 27, 33, 159, 192; and adaptation, 157, 182, 183–84; and Artiguista struggle, 177; and community lands, 172–73; and economic conditions, 173–74, 175, 183; effects of secular regime, 167–69; European concepts of, 163–64; as laborers, 164–65; profits, 175; and purpose of *pueblos*, 161; and race mixing,

172; rebellions, 160, 166; removal from Itapúa, 179; seizure of property, 180; social organization of, 158–59, 160–61, 162, 174; as soldiers, 166, 176, 177–78; and Spanish, 159, 161, 162; as synonym for Paraguayans, 184; wages of 163–64
Guaraní language, 23, 38, 160, 182
Guazapare Indians, 78
Guirior, Manuel, 148–49

Habig, Fr. Marion, x
Hacienda, 19, 51, 68, 82, 89
Hagiography, xiii–xiv, 2
Hallowell, Irving, 135
Hechicero. See Shaman
Helms, Mary, on contact, 135
Herding, 19. *See also* Cattle; Livestock; Ranching
Hides, 169, 180
Hieronymites, 137
Hispanicization, 163. *See also* Acculturation
History: cultural, xi; demographic, 192; ethnohistory, ix, xi, 2, 83, 130, 189, 193, 194; missionaries as agents of, 43; Native American, 43; quantitative, ix; revisionist, 50; social, ix, xi, 8, 189, 194; traditional, ix–xi, 190
Holidays, celebration of, 97. *See also* Festivals
Honduras, 10
Horses, 34, 61, 90, 160, 163
Housing arrangements, 5, 13
Huacaya (Bolivia), 70
Humanity, of mission Indians, 25
Humes Indians, 78
Hunting, 56, 82, 97, 114, 160, 193
Hygiene, decrease in, 13, 123

Ibi, Fr. Gregorio de, 138, 139, 140
Iguembe (Bolivia), 69

Iitujulu, Mount, 136
Ilex paraguaiensis. See Yerba mate
Imperialism, 130, 131
Incest, 84
Indé (Mexico), 82
Indians: as active participants, 131, 132, 133–34, 148, 152, 191, 193; alliances with whites, 54, 159; authorities, 37–38; autonomy, 191; as citizens, 180; communities, 36; as consumers, 66–68; and deserters, 55; docility of, 165; exploited, 68, 71; failure to turn into peasants, 109; importance of economy, 194; as military auxiliaries, 54, 70, 89, 166, 176; and monetary economy, 63, 71, 89, 169; population, compared to mestizos, 160; seizure of property, 180; as spies, 89; survival strategies of, 183; as victims, 190
Individualism, 39
Infanticide, 12, 25
Infantilization, of Indians, 27–29, 45
Inflation, 64
Ingre (Bolivia), 69
Irrigation, 119, 120
Itá (*pueblo de indios*), 159, 176
Itapúa (*pueblo de indios*), 179
Itatí, 179
Itau (mission), 51, 54
Ivo (mission), 51, 60

Jayme, Fr. Antonio, 124
Jesuits, viii, xiii, 1, 9, 11, 26, 35, 178; accusations against Franciscans, 159; to Asia, 24; and combat with devil, 86; compared to Franciscans, 63, 65, 175; complaints about Indians, 95; cultural ideals, 99; destruction of liquor, 84; expulsion of, 27, 33, 97, 158, 159, 161, 166, 169, 182;

Jesuits (cont.)
  flight from former missions, 170; to Guajiros, 132, 144; history of missions, 162; Indian attraction to, 84–85; medical practices of, 93–94; missions among Guaraní, 27, 38, 157, 161, 164–67, 183; missions among Tepehuanes, 77, 87, 96; missions in Nueva Vizcaya, 78; privilege native elites, 163; yerba ventures, 165–66
Jofré, Manuel O., 59, 60, 61
Jova Indians, 98
Jujuy (Argentina), 57
Julián, Fr. Antonio, 132, 144
Justice, system of, 22

King City (California), 113
Kingston (Jamaica), 134
Kinship organization: among Guajiro Indians, 141; among Nueva Vizcaya Indians, 81, 82, 84

Labor: abuses, 56, 68, 193; agricultural, 53, 55, 56, 62, 81, 82, 118, 125, 193; as cause of revolts, 87; as cause of mortality, 123; child, 19, 62–63; conflicts over, 52; construction, 53, 70, 91, 122, 125; demands, 52, 53, 54, 95; European discipline of, 21; European patterns of, 64, 118, 160; forced, 17–18, 20, 21, 45, 50, 57, 89, 94; hiring out, 18, 163; lack of missionary, 20, 22; and loss of old skills, 55; mine, 82, 89; mission Indian, 4, 15, 25, 192; missionary control over, 56, 57, 193; *mitayo*, 160, 164–65, 166; outside of mission, 53, 96, 163, 193; payment for, 53, 56; personal service, 20, 161; and production of surplus, 17, 109, 118, 126; reciprocal, 84; recruitment, 57, 170; and reliance on mission, 70; *repartimiento*, 88; routinization of, 16–17, 18; scarcity of, 56, 57, 68; sexual division of, 19, 53, 55, 81; skilled, 20, 70, 91, 118; specialization, 55, 62; for textiles, 122, 125–26; in *yerba* plantations, 165–66. See also *Encomienda*
La Cruz (mission), 139, 142, 143, 145, 147
Ladino, 95
La Grita (mission), 139, 142
Laguna de Fuentes, 139
Land: concepts of, 17, 112; grants, 68; disputes, 177; distribution of, 17, 58–59, 90–91, 161, 179; usurpations, 172–73
Languages, 38; European, 52; Indian, 23, 38, 160, 182; instruction in Indian, 6; Jesuit refusal to teach Spanish, 166; learning of, on missions, 23; *lingua geral*, 23, 38; as resistance, 41
Lara, Fr. Juan Cuadrado, 137
Latin America, 193
Laziness, missionary perceptions of, 19–20, 95
Leisure time, 53
Liberalism, 20, 179–80
Liberal Party (Bolivia), 58
Liberation theology, 7
Life expectancy, 124
Lingua geral, 23, 38
Livestock, 31, 34, 89–90, 164; in California, 122; economy among Guajiros, 134; gifts of, 89; herding, 19; introduction of, 34, 35, mythicization of, 131; tax on, 180; in temperate zones, 36; trade, 144. See also Cattle; Ranching
López, Carlos Antonio, 178–81, 183

López de Sierra, Cecilio, 144–45, 146
Lowie, Robert, 145
Luiseño Indians (California), 33

Macharetí (mission), 51, 59, 61, 66
Machete, 34, 35
Madrid, 167, 174
Magariños, Manuel Rodríguez, 69
Magic, 86
Maize, 34, 59, 80, 89, 121, 159; alcohol, 84; and cattle, 58; trade in, 82; as tribute, 81
Maleiwa, 141
Malnutrition, 15–16
Manatee, 36
Mancebos de la tierra, 160
Manioc, 15, 16, 34, 159, 182
Maracaibo, 138, 139, 140, 142, 144
Marianismo, 141
Marriage, 92; choice of partners, 25, 93, 96; compliance with, 93; intermarriage, 98; sanctity of, 84
Masquare, 144–45
Matachín dances, 91–92
Mataco Indians (Bolivia), 57
Material culture, retention of Indian, 117–19, 126, 191
Matrilineality, of Guajiros, 130, 141, 145
Maynas region, 11
Mayoruna Indians (Peru), 33
Mbayá Indians, 159
Measles, 12, 84, 123
Medicine, 14, 30, 93
Mendinueta, Pedro, 136, 150
Mendoza, Gerónimo de, 147
Mental illness, 14
Mercedarians, viii, 1, 9
Merchants, 66, 69, 70, 71
Mérida (Venezuela), 139, 142
Mescal, 81, 97
Mesoamerica, vii, 23, 39, 80
Messía de la Cerda, Pedro, 147

Mestizaje, 12, 45, 94
Mestizo: acceptance of, 98; change from Indian, 172; expropriation from, 180; Spanish-Guaraní, 160; work habits in Paraguay, 164
Métraux, Alfred, 34
Mexico: central, 3, 85, 88, 90; northern, vii, ix, x, xii, 3, 6, 10, 26, 190. *See also* Nueva Vizcaya
Mexico City, xiv, 94, 110
Migration, 124; bad habits from, 67; causes of, 68, 96, 98; of Chiriguanos, 57–58, 59, 66; as effect of secularization, 167, 169; of Guaraní Indians, 167, 168, 169–70, 183; of non-Indians to missions, 170–72
Military: draft, 89, 180. *See also* Soldiers
Millenarianism, 42, 87, 88
Mining, 85, 97, 193
Misogyny, of missionaries, 26
The Mission, 7, 157
Missionaries: focus on, 8; conflict with settlers, 52, 57, 71–72, 193; control of Indians, 191, 193; disrespected, 96; fear of Guajiros, 143; as intermediary, 71, 161, 167; lack of protection by, 96; number on mission, 161, 191; question authority of elders, 83; as shaman, 30; stereotype of, 193; temporal power among Guaraní, 161
Missions: advantages of, 32–39; authorities on, 37–39; as ceremonial centers, 97; as commercial enterprises, 63, 119; control over Indian labor, 56, 85; defense, 54; as economic units, 6, 49–79, 110, 119; failure of, 136–37, 147–48; and frontier, 189, 192, 193; functions of, 58; income and expenditures of, 63–65; infrastructure

206   Index

Missions (cont.)
of, 53, 64–65, 70; Jesuit, 158, 183; as labor sources, 51, 52–58, 65, 70–72; as laboratories, 194; land distribution on, 58–59, 90–91; land rental by, 65; leaders of, 88–89; life cycle of, 51–52, 53, 70; as market, 51, 52, 66–68; for military protection, 32, 45, 70, 85; officers of, 83, 162; problems with traditional history, ix–x, 2, 8, 189–90; production on, 58–65, 95, 110, 118; reasons for establishment of, 84–86; recruitment of Indians for, 12; as refuge, 71; secular emphasis of, 126; as subsidizing garrisons, 110, 122–23, 126; terminology regarding, 45; traditional activity of, 115–17, 126. See also *Pueblos de indios*
Mita, 160
Mitayo, 158, 164–65, 166; incorporation into military, 176; village, 161, 168
Monjería, 7
Monogamy, 99; serial, 81
Monroy y Meneses, Fr. Antonio, 142, 144
Monte (wilderness), 82
Monterey (California), 113
Monterey Bay (California), 112
Moral economy, 88
Moreno y Escandón, Antonio, 148
Moriscoti, Juan, 139, 140
Mörner, Magnus, 162
Mortality, 12, 13, 71; among children, 123, 125; compared to European rates, 124–25; justification of, 126; and labor, 192; levels of, 123; and recruitment, 110. See also Demographics, Disease
Motilon Indians, 131, 132

Mulattos, 89, 94, 98
Munducuru Indians, 33
Muniesa, Pedro de, 142
Mura Indians, 33
Music, 25, 92
Mythology: adaptation of, 130; of cattle and herding, 136, 152; matrilineal features of Guajiro, 141–42

Nahuatl, 23
Ñancaroinza (Bolivia), 66
Narváez y la Torre, Antonio de, 139
Nature: alienation from, 31; exploitation of, 29; in Indian religious expression, 30; power over, 30
Nayarit, 10
Neumann, Fr. Joseph, 84
New Granada, 130–56
New Mexico, 147
New Spain. See Mexico
Nordenskiöld, Erland von, 55, 56, 67
North America, 192
Nudity, 25
Nuestra Señora de la Soledad (mission), 109–29
Nuestra Señora de los Remedios (mission), 139–40
Nueva Vizcaya (Mexico), Indians of, 77–100

Obraje, 63
Oliva, Fr. Andrés de, 143, 146
Ollería, Fr. Antonio de, 138, 139
Olocau, Fr. Mariano de, 142
Opata Indians, 33
Orihuela, Fr. Pablo de, 139
Orinoco Valley, 1, 10
Orino mission, 139, 140, 142, 143, 145
Orphans, 58
Otomaca Indians, 138

Panama, ix

Index 207

Paternalism, 43
Pará, 18, 33
Paraguay: economy of missions in, 38; export boom, 169; independence, 174, 177; missions in, xiii, 1, 3, 13, 18, 27, 33, 36, 38, 157–88, 193; Republic of, 158, 178; route to, 54
Paraguayan Congress, 179
Paraná River, 158, 161, 167, 168, 177
Partiñanca (ranch), 68
Passive resistance, 88, 94–97
Pasture, 59, 112; overgrazing of, 69. *See also* Cattle; Livestock
Patriarchy, 130, 141, 191
Patron saint, 162
Payaguá Indians, 159
Payeras, Fr. Mariano, 120
Pearl fishing, 142, 144
Peasants: European, 19; Paraguayan, 182
Pedraza, 149, 150
Peredo, Diego, 140
Pérouse, Jean François de la, 22
Perrin, Michel, 130
Peru, xi, 159
Pestaña y Chumacero, José Xavier, 145
Petén, 10
Phelan, John, xi, 49
Philip V, 144
Pilcomayo River, 54, 69
Pima Indians, 98
Pizarro, José Alonso, 144
Plantations, 18, 19; sugar, xii, 57, 62, 66, 67
Political organization: of Concho Indians, 82; of Nueva Vizcayan Indians, 80
Polygamy, 25, 81, 87
Polytheism, 84, 87
Pongo, 14
Population. *See* Demographics

Portugal, vii, 28
Portuguese expansion, 161, 166, 177
Potosí, 169; Franciscans from, 51, 55, 62, 64, 66
Power: in Indian communities, 83, 175; and spirituality, 30; structure in mission, 36–37
Prayer, 37, 86
Preaching, reaction to, 92
Pregnancy, 123
Presidio, 4, 85
Priesthood, training for, 28
Primitive communism, as myth, 162–63
Principal, 81, 82, 83
Prison, 19
Prisoners, in exchange for tools, 34
Processions, 91
Production, 51, 52, 58–65; by children, 62–63; for market, 19, 71
Proletarianization. *See* Labor
Protector de naturales, 172
Protestants, xii
Provocateurs, Dutch and English, 134
Puebla (Mexico), 49
Pueblo Indians, 33, 147
Pueblos de indios, 19, 157, 163; administrators of, 172; decline of, 178, 179–81; economic conditions of, 173, 174; and encroachment of lands, 172–73; ethnic composition of, 173; as institution, 182; as intermediary, 161; and labor, 170, 175, 176; legal functions of, 182; and López's reforms, 178–81; population of, 170, 172, 177; power on, 175; and taxes, 180; survival of, 177
Pulowi, 141–42
Punishment. *See* Discipline
Puritans, 133

Quechua, 23

Index

Race mixture, 12, 45, 94
Raiding, 88
Rainfall, 119
Ranchería, 80, 82, 84, 94; settlement pattern, 97
Ranching, 55, 68, 177; and assignment of mission lands, 119; methods, of, 61, 68; on Soledad mission, 122. *See also* Cattle; Livestock
Rebellion, 78, 92; Acaxee and Xixime (1601, 1610), 86; against sexual prohibitions, 25; Concho (1640s), 87; first-generation revolts, 86–88; Guajiro, 136–37, 140, 147–50; Guaraní, 160, 166; lack of, 181; leaders of, 87; organization of, 88; and rebelliousness, 28–29; symbolism in, 87; Tarahumara, 87, 98; Tepehuan (1616), 87
Reciprocity, 17, 83
Reclus, Eliseo, 148
Recruiting, for mission, 117, 125, 126; and cultural change, 118; and destruction of Indian population, 124–25; sexual imbalance in, 125
Redistribution, 17
Reducción, viii, xiii, 82, 86, 158
Regidor, 162
Regimentation, 16–21, 39
Religion: as cultural identity, 133; and dramas, 91; elimination of Indian, 113–14; European views of, 30, 40–41, 133; folk, 41; Guajiro, 130; Indian views of, 81; retention of indigenous, 118; rituals, 92; and self-expression, 41. *See also* Christianity
Renters, 180
Repartimiento, 88
Resistance, Indian, xii, 14, 25, 26, 32, 41–43, 45, 86–100, 193;
armed, 33, 42; cultural, 41–42, 43; in Nueva Vizcaya, 77–108; to recruitment, 123; Tarahumara, 98; and trade, 143–44. *See also* Rebellion
Resistant adaptation, 78, 88
Revillagigedo, Conde de (viceroy), 77
Revolt. *See* Rebellion
Ribera, Lázaro de, 157, 174
Ricard, Robert, xi, 49
Rincón mission, 142, 147
Río de la Plata region, 158, 167, 178
Río Hacha (New Granada), 130–56
Riohacha (town), 137, 138, 139, 140, 142, 147, 148, 150
Río Tebicuary, 166, 168, 169, 174
Rites controversy, 24
Rosa de Amaya y Buitrago, Juan de la, 140
Ruiz de Noruego, Bernardo, 146–47
Rustling. *See* Cattle

Sábana del Valle, 149, 150
Sacrifice, among Indians of Nueva Vizcaya, 81, 82
Sacrilege, 22
Saint Francis, 151
Salinan Indians, 112–13
Salinas (Bolivia), 54
Salinas River (California), 113, 120; Valley, 112, 113, 119–20, 126
Salvation, 45, 84
San Agustín de Manaure (mission), 142
San Antonio del Parapití (mission), 51
San Antonio del Pilcomayo (mission), 51
San Antonio de Orino (mission), 139, 140, 142, 143, 145
San Antonio de Padua (mission), 110
San Bartolomé, Valle de, 82
San Buenaventura de Ivo, 51, 60

Index 209

San Carlos Borromeo de Carmelo (Carmel mission), 110, 113
San Diego (California), 33
San Estanislao (mission), 158
San Felipe de Palmarito (mission), 142, 143
San Francisco del Parapití (mission), 51
San Francisco del Pilcomayo (mission), 51
San Ignacio (*pueblo de indios*), 180
San Joaquín (mission), 158, 180
San José del Rincón (mission), 142, 147
San Juan de la Cruz (mission), 139, 142, 143, 145, 147
San Miguel, 168
San Nicholás de los Menores (mission), 139, 142
San Pascual de Boicovo, 51, 64, 66, 70
San Pedro Nolasco, 142
Santa Bárbara (Mexico), 82, 85
Santa Cruz Department (Bolivia), 51
Santa Lucía, 179
Santa Lucia Mountains, 112, 113, 119
Santa María (*pueblo de indios*), 172
Santa Marta (New Granada), 132, 134, 137, 138, 139, 140, 142, 143, 147
Santa Rosa de Cuevo (mission), 51, 53, 55, 59, 60, 64, 65, 66, 70
Santiago (Chile), 169
Santiago (Paraguay), 168
Santiago Papasquiaro (mission), 77
Schooling, 6, 27–28; Eurocentric, 3; of children, 24, 44, 62–63, 92; skills taught through, 55, 91
Schools, 53, 55, 70; distribution of clothing in, 66, 67; flight from, 57; production in, 62–63
Scott, James, 190
Secretario, 162
Secularization, 72, 122, 127, 131, 191–92; of clergy, 176; and cultural change, 118; and economic exploitation, 167–68; and race mixture, 94; resistance to, 96–97; of Tepehuan and Tarahumara missions, 96; unattended, 174
Seed ratio, 121–22
Self-flagellation, 92
Senan, Fr. José, 24
Serra, Fr. Junípero, x, 2, 8, 21
Settlers, 50, 52, 62, 71; contact with missions, 168; demand for mission labor, 56, 166, 193; demand for mission surplus, 119; exploitation of Indians, 68, 71, 193; and forts, 69; increase in, 56; relations with Jesuits, 166
Sexuality, 25–26, 84
Shaman: devil as, 86, 97; as healer, 93–94, 114; leader as, 97; missionary as, 30, 40; among Nueva Vizcayan Indians, 81; struggle with, 86
Shamanism, as resistance, 41, 96
Shaming, 83
Sharecroppers, 180
Sharing of goods, among Chiriguanos, 67
Sheep, 34, 122
Shipek, Florence, 33
Shipyards, 170
Sierra de Salinas, 112, 120
Sierra Gorda (Mexico), 5
Sierra Madre Occidental (Mexico), 78, 80, 86
Silvestre, Francisco, 150
Sinaloa, 80, 98
Sinamaica, 149, 150
Sins, 84
Slavery, 4, 19; African, 4, 19; Indian, 17–18, 32, 34, 81, 82
Smallpox, 12, 84–85, 86, 123, 160
Smuggling. *See* Contraband, Trade
Soap factory, 180
Social history. *See* History: social

Social networks, 84
Soldiers, 5, 17, 42, 50, 69, 92, 109; as coercive force, 85; demand for mission surplus, 122; drafting of, 89, 180; as laborers, 69; and recruitment for missions, 123
Soledad mission, xii, 109–29
Solís Folch de Cardona, Pedro, 132, 146
Sonora, 10, 80, 98, 191
Soria, Fr. José de la, 142, 143
Soul, native beliefs regarding, 82, 92
Sources: archives, xiv; lack of Indian testimonies, 2; histories, xiv; lack of production, 59, 60; *memorias*, 91; problems with, 9, 189–90; reports, xiv; sacramental records, xiv; types of, 193
South, Stanley, 115
South America, ix, 159
Spain, vii, 3, 28
Spanish borderland, x, 2, 189, 192
Spanish language, 38, 166
Spanish Cortes, 124
Spanish Crown, viii, 3, 109, 119, 166; and tasks for pueblos, 170; vassals of, 18
Spanish Main, 134, 137
Spicer, Edward, 190
Spies, mission Indians as, 89
Spirituality. *See* Christianity; Religion
Standard of living, 35
Subsistence activities, 18
Sucre (fort), 69
Sugar cane, 55, 59, 62–63, 160; mill, 180; plantations (Argentina), xii, 57, 62, 66, 67
Suicide, 12
Susnik, Bratislava, 58
Syphilis, 12, 124, 163

Taboos, 84
Tamaulipas, 10

Tannery, 180
Tarahumara, 26, 33, 39, 78, 80–81, 83; and adaptation, 91–92, 94; and Apache governor, 89; and Christianity, 91–92, 93; collaboration of, 89; European perception of, 83, 91; as laborers, 82, 91; and mission as haven, 85–86; rebellion of, 87–88; religious beliefs and rituals of, 81, 82, 84, 97; and resistance to secularization, 96–98; and trade, 95. *See also* Nueva Vizcaya, Indians of
Tarairí (mission), 51, 54, 55, 59, 61, 62, 66, 70
Tarascan Indians, 85
Tarija (Bolivia), 51, 55, 58, 60, 61, 63, 69
Teaching: of languages, 166; of religion, 39. *See also* Schooling
Tebicuary River, 166, 168, 169, 174
Technology, 29, 30; adaptation to new, 160; agricultural, 55, 91; and innovation, 34
Temastian, 83
Temperate zone, missions in, 36
Temporalities, viii
Tepehuan Indians, 77, 78, 80–81; and adaptation, 94; and Christianity, 93; collaboration of, 89; and *encomiendas*, 82; European perception of, 85; rebellion of, 87–99; religious beliefs and rituals of, 81, 82; and secularization of missions, 96; and trade, 9. *See also* Nueva Vizcaya, Indians of
Tesguinada, 84
Texas, x
Textiles, 122; and finance colonization, 125–26; workshops, 170, 180
Theft, 22, 61
Tierra Firme, 138

Index   211

Tiguipa (mission), 51, 59, 70
Timber, 112, 170, 176
Time, concept of, 16–17
Tlaxcalan Indians, 85, 89
Tobacco, 160, 165, 169, 182; factories, 173; stagnation of, 173, 176
Toba Indians (Bolivia), 54, 56
Tobatí (*pueblo de indios*), 159, 172
Todorov, Tzvetan, 133
Tools, 34–35; access to iron, 33–34, impact of new, 36, 55
Topia (Mexico), 85, 87
Towns, and reliance on missions, 70
Trade, 38, 69, 109, 194; Caribbean, 131; collapse of, 183; and cosmology, 135–36; in firearms, 134, 143; Guajiro, 134–35; impeded by Guajiros, 132; by Indians, 82, 91, 95; Jesuit, 165; in mission cattle, 118; in Paraguay, 182–83; pre-Columbian, 84, 91; with settlers, 122–23; utilization of European, 131, 135; in *yerba*, 165–66, 169. *See also* British trade; Dutch trade
Tribute, 140, 170, 179; decline in, 170, 173–74
Tropics, missions in, 36
Trujillo, Fr. Joaquín, 89
Tubare Indians, 78
Tupambae, 161
Tuparaí (*pueblo de indios*), 179
Turtles, Amazon River, 30, 31
Twin Myth, 141
Typhus, 12, 84, 160

United States, vii, x, 192
Uria, Fr. Francisco, 112
Uruguay, 168, 177
Uruguay River, 161, 166, 167

Valencia, 138, 146
Valledupar, 140
Venereal disease, 12, 124, 163

Venezuela, 10
Vera y Fajardo, Juan de, 134
Villalonga, Jorge de, 143
Virginity, 25
Virgin Mary, 92, 97
Visita, 174
Vistabella, Fr. Buenaventura de, 138, 139
Voltaire, 157

Wages, 18, 69, 163; labor obligations of, 164. *See also* Labor
Warfare, 12, 19, 32, 34, 54, 69; change after mission, 54, 83; failure of, to expell Spaniards, 88; against Guajiros, 147–50; and male power, 83; among Nueva Vizcayan Indians, 80–81; participation of mission Indians, 55, 89. *See also* Rebellion
War leaders, 81
Water, lack of, 119; pollution of, 123
Wealth, accumulation of, 162. *See also* Missions: as economic unit
Weaponry, 131, 134–35
"Weapons of the weak," 78, 95
Weaving, 62, 63, 160
Wheat, importance of, 121–22
Whipping. *See* Discipline
Widows, 58
Willemstad (Curaçao), 134
Wine, 35
Witchcraft, against priests, 96
Women: in *cofradías*, 90; exchange for cattle, 136; fertility of, 123; as laborers, 53, 160; lack of confessions, 93; locking up, 124; missionary attitudes toward, 26–27; *mita* labor, 164; and population, 125; roles of, 26; segregation of, 25, 124
Wool, 122
Work, European concept of, 17. *See also* Labor

Xiximee Indians, 78, 85, 86

Yacuiba (Bolivia), 68
Yaguarón (*pueblo de indios*), 159, 180
Yapeyú, 168
Yaqui Indians, 26, 33, 39, 41
Yberá marshlands, 178
Yerbales, 160, 169, 175, 176; decline of, 178
Yerba mate, 160, 164, 165, 167; commerce in, 169; refusal to supply, 174
Ypané, 159
Yuty (*pueblo de indios*), 159

Zuñi Indians, 33

In the Latin American Studies Series

Modern Brazil
Elites and Masses in Historical Perspective
Edited by Michael L. Conniff and Frank D. McCann

The Struggle for Democracy in Chile, 1982–1990
Edited by Paul W. Drake and Iván Jaksic

The New Latin American Mission History
Edited by Erick Langer and Robert H. Jackson

Sexuality and Marriage in Colonial Latin America
Edited by Asunción Lavrin

Spaniards and Indians in Southeastern Mesoamerica
Essays on the History of Ethnic Relations
Edited by Murdo J. MacLeod and Robert Wasserstrom

United States Policy in Latin America
A Quarter Century of Crisis and Challenge, 1961–1986
Edited by John D. Martz

Food, Politics, and Society in Latin America
Edited by John C. Super and Thomas C. Wright

Revolution and Restoration
The Rearrangement of Power in Argentina, 1776–1860
Edited by Mark D. Szuchman and Jonathan C. Brown

Latin American Oil Companies and the Politics of Energy
Edited by John D. Wirth

www.ingramcontent.com/pod-product-compliance
Lightning Source LLC
Chambersburg PA
CBHW022057160426
43198CB00008B/268